Making
it Home

Making it Home

IIIIIIIIIIIIIIIIIIIIIIIIIIIIII

LIFE LESSONS FROM A
SEASON OF LITTLE LEAGUE

TERESA STRASSER

BERKLEY
NEW YORK

BERKLEY
An imprint of Penguin Random House LLC
penguinrandomhouse.com

Copyright © 2023 by Teresa Strasser
Readers Guide copyright © 2023 by Teresa Strasser
Penguin Random House supports copyright. Copyright fuels creativity,
encourages diverse voices, promotes free speech, and creates a vibrant culture.
Thank you for buying an authorized edition of this book and for complying with
copyright laws by not reproducing, scanning, or distributing any part of it in any
form without permission. You are supporting writers and allowing
Penguin Random House to continue to publish books for every reader.

BERKLEY and the BERKLEY & B colophon are registered trademarks of
Penguin Random House LLC.

Library of Congress Cataloging-in-Publication Data

Names: Strasser, Teresa, author.
Title: Making it home: life lessons from a season of little league / Teresa Strasser.
Description: First edition. | New York: Berkley, 2023. |
Identifiers: LCCN 2022050433 (print) | LCCN 2022050434 (ebook) |
ISBN 9780593546086 (trade paperback) | ISBN 9780593546093 (ebook) |
Subjects: LCSH: Grief. | Parents—Death. | Self-doubt. |
Little League Baseball (Organization)
Classification: LCC BF575.G7 S765 2023 (print) | LCC BF575.G7 (ebook) |
DDC 155.9/37—dc23/eng/20230222
LC record available at https://lccn.loc.gov/2022050433
LC ebook record available at https://lccn.loc.gov/2022050434

First Edition: June 2023

Printed in the United States of America
1 3 5 7 9 10 8 6 4 2

Book design by Kristin del Rosario

This book is a work of memoir. It is a true story faithfully based on
the author's best recollections of various events in her life. In some instances,
events and time periods have been compressed or reordered in service of the narrative
and dialogue approximated to match the author's best recollection of those exchanges.
Names and identifying details of certain people mentioned have been changed.

"I don't care if you make me the villain of the piece.
There's nothing more important than art.
Are they going to pay you for this book?
Who's going to play me in the movie?"

—NELSON STRASSER

Making it Home

PROLOGUE

||||||||||||||||||||||||||||

"Baseball, it is said, is only a game. True. And the
Grand Canyon is only a hole in Arizona."

—GEORGE WILL

If I drive down Indian School Road, between Camelback Mountain and the less majestic, but equally formidable, Ingleside Middle School, my head still turns toward the baseball fields, like I'm on a bus tour of Jerusalem passing by the Temple Mount. I can't help feeling like I'm hugging a curve of Phoenix road around some kind of holy place.

CIRCLE K PROUDLY SUPPORTS STATE OF ARIZONA LITTLE LEAGUE, announces a white vinyl sign fastened to a chain-link fence. COURTESY AUTOMOTIVE SUPPORTS ARCADIA LITTLE LEAGUE, too. A tall green wooden scoreboard is hoisted up high by two long beams, erected for the purpose of counting balls, strikes, and outs, tracking innings for the guest and home teams. The Diamondbacks logo, a giant red capital *A*, sits atop the scoreboard, which is operational only one magical night a year, the night of the championships, when you can squint through the desert sky and tally the evolving possibilities.

For the most part, though, we had to keep score for ourselves, and that's what we did, my dad and I, sitting along the first-base line at those three fields behind Ingleside Middle School.

"Morgan would've gotten that ground ball." My dad would grimace, his watering, twitchy eyes on the field. "He never missed a grounder at first. You have to play the bounce. Don't let the bounce play you."

Morgan was my older brother, a lights-out, fastball-loving lefty who was a baseball prodigy until he slid into a mysterious hitting slump that nobody could understand or cure. He stopped playing at age thirteen and, relevant to this story, he stopped living at age forty-seven. In between, he was a juvenile delinquent, passed the California State Bar exam on the first try, taught himself how to use a manual-focus Nikon he bought with money he earned parking cars. He fell in love with an Argentine economist named Laura, with whom he had two children. Both kids were still small on the stormy night he died on a rented hospital bed in the basement. Laura curled up next to his body for hours, until the snow slowed to a delicate flurry. A couple of guys finally showed up, wrapped him in a plain sheet, belted his body to a gurney, and rolled him down a plywood ramp into a nondescript van and out into the blustery blackness.

When I drive by Ingleside Middle School, I refuse to know it's just a cluster of standard-issue boxy public school buildings, beige with faded red trim. Next to that school are the neighborhood diamonds. For me, those middle school baseball fields—the red dirt under the bleachers dotted with small pine cones and forgotten Drumstick wrappers—are sacred ground.

During the course of a certain season my oldest son played there, I mourned my dead brother, who had died of spinal cancer. I mourned the sibling relationship with him I never got to have after our parents divorced and divided us, King Solomon–style, an event that happened before my conscious memory, but a separation that came alive that spring in every cell of my body.

Then, in these bleachers and along these sidelines, I mourned my mom, who died four months to the day after my brother.

And it's here, in the desert, alongside this busy, winding street, that I sat with my dad as my husband coached, holding our breaths together at every full count. And it's here, unable to detach from the whims and bounces of a baseball, that I came to know the terrible, beautiful, agonizing truth, that there are forces a parent can't control.

"Who has it better than we do?" my dad'd ask, after his grandson connected on an 0-2 count. He'd raise his bushy eyebrows, throw back his head, and cackle before covering his mouth with his bandana, remembering the conspicuous gap where his right incisor and canine used to be.

"Nobody," I'd answer, our call-and-response.

We were a congregation of two in this chapel of chalk lines and regulated dimensions, where fair was fair and foul was foul and rules were rules. Things didn't go out of order, like a father outliving his son. And at least when it came to baseball, we were finally on the same team.

"This batting order makes no sense," I'd whisper, shoulder to shoulder with my trailer-park pops.

"I know. Sorry, but the kid in the two hole can't hit."

"Couldn't hit water if he fell out of a boat. Damn, I can't believe I just said that about a third grader. I'm an awful person, Dad."

"You're a monster," he'd say, before I punched his bony upper arm.

Little League baseball gave me a way to be with my dad in all his eccentric multitudes—the bankruptcy and abiding compulsion to invest in hopeless schemes and plots of land, the evil stepmother he'd foisted on us, the slapdash parenting, the divvying up of his children.

Letting him be broken was a thing I learned to do as the wildly unpredictable physics of baseball thrust us into a mutual foxhole. The ballpark seemed to be the only place it was safe to fully experience, inning after inning, the colossal ways the world could fuck you over and the vast possibilities for redemption.

The Great American Pastime was also a kind of nirvana for Dad. A former mechanic with no desire to talk death, Nelson Strasser processed his shit by riding the rhythm of sitting in bleachers and camp chairs with his daughter.

I know what you might be thinking: There are Jewish mechanics? Not many. I've never met another.

He was a terrible businessman, but at least as an auto mechanic he never had a boss, some square who could fire him for refusing to wear a tie. This was the case with his first job out of college, working for the Los Angeles Health Department. His duties there involved the contact tracing of suspected syphilis cases, ferreting out unfortunates in dark bars. I consider it a damn shame he lost that gig. My dad is exactly the guy you'd want calmly telling you about your syphilis, then quoting Camus, then sticking around to watch the last inning of the Dodgers game before grandly paying for your beer, even if he couldn't expense it.

I didn't know much about baseball fundamentals, but I would learn. It was grief or baseball, and we'd take baseball every time.

"You can't protect your kids from life," my dad would say as we sank into the depths of darkness over a strikeout.

He only talked about baseball, but I knew what he meant.

When I snap my head to take in the open-air sanctuary of the ballpark, I praise Jesus, Moses, Elvis, the Buddha, and the Babe for that season, even on the days it drove my dad to hit the Kirkland tequila before noon. I give praise to the baseball gods, who made it possible to accept that all of us will swing and miss. But if we're lucky, by the end of the game, we'll be covered in dirt and bruises because we played so hard, played with our whole hearts, even when it hurt. We will relish all the bruises we got rounding the bases, headed toward home.

This is the season my dad and I conduct a grief group of two, just us, in our striped beach chairs lined up directly behind the first-base line, so my dad can see every play, despite his crappy vision and the eye spasms he has developed over the past few years.

This group will meet at the Ingleside Middle School in Phoenix, Arizona.

There are no therapeutically trained facilitators and there are no rules, other than those dictated by the Little League of America and the human heart.

||||||||||||||||||||||||||||||

CHAPTER ONE

Somewhere Outside Prescott, Arizona

"We made too many of the wrong mistakes."

—YOGI BERRA

A lanky man with a weathered face at a High Country coffee shop gestured with his impossibly long arm toward the desk in his office and pointed his finger toward that desk, made from the front half of an old Buick. It was blue, a shade somewhere between Arizona midday sky and roadside-tourist-shop turquoise.

The grizzled barista regarded my dad, then me.

"You should take her picture in front of that desk. Naked," said the man, backing up toward the counter with a hitch in his step, and cheeks so deeply sunken and overly tan, they seemed almost unstable, sinkholes on the verge of collapse.

"That would be awkward. Because I'm his daughter," I said, understanding how tricky the world was, my dad and me in masks.

It was the pandemic summer, and we left Phoenix and the melting black asphalt of our neighborhood every weekend for Sedona, Flagstaff, Payson, Cottonwood, anywhere a few degrees cooler with a decent motel pool and a field large enough to shag pop-ups or hold a Wiffle ball home-run derby. We always brought my dad, who sat in the back of our Ford Expedition with the kids, wearing the keys to his mobile home around his neck on a lanyard, his black vinyl fanny pack hovering above his seat belt. We busted his chops about the omnipresence of his fanny pack, but it was all worth it when the boys needed a wet wipe and he would produce one from within a small Tupperware container, popping the red lid with glee and a sense of purpose. When it was his turn to pick a song, he'd sometimes surprise us. Sure, there were the Bob Dylan and Joan Baez tunes you'd expect from an old Jewish guy who considered himself a radical, but he'd sprinkle in some syrupy songs, too, a sparklingly wholesome Marty Robbins crooning about the prom, "*A white sport coat, and a pink carnation, I'm in a blue, blue mood.*"

Those were the palate cleansers between darker voices.

"Leonard Cohen is a genius," he'd remind us. "Listen, listen, quiet. This is the part." And he'd shush the boys and sing/talk a duet with Leonard. "'*There is a crack, a crack in everything. That's how the light gets in.*' How does anyone even think of that? And he lost all his money. Did you know that? Someone went to jail for embezzling it. Smartest guy in the world. 'Hallelujah' is the best song ever written. *Loses everything.*"

"How much, Grandpa? Like how much did 'Hallelujah' guy get stolen?" asked Nate. "Thousands of dollars?"

"*Hah!* No, Natey. Millions. He lost almost ten million dollars," said my dad, staring out the window, watching the pines go by, a hint of a smile.

"You're telling me you can make millions of dollars writing stupid songs? That's like as much as MLB players make."

"For real, dude. Genius songwriters like Leonard Cohen can make millions, but want to know what he had after writing all those songs? Bubkes. That's Jewish for 'nothing.' He had to go back on the road at seventy-three. Can you imagine? It was his manager, who was maybe also his girlfriend. Anyway I think she stole it, went to the slammer, but he never got back that money."

That was the crack that let the light in for my dad.

He had also lost all his money, not the type of fortune you earn writing about secret chords and baffled kings, but the type a working-class guy should've socked away after all those decades rebuilding alternators and generators in his own shop, Delta Battery, first located at the end of an industrial strip mall on a forever-smoggy stretch of the San Fernando Valley, then later, on a nowhere road in Santa Rosa, a couple of hours north of San Francisco. Carol complained that there was too much smog for her in the Valley, so they relocated about five years after my parents split. The move didn't change things much. The bus trip was shorter for me, but the custody arrangements were the same: monthly visits. Dad sold the old Delta Battery and opened a new one. Sometimes he had one guy working for him, sometimes four or five. There was always cash in his faded brown leather wallet, shoved into the back pocket of the navy uniform pants he wore with a matching Dickies shirt, NELSON stitched onto the front in red thread. He wrote receipts by hand, pressing down hard on a clipboard to make copies through sheets of carbon paper, handing the pink one at the bottom to the customer, remnants of brake carbon and engine grease under his nails, no matter how much he scrubbed his hands with the pint-size plastic tub of pumice scrub precariously balanced on Delta Battery's tiny bathroom sink.

"Sir, the Accord is ready," he'd say, pointing to a parked car out front. "Bring it back if you have any problems. And if you do need to bring it back, no charge." He'd hand over the pink receipt, folded: *$78, rebuild, Accord starter, parts and 2 hours labor.* "TONY! TOOOOONY! Where's Tony? TONY! Bring around the Cutlass," he'd shout over the din of machinery, noticing a customer patiently waiting, hands in the pockets of his ironed khakis, staring at the framed school photos of my brother and me on the wall. "JOSÉ! JOSÉ!" he'd bellow, followed by a bunch of words in Spanish I didn't understand, other than "*gracias*" and "Cutlass."

"Your Cutlass is ready, sir."

He'd call every male customer "sir," and he never charged any-one for a "bring back," two things that delighted me on those Sat-urdays when my dad had me for the weekend, when I would pretend bolts were diamond rings and force the sweating, over-whelmed mechanics to stop and look at how I'd arranged them on my fingers. "Sir" was a formal gesture, a perky nod toward tradi-tion, a respect for life's chain of command.

Every time he'd call someone "sir," it felt like a break from our family's strangeness, the way we lived, the unusual custody arrange-ment, the fact that my dad had won legal custody of me but re-turned me to my mom, the grease always under our nails even when you couldn't see it. That word, not intoned unctuously but delivered with just enough subservience, offered a glimpse at a version of my dad who could operate in the polite world. It was a smooth dollop of rosy-cheeked, 1950s full-service gas station decency, someone in a white sport coat and a pink carnation getting ready for the dance. This chirpy, upbeat civility was also deployed for police officers, so I never minded when we got pulled over. "Sir, I'm sorry. That was my fault. I didn't know where I was going and I shouldn't have made that illegal U-turn." To me it was a magical spell he cast.

I sat in the passenger seat still and quiet, taking in my dad's genuine disappointment with himself as communicated to the cop leaning into the car window, his true remorse about inconvenienc-ing the California Highway Patrol. He never once got a ticket, and every time a police officer said, "You and your daughter have a great day," and loped back to his black-and-white, I knew they saw what I saw and that it was real. My dad was good. He was guarantee-your-car-repair good.

Because he never did charge a customer for a "bring back," I knew that my dad, despite everything, was the hero of the story. He was the mechanic you returned to, year after year. The man with his name stitched over his heart had won me, given me away, and taken me back for a weekend a month, and now I could relax, because despite this confusing sequence of parental events, he was better than anyone else's dad and their manicured hands and corner offices. I was this mechanic's daughter, and even Johnny Law knew to back down off a ticket for this guy, his nervous, frizzy-haired daughter wide-eyed in the passenger seat.

I wasn't yet four when I started going back and forth between my parents, flying solo from San Francisco to my dad in Santa Monica, then later, when flights became too expensive, taking the Greyhound bus. Later I took a commuter bus across the Golden Gate Bridge to the gloomy house in Santa Rosa where he'd moved with Carol, my stepmother—whose wisdom, gleaned from completing three-quarters of a degree in psychology from junior college, had persuaded my dad to return me to my mom while keeping my brother.

Carol ran through the hateful-stepmother checklist pretty thoroughly.

She was jealous, critical, shit talking. She didn't feed us or take us anywhere when my dad wasn't around, isolating us almost completely. She assigned a long list of heavy household chores, then lorded over them with evil-stepmother glee, screeching and screaming if we left a crumb in the sink or wrapped the vacuum cord incorrectly. She wanted every second of my dad's time and every dime of his money, and we were just messy-haired wild cretins she had to keep away from all that was hers.

"Why should you pay for half of a fifteen-dollar haircut for *her*, Nelson? Let her mom pay."

According to her, it was too bad, but I was mediocre, rude, a dullard, and later a teenage kleptomaniac (a story she invented and stuck to for years). As for my brother, she regularly warned my dad, loud enough for us to hear, that he was a sociopath. "No, scratch that," she'd say, probably a psychopath, in her clinical opinion. She said we were both filthy, fat, thoughtless, disturbed, and of course spoiled; the Prince and Princess, she called us, though we did more housework than any kids we knew. She said my dad shouldn't pay attention to us, or he'd risk making us even worse, even more spoiled rotten. And that thought worried him, because Carol was almost an actual, real therapist.

From the time I was six, I remember that unless we were alone, she referenced me only in the third person, as in "Nelson, I'm sorry, but she's getting fat. Her legs look thick and it's getting worse."

Or "She always looks so dirty, Nelson. She shouldn't be this dirty at the table. She's uncouth and rude and I'm going to lose my appetite."

"There was just something wrong between you and your dad. You were too close and I knew it wasn't healthy. That's why you live with your mom. You can thank me."

"She doesn't need to have your attention every single second! SHE SHOULD DO THINGS BY HERSELF!"

"There are two kinds of love. The kind of love your father has for me, and the kind he has for you. The kind he has for me is more important."

"There's a secret about you but I'm not going to tell you because you aren't ready to hear it."

I remember running this one by my mom, because I'd analyzed all the possibilities, and the only scenario that could rise to this operatic level was that I must have been adopted. My brother and I looked so much alike, we'd often tell people we were twins just to see if they'd believe us. We had the same freckled long noses and heavy eyelids and calcium spots on our front teeth. "Oh, she's just messing with you," explained my mom with a pained expression, looking away, her mouth tense. "Because she's jealous of you. Jealous of a kid. She's a very broken person."

As to what broke her, my mom said Carol had been molested by her father as a kid. At least, that's what Carol used to say when they all met, at a drug rehab center turned cult that invited middle-class nonaddicts to participate in weekly group therapy sessions. "The whole thing was they'd just yell at you and tell you what an asshole you were," Mom explained. "It was supposed to help you and be this big utopia, but those people turned out to be thieves and idiots. Carol told the group about her dad, all the awful things he did. I believe she was telling the truth, absolutely. That's why she's all screwed up. Her childhood really did a number on her. So that's all she knows, and that's all she sees."

My mom shot me a look as I bit my thumbnail. All my nails were chewed raw. I placed both hands on our yellow Formica kitchen table so I wouldn't be tempted to draw them back up. "You know I'm not a big fan of your father," she said, leaning toward me. "But this business of you and your dad being too close, it's Carol's thing. It's about *her*, not you."

―――――――――――

My dad worked until noon every Saturday, and I listened to the sounds of that house, waiting for him to come home so we could go to the movies or rent poetry records from the library.

My ears were tuned to the sound of his red Delta Battery pickup truck slowing down over the rocks in the driveway, to the soft clack of Carol's espadrilles in the kitchen, to her every move, in fact, so I could stay off her radar, watching reruns of *Gomer Pyle* and *Alice* on a small black-and-white TV with my brother. We scampered out to get food only when we heard the sliding door to the backyard open and knew Carol would be out there tending to her eggplants and tomatoes. ("Carol is an organic gardener," my dad would brag to his family. "We have a wood-chipping machine for composting. She knows how to do all that stuff. Tomatoes you buy at the store? They're inedible. You should taste the ones Carol grows.") She never visited my dad's family, but when her name came up, my aunts whispered about the machine, how it cost thousands, and how I had shown up to my grandparents' house on a Greyhound bus, without even a swimsuit. My aunts had to take me to JCPenney, where they bought me a blue one-piece with yellow trim that had a round cut-out in the back, the same exact one my cousins had, and we all had matching circular tan lines and I loved that suit, even though I knew from walking past the kitchen real slow, so I could listen to my aunts, that Carol's big wood-chipping machine had shredded and decomposed my dad's Delta Battery cash.

Carol haunted the house when she wasn't tending her tomatoes, appearing suddenly in a doorway to ask me if I knew I had left crumbs in the sink, or to tell me, "I know why you didn't rinse the dishes properly, which you never do. You're trying to poison us. It's called passive-aggressive, leaving the dish soap chemicals. I've discussed it with your father." I was barely tall enough to reach the sink, yet there was no convincing her I wasn't passive-aggressively dooming her with suds of Dawn. Better to lie low until dad got home, peeled the lid off his Dos Equis, showered, and provided a steady if spineless buffer.

As an adult, I demanded an explanation for why he'd left us with someone cruel. "I don't really remember any of that, Teresa. That was a long time ago," he'd say, changing the subject, like the whole thing was the plot of a movie he took us to on a Saturday afternoon decades earlier. I wanted to both forget and to remember, to delete the whole thing and to animate every frame of it, to make him pay and to grandly forgive the debt. She was a ghost now, dead and gone a decade before my brother died, a death I mourned not a single second. But I was still listening for the sound of her espadrilles on the carpet coming for me.

Back in the Arizona High Country, the wizened barista ambled behind a case of baked goods.

I felt for the scarecrow of a man, in his empty roadside coffee shop, so I let it ride, about the car desk and the naked photo. This is what passes for a compliment in these parts. You take what you can get.

When we spotted this little place, we imagined freshly baked blueberry muffins, but there were just a few rows of prepackaged chocolate chip cookies on display between the proprietor and us.

He wiped the glass counter once with an old rag, giving himself a beat to calibrate his own regret. We wordlessly decided that settling this guy's hash was pointless. We weren't going to shame him or give him a lecture on feminism; we were going to treat him like the little brown bird with blue-tipped wings my dad had spied earlier that morning in a low pine tree as we walked around Lynx Lake. We observed him in his natural habitat, and we let him be.

The man's hair was straight, bleached somewhere between platinum blond and professional wrestler, and he shook it briefly like he was trying to erase himself.

"Be good to your dad, now," he said. "Always be nice to your dad."

Throwing the rag over his shoulder, he turned his back to us and reached for a bottle of cherry syrup high on a shelf. "I'm going to make you something nice. Smoothies are bullshit." As he whipped up a drink, grabbing ingredients with his endless arms, he told us he hated Jane Fonda. I can't remember why, or how it came up, but I had noticed a patch sewn on his denim jacket, something that made me think he'd been to Vietnam, probably had a bad taste in his mouth about Hanoi Jane. I knew my dad had protested against that war and railed against all wars, but I knew we'd tacitly agreed on letting this ride, too.

We hadn't been to war, couldn't possibly understand, but we knew wounds.

The fleshy crater from one of my brother's spinal surgeries was too deep and wide to close, so they connected the maw of pulp from his insides with a drainage tube to a portable vacuum pump. My brother had to wheel around with that contraption on his lap, a small square machine suctioning the wound so the edges might finally come together. It made a steady whirring sound, sitting on my brother's lap like a rebuilt alternator.

That wound never did close.

He always looked unstable to me in his motorized wheelchair, which he used the last six months of his life, teetering along, his little kids riding alongside him on their bicycles when we'd roll him down a plywood ramp to the cul-de-sac outside, the younger with her training wheels clopping loudly. He winced every time his chair hit a bump or a rock. The narcotics were making him feel off-balance and weren't doing so much for the pain anyway. Because he'd had a stroke, either from the cancer or from the cancer treatment, he wore white compression socks up over his knees. The doctors said the socks would keep blood from stagnating in his lower legs, where it could form a clot, especially because his legs were no longer mobile. The tumor had eaten away at whatever nerves controlled their movement. A blood clot, they said, could cause another stroke, or part of a clot could break loose, travel through his bloodstream, and kill him within minutes. Over the socks, he wore black sandals with Velcro straps that I'd purchased at his wife's request. When the receipt for the orthopedic sandals hit my inbox, I deleted it as fast as I could. My big brother could no longer tie his own shoes.

Steroids had changed his face, distorting it, inflating the flesh around his jaw and near his ears, thickening the area under his chin, and his torso was leaning to the right, probably to prevent the wound from jostling against the chair. On one of my last visits, I spent hours trying to find him a better wheelchair, because I just knew the insurance company must have given him the cheapest one, those cheap bastards, and that was the problem. If he winced in the cu-de-sac, or nervously glanced at Laura to see if she had another pain pill while rolling across the Key Bridge, over the Potomac, it was the chair. I was a kvetch and he was a stoic; I was his sister, and I wasn't going to let him suffer because of some heartless healthcare bureaucracy's penny-squeezing algorithms.

After calling around and looking online, I realized his too tall-looking power chair with midwheel drive and a tight turning radius was actually a solid wheelchair. I would have spent my last dime on a top-of-the-line brand, I would have sold my car, my house, and my soul, as I sat working on my laptop with my notebook open, scribbling down pages of illegible notes about the relative merits of various motorized chairs, but it seemed it wasn't the chair as much as it was the dying. The dying wasn't going to be smooth. And I couldn't throw money at it.

I watched his daughter screech by him, ringing her purple bell, "Look, Daddy! Look! I'm going faster than you." She was five and spoke with more than a hint of her mother's Argentine accent.

———————

The barista handed each of us a tall plastic cup, whipped cream domed over the top. "This one's on me," he announced, handing it over. "Because you're good to your dad."

"She is," said my pops, taking his drink. "I wasn't a good father. I was a terrible father, but she's a great daughter."

Boom.

The coffee shop and everything in it turned still tableau, like we were plastic people and plastic furniture in a snow globe, except instead of snow shaking down through glitter water, there was only dust dancing in columns of high desert sunlight.

He hadn't said that to me, ever. And now he'd shared it through a desiccated High Country coffee purveyor. I glanced around at a vintage stove stocked with sugar packets and stacks of periodicals. "I hope I'm making up for it now," he added, his back turned, looking down at some earrings for sale on a black velvet display case, his volume carefully set.

The level said, *I want only you to hear this; I am an old man and I can't drink from your mug of shitty childhood memories. I can only say sorry, in this no-man's-land, with God's oldest barista, in God's country, where the tall pines know I meant well.*

And that confession, uttered somewhere outside Prescott, Arizona, was possible only because of the Arcadia Little League season that had ended exactly one year before. The words landed quietly, somewhere between a stack of yellowing copies of *High Country Hunter, Northern Arizona's Resource for Big Game Hunts* and the dusty inner hermitage where I store my secret wishes.

The man brushed his hair away from his face with his forearm. "Try it," he urged, and I was scared not to, scared he would know how much I love both smoothies and Jane Fonda.

"Oh, this is amazing," I pronounced, lifting the concoction with one hand, elbowing the door open with the other. We stepped outside, gave each other a look, joked about the man and the Buick desk, which we had to admit was an impressive piece of furniture, despite the creepy way he introduced it. The drink was somehow even sweeter than I'd expected, though I knew its main components were cherry syrup and whipped cream. It was the beverage form of one of Dad's 1950s songs. *A white sport coat and a pink carnation, I'm in a blue, blue mood.*

We returned to the car and gave the drinks to the boys, then seven and ten years old, nestled into the back seat with blankets and pillows. Andrew, the younger, a shirtless waif of a thing, took a long sip and handed it back. "I don't want to be rude, but I don't like it." We headed back onto the highway, taking I-17 South through the mountains.

Andrew looked out the window and said, "The trees are like waterfalls of trees down the hills," a phrase my dad repeated for months after that, because his grandson was a genius, his lyrical observations of the natural world somewhere between Henry David Thoreau and Leonard Goddamn Cohen. I figured the kid had just lucked into a decent string of words, but I let my dad have it. "*Nachas*," he would say, using a Yiddish word that has no perfect English translation but essentially describes an explosion of pride or gratification often used in regard to children. "They are *nachas* machines, these two!"

It had been about a two-mile walk around Lynx Lake that morning. Dad wore his beige hiking shirt and the same Nike sneakers he'd worn in one version or another for decades. He exhaled with every few steps around the lake, pursing his lips to push out staccato breaths.

"Did you see all the mansions when we drove by the golf course out here? And these people have boats. *Boats.*"

We traversed the lake's curves, shaded by a cool forest of ponderosa pines. "Boats," he repeated, disgusted. My husband, Daniel, and I had theorized that most of my dad's disdain for the very wealthy came from a good-hearted sense that it just wasn't fair to "screw the poor," as he'd put it. But some of his egalitarian ardor was just plain jealousy, and embarrassment that he'd never learned how to play the game.

Back when computers were a new thing, he had found some local programmer and paid him to painstakingly log photos of alternators, generators, and starters for a new software program he conceived to help mechanics visualize parts. It was going to make us all rich. But that same programmer my dad had found by placing a classified ad in the *Santa Rosa Press Democrat* was hired by a company in Silicon Valley to do the very same thing, and that was that. His savings were gone and there were whispers about taking a line of credit on his house.

"Carol is going to make big bucks once she gets her therapy license," my dad had boasted. "She's really good. She can take one look at you and tell you exactly why you're crazy. She'll make at least fifty dollars an hour. I'm paying for the classes, but she's going to pay me back, and then some!" On the day of her licensing exam, she got as far as the parking lot but never left the car.

Later, after Carol died, he sold the triple-mortgaged house and bought a plot of land in the woods of Northern California. "Hundreds of acres of forest will be right in my own backyard." He beamed. He fell too in love with the square of earth, which he'd purchased the very day he'd first driven by it, to risk having it evaluated, dreamily removing himself from a world of land clearances, utilities, permits, and drainage. "I paid a hundred grand for it. I won't take a penny less than 75K," we'd overheard him sternly tell his only prospective buyer before the call dropped.

The art of his deals looked like the smeared handprints of a jittery child, only the paint wasn't washable and the thumbprints somehow ended up on the curtains and the bedspread.

Dad then sank what cash he could raise into yet another property. He asked me to cosign on that loan, and I did. Predictably, the bank foreclosed after six months of him sending in "most" of the mortgage payment.

"What did you think was going to happen, Dad?" I yelled into the phone, walking around and around a track at the park, pushing Nate, then a few months old, in his stroller. I turned up the white noise coming out of a battery-powered sheep and tucked the plush toy into the crook of my infant's neck. "What, did you think the bank was going to be like, *Sure, this guy seems like he's trying. Let's not sweat the details*? It's a bank, Dad. They're in the business of sweating details. YOU JUST PUT YOUR FUCKING HEAD IN THE SAND AND NOW I'M SCREWED. WHY?"

"Stop yelling at me. I don't know. I sent them almost all the money every month. That's all I had. It's done now and I can't undo it, so what do you want me to say?"

"Dad, you're always going on and on about the 'unexamined life' not being worth living, and yet nobody examines their life less than you. You keep losing everything and now you dragged me down with you. I have a baby to think about and bad credit for the next seven years because *you were an idiot*. I couldn't finance a sandwich at this point, even though I paid every student loan bill on time. You really messed things up for me," I sobbed, sleep-deprived. "And the thing that really gets me is that you're the parent. You should be looking out for *me*, not the other way around."

"I can't help it. I'm a Strasser," he said with resignation. His father had been a vacuum cleaner salesman before starting some kind of swap meet that went bust.

"We went from the penthouse to the shithouse. We lived a mile south of Ventura, toward Mulholland Drive, in the mountains. We had a pool and a new Cadillac—a Jew canoe. You can only say that if you're Jewish, so I get a pass. Then we moved to Van Nuys. It was a long way down into the armpit of the Valley," my dad moaned. "I had to change schools. My dad was so depressed, he didn't get out of bed for months."

"Uh-huh. What does this have to do with anything?"

"I'm just doing what he did. We aren't good with money."

"Really? The blame-your-parents thing? BOO-HOO. You're a grown-up and they're both dead and gone, so come up with something better." I lashed out, but maybe he was right.

Whether or not it was in the blood or a product of patterning, "he has to zero himself out," as Daniel framed it. My dad chased the black into the red as consciously as a brainless pea plant turns toward the light. The accountancy made sense when he was broke; he was nothing and he should have nothing. Losing it all balanced his books. Daniel had been right about my dad's magnetic pull in the direction of financial ruin, a fact he pointed out lovingly but also too late. I had cosigned on the loan just before I met Daniel, when there was nobody to talk me out of being my father's daughter.

"Well, Dad, I guess I'm also a Strasser. I had to be a big shot, swoop in to save you, not pay too much attention to the fine print. Cosigning is the same thing as signing."

Neither of us was any good at math; that had always been Morgan's realm. We had tumbled into a world of numbers we couldn't wrestle down, irregular payments, accrued interest, late fees, deeds, and debts. I didn't know who owed what. I just wanted to scream at my dad from a bottomless well of volcanic sorrow and little-kid rage, the muck now burbling up through this fissure. I had stopped talking to my dad a few times, but This Was *It*. Okay, maybe there would be one or two rambling emails about his refusal to be an adult, his failure to warn or protect me from this mess, a mess I knew in my heart didn't really matter. The house, my credit. The *real* mess began even before my conscious memories; it was the swamp underneath, thick with evil-stepmother scar tissue and the simple fact that I was a go-back, a return. No matter how good-natured I'd tried to act about it, and no matter how, in fact, lots of fathers ditch their kids outright and he never did, the truth remained. Like that patch of woods with craggy angles and thickets of stumpy trees, there just didn't seem to be a way to live there. He'd fought for me and he'd won full custody in California's epic *Strasser v. Strasser* case, but after only a few months he'd given me back to my mom. It never became official, because it was too humiliating to formalize and probably way too expensive. The mess was dad reciting poetry along with vinyl records from the library as we sat on the couch enthralled, likely surrounded by minuscule flecks of broken glass from one of Carol's titanic lamp-throwing shit fits. The mess was something you wanted to get rid of in what my dad used to call a "fire sale," and the debt, incalculable.

I was done with my dad. Then my brother got sick for the second and last time.

||||||||||||||||||||||||||||

CHAPTER TWO

The Draft

"Each person's grief is as unique as their fingerprint.
But what everyone has in common is that
no matter how they grieve, they share a need
for their grief to be witnessed."

—DAVID KESSLER,
FINDING MEANING: THE SIXTH STAGE OF GRIEF

"Come here, kid," barks the gruff scout sent from official Little
League headquarters to rank about 120 players on a scale of 1 to 5,
assessing their speed, hitting, catching, and throwing, with individual numerical values in all categories.

Nate—the second-tallest kid in his third-grade class—looks
like he needs to grow into his wide, flat platypus feet. He has just
stretched his legs, twice as thick as his rangy arms, to catch a high
throw at first while keeping his left cleat on the bag. That was the
last of the drills. The man jots something down on his clipboard
before bending down from his waist, placing a beefy hand on top
of Nate's baseball hat, and mumbling, with a chuckle, "Looks like
you're the Chosen One."

It's hard to know what Nate registers, because he's a serious kid,
and sparse when it comes to chitchat. All three pitches he'd thrown
to the Little League volunteer mom—she'd played catcher at Arizona State University—were strikes, right down the middle. During the hitting portion of the tryout, his stance looked solid, elbows

up, front foot dancing right on time, as the ball left the pitching machine set up on the mound. When it came time to shag a fly ball, shot from that same ancient pitching machine into the sky and toward center field, his attempt passed what my husband called the "eyeball test," though he didn't catch it.

Daniel is watching the tryouts carefully. For the first time in his Little League coaching career, he will be responsible for drafting his own team. Before this season, the league assigned you players and you did the best with what you got, daisy-pickers or studs.

HERE'S HOW IT WORKS AT ARCADIA LITTLE LEAGUE:

Coed T-ball (ages 4–5): all kids bat every inning off a tee, no outs are recorded, no score is kept, defensive coaching strategy consists of screaming, "SAME TEAM!" when two infielders are wrestling over a ball in the dirt

Baseball Farm A (age 6): coaches pitch

Baseball Farm AA (age 7): players bat off a pitching machine

Baseball Farm AAA (age 8): kids pitch 1–2 innings before the pitching machine is rolled onto the mound, outs are recorded, score is kept, shit is getting real

Minors (ages 9–10): kids pitch all six innings, players are officially evaluated and ranked, coaches draft teams, and a postseason, single-elimination tournament determines a champion

Majors (ages 11–12): exactly like the Minors, but with more puberty

The Minors is the dividing line in Little League. This is basically how baseball is going to look from here on out.

Kids are going to remember this season. It's going to leave cleat marks in the soft dirt of their little-boy souls. And Daniel knows it. He and his buddies from the old neighborhood, a suburb outside Philadelphia, have to live with their second-place finish in the finals of the Roychester Little League championship. "My pitching was solidly above average," he once explained to me, his version of boasting. "But our ace went on vacation the weekend of the finals. Our bullpen was decimated. It still stings," he said, joking and not joking.

Daniel was still pitching after Little League and into high school before he tore all the ligaments in his ankle tripping over a sprinkler during practice. The ankle recovered, but by senior year of high school—when he weighed 155 pounds at a height of almost six foot four—his playing time was limited.

By the time I met him on a Friday night in West Hollywood, we were both thirty-six. He'd filled out. I was dazzled, not because he was a professional athlete (or even a key member of the second-place Roychester Royals), or the lead singer of a band, or a stand-up comedian, but because *he had dental insurance*. Everyone I knew in Hollywood was there to be something special, but this guy was steady and unassuming. He was happy to be a background player—with healthy gums. "He's tall and he has dental insurance," I told my friends breathlessly at brunch the next day. "I have no idea what he does. Something about long-term leasing contracts for software. It's so dull it could be a cover. He's probably a hit man for the CIA." But he wasn't, and that's what made him so exotic to me. I came from chaos. He came from suburbs. He had a normcore sex appeal that only a Gen X latchkey kid raised on convenience store burritos could understand.

Daniel was by no means a titan of industry, but he carried no debt, not so much as an overdue parking ticket. Before our first date, he texted to let me know he'd be five minutes late. He hasn't been late for anything since. So I married him, and now I root for the Philadelphia Phillies. And my husband is the Little League coach with a laptop, a backup charger, and a *Moneyball* mindset.

Attentive scouting, careful analysis, and the identification of undervalued players will matter. And that's why Daniel doesn't wholly trust the assessments of this official league scout, not as much as he trusts his own meticulous data collection and organization.

Spreadsheets are his love language.

When I first found out my brother was terminal, I became overwhelmed trying to find a grief counselor.

"I need a therapist to deal with the frustration of finding a therapist," I told Daniel, putting my hand over my face.

"Give me everything you have," he said. I turned over my notes, scribbles on the back of a school flyer.

The next day, Daniel handed me the "Grief Counselor Options Spreadsheet." Columns included: Contact Information, Proximity to Home (in terms of mileage and average drive time), Ratings, Specialties, Training, and Cost. Swirling sadness was gathered up and harnessed, transformed into a grid I could hold in my hand. To his mind, you could cry about swirling sadness when you got there, but before that, you'd need to know where you were going. It's the best love letter I've ever received.

So no surprise Daniel was paying attention to every kid, every drill, and that's why it turned out to be a blessing that Gavin Porter[*] went to urgent care before the official league scout could give him a ranking.

---

[*] Descriptions of games are based on my best recollections and my husband's detailed notes. All the Little Leaguers (and coaches) in this story are based on real people, both from this season and from previous seasons, but names have been changed and identifying details have been adjusted to respect the privacy of people who had no idea some coach's wife was going to write about them later.

During the pop-fly drill, Gavin had managed to get under the ball, with his compact body and athlete's devotion. But when he reached up to catch it, the ball was a dive-bombing falcon, wings tucked, an apex predator swooping toward his forehead, where it left an imprint of the baseball's stitches and a swelling knot.

Urgent care declared the kid concussion-negative.

He was fine, but he would have to finish his tryout in the parking lot of the Camelback Christian Church the night of the draft, after the league had already handed out copies of their rankings. And nobody pays attention to parking-lot tryouts, except the one guy with his own spreadsheet, a marvel evolving in real time.

After tryouts, my dad rides his bike over from the Riviera Mobile-home Park for adults fifty-five and older. He lives just a few miles away from us, in a single-wide he bought for two thousand dollars cash after my brother died. He got the money by selling the pickup truck he drove to Phoenix, taking the first cash offer in response to his Craigslist post.

I hear him open the side gate, wedge his bicycle in between the deck chairs on our back patio, and let himself in with the key around his neck. "Hi, guys," he calls out, announcing himself, leaving his cycling shoes outside, entering in sock feet. "I was in the neighborhood. I had to pick up a part for my tire pump from the Bike Barn, and it's just around the corner."

I know he just wonders how the tryout went.

He scurries from the pantry to the kitchen table with a box of Snyder's hard pretzels and one of the nonalcoholic beers I stock for him. "Don't get the expensive kind," he says, holding up the beer. "I don't need the Beck's. Just get the cheaper kind, domestic. These are too much money. I just like a little something fizzy with my nosh."

Andrew sits on his grandpa's lap for a minute, gnaws on a pretzel, then runs out back to practice taking hacks with a giant red plastic bat, attempting to hit a Wiffle ball off a blue Little Tikes tee. I hear Daniel open the window and remind him, "Don't use the fat bat. You can use the yellow one; I've seen you do it." Andrew has been busted and he knows it, but he wants to see if he can crush the ball, send it soaring over our roof like his big brother does. The yellow bat is skinny, and that means the unsatisfying and frustrating toil of executing a perfectly level swing.

Daniel has one eye on Andrew as the scrawny child slowly and deliberately arranges himself. "Get your hands up toward your back shoulder. More. Keep that left elbow in tight, close to your body when you swing. Swing all the way through and keep your head on it," he says through the window screen, observing long enough for Andrew to hit a line drive, *whoosh*. The plastic orb nails the tree swing with a satisfying *clack*.

"Dad, the Beck's is only a few cents more a bottle. You said the domestic was swill. Life is too short for swill, so just enjoy it," I say, but I know he can't, because in his mind the price differential is just too grand, and this imported beer is a luxury he doesn't need or deserve, and one day I might need that eighty-seven cents. He works the pretzel around to the side of his mouth where all the teeth are intact and bites down hard, whittling it down into manageable fragments.

"What does it mean when someone says 'the Chosen One'? What is that? Is that good?" Nate asks his grandpa.

Grandpa answers, "The Chosen One. I think that's something from the Bible."

He sips his too fancy beer. "And they call the Jews the Chosen People. My cousin Steve used to joke that God chose the Jews. He chose them for slavery. Then he chose them for the Holocaust. Choose someone else, God!" Careful the pretzel has been cleared from the side of his mouth, he laughs, a big, loud series of open sounds, the laugh of a child who has just waited patiently for you to select the spring-loaded slice of gum in the novelty pack, the one that snaps right back into the package.

"And it's a book written by Chaim Potok," he adds.

"He's Jewish," I chime in.

"Yup, Jewish," he agrees. (I'm careful to include this information about any person of note when I'm talking to my kids, trying to make up for marrying a Catholic and not sending them to Hebrew school.) My dad was not a religious man, but he also never failed to mention that Hall of Fame pitcher Sandy Koufax was one of us, maybe the best one of us ever.

"Koufax threw hundred-mile-an-hour fastballs," the old man had told my boys before the season began. "His heater was *blistering*." Grandpa's voice got breathy, like he was telling a ghost story. "And Koufax threw a curveball so . . . *nasty* . . . that Mickey Mantle struck out looking! This is *Mickey Mantle* we're talking about, greatest switch-hitter in baseball history. You know what the Mick does? He turns to his catcher and says—excuse my French—'How the fuck is anybody supposed to hit that shit?' and he walks back to the dugout."

"How the fuck?" repeated Andrew, giggling.

Nate warned, "Don't say the f-word outside the house."

"Seriously, don't," I added. "Pretend like we're fucking classy. Excuse my French."

As an adult, my dad has never belonged to a synagogue other than the temple of retired Jewish mechanics who sing along to Leonard Cohen. Still, the fact that Koufax famously sat out game one of the 1965 World Series because it fell on Yom Kippur made even the most secular Jew bow his head. It's the holiest day of the year in Judaism, the Day of Atonement. You're supposed to spend it in prayer, repenting the sins you committed in the past year and asking forgiveness of God and anyone else you screwed over. You reflect on your past screwups to prevent future screwups. Repentance has the divine power of a Koufax curveball.

By the way, on Yom Kippur, you don't just seek forgiveness; you offer it, too.

"What if you try to forgive someone but you just can't?" I once asked a rabbi, thinking of Carol.

"You try again," said the rabbi.

My mind goes back to the novel *The Chosen*, which, it occurs to me, opens with a baseball scene, though I don't remember much else about it. "Dad, isn't there a baseball game in that book where one kid gets hit in the eye?"

"Right," Dad says, looking off, taking another big, expensive sip. "The kid is Orthodox, but he's really good at baseball. Who was that actor?"

"Robby Benson?"

"Robby Benson! What ever happened to that guy?"

"He's directing," I say, brushing crumbs from the old man's sleeve.

"Why did you ask about the Chosen One, Natey?" Dad inquires.

Nate does the thing where he leans back in his chair, leans it right to the point where he isn't sure he can maintain the fulcrum.

"The baseball guy said that. At the tryout. The scout guy."

"Well, in that context, it means you're good at something. It's a compliment," Grandpa explains.

"Okay," Nate says, releasing the chair and drifting away to trade yellow bat swings with his brother in the yard.

My dad leans forward. "ARE YOU KIDDING ME? The scout

called Nate the Chosen One? Daniel, did you hear the scout say that?"

Daniel turns off the garbage disposal and nods. "That's what the guy said."

My dad looks at me, leans in closer, and repeats the words again, an incantation over a nonalcoholic beer. "The Chosen One," he whispers.

The Chosen One, my dad and I would text each other, all that week.

———————

In a drab community meeting room at the Camelback Christian Church, sixteen managers are drafting teams. The room is subdivided with a partition, and there are folding card tables covered with pizza boxes, their lids flipped open, sending the smell of pepperoni into the air to compete with the stale scent of beige church carpet.

"Let's not turn this into a four-hour thing," grouses Calvin Palowski, the long-suffering commissioner of the Arcadia Little League.

"Guys, if it's your turn, just be ready. Do not be the guy who tries to draft the player that's already been picked, okay? If you do that, you get a warning, and the next time you just get the next best available pick and we move on."

In parallel with the player draft is the jersey draft, going in reverse order on the other side of the partition. Because the Arizona Diamondbacks donated the uniforms, every team is the Diamondbacks, with jerseys of different patterns and hues. Coach Damon Bennett is gumming up the jersey draft, taking forever, picking up jerseys, holding them far away from his body, then close to his eyes. "Can someone help me?" he begs. "I'm color-blind," he tells Daniel. "My wife is going to kill me if I end up with something ugly."

Daniel advises him to avoid the pea green, which he does, but in the commotion, poor Bennett ends up with a bag of neon yellow-green jerseys, a draft choice that will get his balls busted all season. Daniel falls in love with the purple pin-striped jerseys, a hint of Yankee without all the baggage, somewhere between the snooze of flat gray and the abysmal accident of Bennett and his chartreuse.

Before he left for the draft, Daniel explained his strategy to me: "Not just the early rounds matter in a draft. Mistakes are made at the bottom, in the final rounds. If a kid has 1.5s across the board, but a 2 in speed, maybe that kids gets on first base taking a walk and then makes it to second on a passed ball. That kid isn't going to be a black hole in your lineup. There's hope."

Each coach automatically gets his own son on his team, so, for his first-round pick, Daniel takes Leo, one of the oldest players, a fact that edges out others with a similar ranking. Maturity is a factor in his calculations.

The draft goes on until it's time for Daniel's second-round selection, and there's no hesitation and no paper shuffling: "GAVIN PORTER," he bellows. All the other coaches were shooting the shit during his parking-lot tryout while Daniel noticed Gavin had a cannon for an arm and a sweet, percussive swing. Forget the fact that his forehead was still swollen because he caught a fly ball with it.

Daniel calls me from the car on the way home, jubilant. "I was the only person with my laptop. Everyone else just had a printout from the league, or NOTHING. Some of the coaches had NOTHING," he tells me, aghast.

He's as fired up as I have ever heard him, at least since the Phillies made it to the World Series.

"I don't want to congratulate myself too much, but Gavin was the steal of the century. No way he's a second-rounder. I almost,

almost, waited until the third round, but I didn't want to get greedy. I got Easton Cage in the final round. So what if his glove is weak? When he hits the ball, he hits it hard."

"And he has a good baseball name."

"He has a *great* baseball name," Daniel says. "Every single Purple Pinstripe is capable of making a play."

"Nice. I knew you'd *Moneyball* it." I could feel my face smiling hard.

"Maybe people judge me for putting too much time into this, but I don't care. I think I just *won* this draft."

———————

My mom died in the palliative care wing of UCSF. (She didn't trust the medical care in her local hospital since they'd issued her husband Ron's death certificate declaring him to be a Caucasian man who died of pneumonia, when in fact he was a Black man who died of kidney failure.) As she lay with her hair splayed out on the bleached-white pillowcase, her last words were about my husband. "Who is that man? Name of that man?" she asked me in the final morphine tunnel headed God knows where. I proffered the names of my dad, my long-dead stepfather, her dad, her brother. She shook her head. I was too scared to include my brother. Morgan was a name I couldn't say in that room, with the big window looking out on Parnassus Avenue, the chocolate See's lollipop I had bought in the first-floor gift shop waiting, stick up, in a white foam cup on her tray. What if she'd forgotten he'd died? This was no time to remind her. Even the hard-science infectious disease specialists admitted that there was a good chance she was dying of a broken heart instead of C. diff, a bacterium common in healthcare settings. At first there was a kidney problem, and then her bladder swelled and stopped working; nobody knew why. Within weeks, she had surgery, and the opening in her abdomen left the door open to the germ, and she was in no condition to fight it. I had never been good at talking to my mom, and I didn't want to bobble this last interface by reminding her of the son she'd lost twice in one lifetime. She raised one arm, the skin fragile and thin. "Tall," she said, her eyes pleading with me to please guess the clue in this game of deathbed charades.

"Daniel?" I asked, handing over the lollipop that had been waiting in the cup.

"Lucky," she said, pointing to me. And that's how my mother got the last word, literally.

I knew when she said I was lucky it wasn't a compliment; it was a reminder and a warning: *I know you. Don't fly off the handle and pick fights and say nasty things you can't take back, and don't take him for granted or not notice when you hurt his feelings, because he won't complain about it. Be careful throwing fits and slamming doors. Keep your shit together, because I'm leaving you here with someone good and patient and decent, and maybe I'm not the most maternal, but I am inches from nothingness, where maybe I'll see my dead child and maybe I won't, and I know what I'm talking about.*

After she died, I was the only one left to clean out her condo.

In her nightstand, I found a manila envelope. Inside was a twenty-five-page "Petition for Writ of Mandate," with a typed cover letter on yellowing stationery from Berman, Hanover & Schneider, Inc.

I was three and my brother was five when my parents fought over us on a clear, cool day at Los Angeles County Superior Court, where my father won full custody.

He remembers her sobbing on a bench in the hallway of the courthouse. He had to walk right by her, weeping in a flowy dress and knee-high cowhide boots. She was twenty-nine years old, an underachieving former UCLA math genius turned hippie. She had a decent government job. She had no criminal history. And yet she'd just lost all parental rights.

She appealed the court's decision and lost again, despite the efforts of Harvey A. Schneider.

My dad, realizing he had overplayed his hand and was in over his head, gave me back to my mother a few months later. His new girlfriend, Carol, seemed to have all the answers. She said the father should keep the boy. The mother should take the girl. That was our family's entire draft.

I don't remember much about living with my dad, just the way his work boots were always outside his bedroom door, and the deep attachment I had to our babysitter, Ynez, who let me sit in her lap for hours, chewing the chicken off a wing she'd cooked. But my mom had already become unfamiliar, and I was nervous around her.

She didn't use a singsong voice like Ynez. And she didn't hug. I was reassured on my first night in San Francisco only after my mom handed me a mug full of hot chocolate with a few miniature marshmallows floating on top. That was now home. I'd have to focus on the sweet parts, even though all the people who had populated my world were gone.

So that's how I lost my brother for the first time. And that's how I came to grow up as an only child, with a full biological sibling in another city I saw once every month or two, and for a week in summer, and sometimes on holidays.

According to the writ in my mom's nightstand, the judge said she had "placed her career ahead of her children" by leaving them with their father for six months to attend job training out of state. Also, my mom's new job would be in Chicago, and "the weather in Chicago is less preferable to the weather in Los Angeles." My mom had told me that the judge had a brother who died of pneumonia, which he caught during a particularly deadly Chicago winter.

That judge was "a sexist, bullshit motherfucker," according to my mom. If she ever forgave him, she sure kept the evidence of his bullshit close.

After those pages failed to persuade the judge, she moved to San Francisco, because Chicago was now too far away from her kids. She couldn't take us with her, as she had planned. Instead of starting in a fancy management position with the federal government's Social Security office in Illinois, she'd be working at the Disability Quality Branch on Van Ness Avenue in San Francisco, reviewing disability applications, making sure examiners followed correct policies and procedures. To her, it was repetitive and dull, but at least nobody in the Bay Area knew she had lost her kids. The federal government was quick to find her the gig, because even though she lacked ambition—her sole professional goal was to earn enough to support two kids as a single mom, working as few hours as possible—she was valuable. She had a mathematician's mind, catching mistakes in case files and breezing through her work.

San Francisco was also far from her European immigrant parents, who barely spoke English but knew enough to be humiliated by what had happened in court. The city was far from all the bourgeois marrieds suffocating in cookie-cutter houses in the San Fernando Valley. In San Francisco, all her new friends were either divorced like she was or had moved there to be close to the Castro district, the world's hilliest and most beautiful gay mecca.

Having custody of one of her kids was better than having neither one; it was less embarrassing. But, in practice, she wasn't cut out for motherhood. Doing kid stuff was a drag. She spent as little time as possible on parenting; she never took me to a children's movie, or played on the floor with me, or colored, or drove me anywhere. I could tag along with her, but she never went where she didn't want to go. Later, she paid for ballet lessons and a bus pass, and she figured that was good enough. By fourth grade, I took the bus to school, took another bus to ballet after school, and then took the streetcar home. When the Academy of Ballet let out, all the girls bounded down the stairs to a row of cars waiting in the dark, hazards on, eagerly opening passenger doors for daughters in leotards and buns. I never looked into those cars; I just soldiered past them four days a week, year after year, toward the island in the middle of the intersection of Church and Market, where I waited for the J Church in the sharp wind, with my backpack and my ballet bag. The streetlights created a safe patch of light there. Men gathered in front of the liquor store on Market Street, where if I had a dime I'd buy a pack of Now and Later candies, which were dense and chewy and would keep me company until the streetcar arrived, and sometimes the whole way home. My mom didn't believe in inconveniencing herself to bend to the needs of a child any more than she had to, not for a second, even though she loved me. She lit up when I won a poetry contest or the spelling bee, but she didn't give rides, or let me sit on her lap, or braid my hair, or worry much about all the time I spent alone, or ask me about my day, who was mean and who was nice or what I'd learned. I think I still want those things from my dead mom. But back then I didn't know I could want those things. I just did what I had to do to make it home to the place my mom had bought for us on a steep hill near a fire station.

She'd borrowed money from her parents, who owned a liquor store in Los Angeles, for a down payment on our small flat.

Like lots of San Francisco apartments, ours was in a building with a brick stoop on the sidewalk. At the top of the staircase to our flat was a hand crank that opened the front door, an oddity of old Victorian buildings. My mom would stand on the landing above the tall flight of stairs and pull the rusty lever.

"There's a Black man up here. And I'm not wearing any pants," she'd announce casually, peering down the staircase, all long legs and jet-black hair. She wanted to make sure everyone understood what the large Black man was doing in our house, that he lived there, that he wasn't some kind of intruder, that he was her man, and she also wanted to let you know she wouldn't be bothering with the establishment's requirement to wear pants, not in her own home, anyway. Nothing was as liberating as waltzing through her flat in a long V-neck T-shirt and full-coverage cotton panties.

The Black man was her boyfriend, who later became my stepfather. I loved Ron as much as I hated Carol, though he didn't move in with us until just before I started high school.

One day he came over to take the vacuum cleaner she no longer needed; she'd gotten a new one. He was working at the same federal government office as my mom, the first day job he'd ever had after a lifetime as a professional trumpet player.

He came over to pick up the vacuum cleaner and then he lingered, a sweet, round man with a dark beard across his wide cheeks, his clothes immaculate and pressed.

After that, he invited her out to see live music, and she came home giddy, dancing with me around the living room. A few dates later, she realized he had hardwood floors and didn't need a vacuum cleaner. "He went to all that trouble just to ask me out," she bragged, beaming. Six months later, he moved in with us. He brought a tiny rag doll of a tabby kitten named Gizmo, and a whole bunch of music, not just the horn section from his band, which rehearsed in our living room a couple of times a week, but also a stack of record albums, mostly by the Motown groups with whom he had played years earlier. There were also records by people I'd never heard of, like Cissy Houston, George Benson, and Keith Sweat. His stack joined my mom's records, Carole King and Cat Stevens leaning up against the Four Tops, Ashford & Simpson.

Where my mother was wound tight, Ron was patient. He taught me how to drive without ever once raising his voice. He never intruded when it came to parenting, and he wasn't a big talker in general. He cooked for us on Sunday mornings, frying bacon and pulling biscuits from the oven during commercial breaks from football games or the Westerns he always watched. If he ever screamed, it was only because the Oakland Raiders were losing. He was a warm breeze, like an Isley Brothers tune from one of his old records, blowing through our house along with the smell of biscuits, Gizmo asleep in a patch of sunlight on the sofa. When I was upset about something, he made a huge pot of chicken and dumplings, stirring it for hours in a big steel pot. He didn't try to make anything better with words, but I understood what he meant, standing over the stove to make my favorite food. The balls of dense dough floating in broth, all the time it took to slice the carrots and celery, an adult burning all these calories just for me.

My mom had left me to raise myself, which was fine until I got older, and for reasons I don't understand even now, she changed. She'd fly into hysterics if I forgot to call her from a friend's house or let her know just where I was. *Now you're worried about me?* I thought, confused by the turnabout. *The time to worry about me was when I was in ponytails, waiting for a city streetcar in a rainstorm past dark, or clocking the creeps at a Greyhound station stop in San Luis Obispo. Let's not pretend that we are this family, that you are this mom. Normal. You didn't care about me when doing so meant tedium or sacrifice, and now I can't be bothered to check in with you as to my whereabouts. You already picked a lane. You wanted me to be a little adult and I did that. So leave me the fuck alone.* She was always apoplectic when I broke one of her ceramic garage-sale collectible plates, or if I lost a sweater or a book or anything else. Those things were household felonies, and she'd be cold to me for days. I know now that kids break things and kids lose things. Even kids who feel okay about the amount of mothering they get forget to call home. I kept stacks of journals in junior high, page after page, mostly about how my mom was a bitch because she wouldn't let me hang out with the boy I met at Fisherman's Wharf who lived in a group home or someone's big sister she thought was bad news, or because she screamed at me over how worried I made her when I forgot to call.

Once, when Nate was two years old, my mom came to visit and I took her to our neighborhood playground. He played in the sand, grumpy and runny-nosed, trying to steal some other kid's pail because I forgot to bring one. Nearby, a mom was twirling her son in the air, holding him under his armpits, spinning faster and faster. They both had long brown hair, flying outward. The mom wore flouncy white pants, bare feet, and a euphoric grin. She sang out, "Faster! Faster! Let's go faster!" as the little long-haired boy let out a series of wild giggles.

"See that lady?" My mom looked toward the spinning, singing, flouncy-pants woman. "She's a natural. *We aren't naturals.*" I said nothing. Because I knew my mom to be the smartest person I'd ever met, I believed her. I wanted to be mad at her for lumping us together, two moms who didn't know how to invent spinning games or make kids chortle or remember the sand toys.

But I figured out how to mom. She never did.

There was also the matter of her delicate moods. She was probably just not wired to be all that happy, even *before* ending up a single mom who just wasn't a *natural*.

And things were always worse after she broke up with one of her boyfriends.

When the self-published, turtleneck-wearing, mustachioed poet from Berkeley called things off, she stayed in bed for a week and didn't buy groceries. There was another loser boyfriend named Fish who played "rocket ship" with our cat, flinging it off a beanbag chair. And there was a squat lawyer guy with thick glasses who took us to a fancy hotel brunch downtown. I recall mint jelly, which I'd never seen before, and the man giving me an Ernie doll, in blue pants and a striped shirt. I was way too old and sophisticated for a *Sesame Street* doll, and I rolled my eyes and laughed at the doll when I opened it. Mom made me wait outside for the rest of the meal. She stonewalled me for weeks after that, and soon the lawyer was gone. There was Malcolm, who painted in an artist's loft by the water but slept in a white van. I still have a photo of my mom in a bikini top and denim shorts, one hand leaning on that van, grinning in the wind. And that's where Malcolm ended up, somewhere in the wind. I'd been at the loft: paints and easels and canvases, creaky narrow metal staircases, rusty nails and other tetanus hazards, commune dropouts and chronic burnouts. My mom was smitten with Malcolm and his whole scene, but I think even he could see it was no place for a kid.

Ron stepped into the tension and loneliness that was our household—just my mom and me—and he transformed it. He brought the Earth to our Wind and Fire.

My brother moved in with us just after Ron did. So our unusual family situation became even harder to explain.

The timeline went like this: My mom left my dad because marriage was boring and conventional and my dad was tuned out. She relocated to Chicago for six months to train for a better job, to make enough money to be a single mom. She planned to send for us and had already found an apartment. But her plan was thwarted by a sexist, bullshit, motherfucking judge who took her kids. She abandoned her Chicago plan and moved to San Francisco, to be closer to the kids she lost. But her clueless ex-husband couldn't raise the two kids, and he gave me back six months later. For almost a decade, it went like that, my brother and me growing up in separate cities. By junior high, my brother was getting into trouble: bad grades, fights at school. He was moody and quiet and had no friends. So my dad gave *him* back, years after he'd first given me back. But by that time, Morgan was a teenager, and most of the time he just went into his room and shut the door. It was too late for us to be siblings like I'd always wanted us to be, but I was still relieved when he showed up. I was relieved because my mom got him into a special private school, and found him a child psychologist in Berkeley, and drove him over the bridge twice a week, and things started to get better. My dad came to visit once a month. He'd linger until we were almost late to the movies because even my dad loved hanging out with Ron, talking about the Raiders or asking about his days touring as a trumpet player.

Ron didn't tell my dad or us the bad things; he told those only to my mom. "Sometimes," she once revealed to me in a hushed voice, "Ron would get pulled over by police, driving to a gig with his bandmates, and the police would make him play his trumpet. They made him play right there on the side of the road, to prove it was his instrument, to prove he didn't steal it." Whatever he'd gone through, he wasn't about to get rattled by a screwed-up teenager and his needy, goody-goody little sister.

Las Vegas was a logical move after they retired. Even when his "lip" for blowing his horn wasn't what it used to be, Ron could still sip a Crown Royal and sit in with casino bar bands all over town. My mom was in her element, too. "I just get on a floatie at the pool and eat a quarter of a pot brownie and float around. What's better?"

Vegas had just as many characters as the Bay Area, only you could get a deep tan while you floated in and among them. "I have this friend from the dog park, and she's a stripper. Her dog is named Velvet. Isn't that a hoot?" Mom asked me on the phone from her floatie.

"That is a hoot," I responded. "And it beats yelling 'Hey, G-String, fetch!'"

"Oh, *you*."

They had the town wired. "We know where you can get ninety-nine-cent shrimp cocktail on Tuesday nights and free hot dogs on Sundays. And my friend from the pool is married to a pit boss. He gets us free drinks anytime," she told me. The worst people were boring people, and the pay-by-the-month joint where they stayed when they first moved to Vegas didn't feature many. "Did I tell you about the Elvis impersonator I met at the pool? Ron and I like to go see his show at the Tropicana. They serve these mudslide drinks, you know, chocolate and booze, and Ron always gets me one in a big, fancy tourist cup."

"Don't let that get good to you," Ron would always joke about the mudslide, because he knew she was a lightweight. When she had just enough to get tipsy, she'd hand over the big tourist cup to Ron and then sit right up next to him, tilt her head on his shoulder. And at some point he'd run all the way out to the car in some giant parking garage to fetch her sweater, because it always got cold in casinos, and because she always forgot it. But even in Vegas, there were things she didn't forget, never could and never would. The court had taken her kids from her. If it wasn't on her mind in casino lounges and floating buzzed around the pool, the evidence of how it went down was never far from her, not ever.

That envelope containing my mother's custody appeal survived four moves in Las Vegas, Ron's death from kidney failure, and the birth of her first grandchild, Nate, followed by a celebration to which she wasn't invited. I was pissed off at her for one reason or another, though Daniel forged a truce by the day of the baby's circumcision. Those pages survived my brother's first bout with cancer, his death seven years later, and my mother's swift turn from hearty, Schnauzer-walking, bridge-playing, casino-buffet connoisseur to another cold stiff in the morgue.

It was an heirloom she never showed me, but left for me to find. A grudge handed down. Proof that we'd been taken, not given away. I never doubted her story, but something about seeing it, typed out exactly how she'd explained it, preserved and pristine, made me realize it wasn't just some bad break she'd caught before I could remember anything about the world; it was a bright line dividing her life. There was before and after that bullshit mother-fucker took her kids. Then there was another bright line, before and after cancer took her son away from her for a second time and would never give him back.

———————

Whenever I visited my dad in the spring, Saturdays were for Morgan's Little League games.

During those games, as I walked along the lowest bleacher, pretending it was a balance beam and dipping my foot below it, I would stop cold to watch my brother at bat, too anxious to look at him directly, but observing him out of the corner of my eye, looking down at my Keds between pitches, adjusting the ponytails I had done myself.

Morgan was wiry, with dark eyes and a quick swing. When I saw him glare down the pitcher, I did a thing that I might now call praying.

I needed something good to happen for my brother. I felt heavy with the guilt that he was stuck with Carol while I got Mom, who was at least our real mom and didn't hate us. Our dad hung the moon—but he didn't have much time for moon hanging, because he was rebuilding car parts six days a week. And while he was at Delta Battery, Carol was in charge. You ate only when she deigned to feed you. You did your chores and hid.

It was clear to me, my brother had ended up on the worse team. I felt sick about it. And I wished his bat to the ball.

———————

Driving my dad to the first Purple Pinstripes practice, I notice him nervously resting his hairy hands on his fanny pack.

"When Morgan was an all-star, at the state tournament, we faced this pitcher. Kid was throwing *seventy*, T. He looked like an eighteen-year-old. He had arms like *this*," my dad says, holding his fingers around his bony biceps, way out. "Nobody could hit those pitches but Morgan. He was the youngest, but he knew how to connect on a fastball.

"The next year he made the all-star team again, but he didn't play. He was terrible. He just lost it."

"It was his vision, Dad. I bet that was it." Around that time, my brother started wearing unfashionable wire glasses. They looked like the kind you'd be issued at juvenile hall.

Dad just shrugs. "I thought he'd make it to the bigs. Somebody has to. Why not him?"

I drive and he stares vacantly at the horizon. To the north, the two behemoth rock formations that make up Camelback Mountain etch the sleepy dromedary shape for which they were named into a still and sapphire sky. My dad sighs.

We pull into the parking lot of Ingleside.

"The way he came up to the plate, he always looked confident. Same as Nate does. And they have the same birthday, September twenty-fourth. Both lefties," he adds, sitting still, even though I've turned off the car. Everything I know about losing a child is nothing at all, and when I try to imagine it, it's a thought experiment too bleak to carry through. I hang with him, though, even if it seems like every single therapist on Daniel's "Grief Counselor Options Spreadsheet" would tell my dad this is no way to grieve, that he should stop comparing the boy to his dead son.

He hasn't talked about my brother much since the funeral, when we'd all held hands in the living room where Morgan and his wife had stayed up late, watching their shows.

I know about the late-night television dates because I could sometimes hear them giggling when I stayed there to help out through his illness. I could hear Morgan explaining to Laura the English idioms and pop-culture references she didn't get. He'd make fun of her for not comprehending some allusion to *The Brady Bunch* and she'd punch his arm, purring, "Morrrrrgan," with her Argentine accent.

"Ouch," he'd say dramatically, but trying to keep his voice down. "You better be careful. You don't know your own strength. *Ouch!*" Laura was strong. She had been a junior tennis champion in Argentina. My brother, even toward the end, was thick and barrel-chested, but she could move him from the bed to an easy chair using a rented hydraulic lift with a manual crank. Private about his bathroom affairs, he never wanted part-time hospice helpers to change his diaper, so Laura managed to do it herself, muscling him to his side, sliding the diaper from underneath him, and cleaning him thoroughly, all without wincing. Then, after changing the diaper of her dying husband, she returned to writing work emails about microloans in developing countries.

In the wake of his death, we gathered in that living room, his immediate family and a couple of close friends, along with some of Laura's cousins who drove down from Detroit and a sugar-hearted hospice lady with a sensible pixie cut and a cable-knit cardigan. We put rocks into a vase we passed around as we each shared a favorite memory.

It's hard to explain my brother, to make him a character in this book, because to me there were several versions of him.

There was the explosive, angry elementary school kid who was almost expelled from school for fighting.

"I'll never forget one of Morgan's report cards. It was a full house. He had three Ds and two Fs!" said my dad, putting his rock into the vase. "The school guidance counselor tested him and told me he was loaded. So I thought, *Oh, great, he's on drugs, too.* But she meant he was loaded with academic ability." We let out an overenthusiastic funeral laugh. "I guess she was right. He turned things around when he moved in with his mom. He graduated second in his class in high school, then went to UC Berkeley, that's a real good school."

There was the teenage version of my brother. He had those awful glasses and skin red and flaring with acne. That version was antisocial, didn't know how to talk to people, cracked his knuckles all the time, and didn't know how to dress or do his hair. He didn't have a light touch or any jokes in his arsenal, was dark and serious, long black bangs always in his eyes. He was overly competitive, even at four square or cards or Ping-Pong or tetherball. He listened to baseball games on the radio. Then he moved in with us and made a best friend. He and Phillip would sit in his room for hours, messing with a Commodore 64 home computer or playing Dungeons & Dragons. They played on the volleyball and tennis teams together at the special private school that catered to gifted kids and troubled kids and foreign students, like Phillip, who came from Germany. This was when I first heard laughter coming out of Morgan's room, my brother wheezing and barely able to catch his breath when Phillip imitated their English teacher, a perfect impression he did even after they were both grown-ups, somehow even mimicking the teacher's lazy eye.

"Your brother was like a brother to me," said Phillip, looking toward me shyly, putting his rock in the vase. They had remained close. Phillip and his wife lived around the corner. They walked to the funeral.

The lawyer version of my brother was mild-mannered and gentle. He didn't bill by the hour or anything. He worked for the government doing estate law, catching ultrarich families trying to cheat on their taxes, and then negotiating settlements based on complicated algorithms. He lived wherever the government sent him: Fresno, Cincinnati, and finally Arlington, Virginia. He wore Skechers and didn't call attention to himself. Over the years, he had two different girlfriends named Michelle (Dad called the second one "Two-ee.") But he never lived with anyone until Laura. He went on camping trips with Phil, taking nature photos with his Nikon. He did my dad's taxes and called him every Sunday night. He liked doing things by himself, same as I did. After college, he traveled to Europe alone, taking trains from city to city, staying in hostels. At a train station in France, a thief stole his money and passport, and that's when a family he met at the station took him in, let him stay at their house for a week, taking him to the embassy to get a new passport. We weren't surprised when that happened. That version of my brother was guileless and soft-spoken. He drew people in, even though he didn't have a big, loud personality. You wanted to help him. He stayed in touch with that French family for years.

Unfortunately, the cancer version of my brother is the one I knew best. That version was also reserved and private, but he let me help him. He didn't have much choice. That's when I spent the most time with my brother. My job was usually to stand guard in case of a medical emergency so Laura could work. I also ran errands, picking up a six-pack of Ensure from CVS on a rainy night, bringing extra clothes or blankets to a hospital or rehabilitation facility, buying extra phone chargers at Target. I never did have to preside over any emergencies. Mostly, I just sat with my brother and we watched movies or sports. I flew back and forth whenever I could. I got to know him in a new way then, not from exchanging ideas or having deep conversations about life and death, but just the kind of knowing you get from spending time in the same room. I observed him, the way he never complained, the way he never got irritated by a nurse forgetting his pain meds or water, the way he never got nasty or cross with anyone, the way he never stopped thinking he'd live. He was willing to try any treatment, no matter how much it might hurt.

Eventually Cancer Brother knew he was dying. Dying Brother

was scared. "I'm not meant for this. I'm not strong," he told me once. But he clearly was.

And of course there was baseball Morgan, who was extraordinary. Until he wasn't.

"Think about it, Dad," I say as cars pull up around us, trunks opening, boys lacing up their spikes as they lean on bumpers. "Every Little League kid wants to be in the MLB. But how many end up there?" This is our habitual riff about Morgan. I've got nothing to fix things for that little kid who walked up to the plate and just stopped hitting. And I've got nothing to fix things for his father.

"He had a good run," I say, as I always do. I never know how else to end the scene.

Then my dad picks up his cue. "He did," he says, with his usual lackluster delivery. Dad isn't about to scream out to the heavens, or to me. If he started screaming he might never stop, and then he'd miss baseball practice.

As we walk toward the bleachers, Dad and I say we'll just stay for a few minutes, take a look at the team. But we both know the second we settle into our chairs that we aren't leaving. "Are we the weirdos who watch an entire Little League practice?"

"Oh yeah. We are those weirdos," he counters, with relish.

Leo is at shortstop, wearing slick baseball sunglasses, the shades tinted yellow. He's undersize, but the way he sweeps up a ground ball, underhanded, then throws a dot to second, makes me inhale deeply. "God, Dad. These older kids are good."

Our catcher is Finn, a shy kid with an already deepening voice. Gavin is pitching, but not well enough for his mom. She yells, "Throw it, don't guide it!" from behind the fence on the third-base line.

I notice big Easton Cage out in left. He has soft features, a face that's gushy and cherubic. His elfin ears point upward along the sides of his hat. I can see Easton isn't likely to catch anything that doesn't fall into his glove, but he is ours, the last pick of the Purple Pinstripes.

Isaiah is at third. His eyes are light brown, almost the same color as his skin, but slightly more golden. He wears long white baseball pants instead of knee-highs and looks like he always knows a secret. Graham Miller, an engineer's son who will become our backup catcher, hits a dribbler to third and Isaiah fields it clean, throws it to Nate, who is now manning first. "You see that, Coach?" Isaiah asks Daniel. "Smooth. I love third base. You should keep me here." Isaiah's mom has a nursing shift at the VA hospital that's about to start, but I see her linger and watch and pretend not to before speed-walking out to her car in her ice-blue sneakers, her head craned backward toward the diamond. Kai's dad is also lingering, a hulking, hefty guy in a plaid shirt. His kid is the best soccer player in the third grade and maybe the entire district. "Mom, he *is* speed," said Nate after practice, awestruck. Kai looks like a designated runner to us if we ever saw one. His dad will good-naturedly keep score at almost every Purple Pinstripes game with a stubby pencil, marking up the official score sheet bound in a spiral notebook.

Daniel takes over for Gavin, careful not to overpitch the boy.

He lobs pitches from behind a protective L-shaped steel screen with nylon netting. This way, he won't get tagged by a hard-hit line drive. Coach doesn't know exactly how this batting order is going to shake out, but Grandpa can see that it will.

"You see the top of our lineup? We got a Murderers' Row out here," he says, grandly and loudly, before I shush him. Team Chartreuse is practicing on the opposite field, and I don't want to get caught bragging with my pops.

He lowers his voice to the level of a private "amen," the kind you say to yourself just in case anyone is keeping score.

"I don't want to get smug, but these kids can play. Daniel knows what he's doing."

A warm wind blows my hair in front of my eyes. "Should we head out, Dad?"

"Can we just hang out until the end?" I nod. "Oh goody! Look. Nate's up next."

Nate's first cut misses. "You're late," Daniel points out, placing his hands on his hips. "Step out sooner." Nate takes a beat, inhales the correction into his muscles and bones. He connects on his dad's next throw, bashing one out to center. Curly-haired Wyatt Reyes is ably captaining the outfield, but he can't get to this one in time. We watch the ball land and then roll across the grass, toward the fence, toward the rocks forming a giant sleeping camel far away in the distance.

"Who has it better than we do?" asks the old man, flashing his gums and raising his bushy eyebrows.

"Nobody, Dad."

||||||||||||||||||||||||||||

CHAPTER THREE

Staying Inside

"Never give up and sit down and grieve.
Find another way."

—SATCHEL PAIGE

"Just sense into your toes," says the voice.

I'm on the floor in my closet, the lights out, feeling my toes. There's no right way to feel into my toes, says the soothing man speaking from my phone, which is beside me under a row of coats, next to a pair of ancient sheepskin slippers. I might feel tingling, or burning, or nothing.

Without wiggling my toes, I can't sense much, maybe some cool closet air on the skin of my baby toe, maybe a light pulsing.

Whatever is there, my only job is to sense it, not to name it or understand it or change it.

"What you are feeling is what you are feeling," says Jon Kabat-Zinn, author of *Full Catastrophe Living: Using the Wisdom of Your Body and Mind to Face Stress, Pain, and Illness*. It's a seven-hundred-page book about mindfulness. And if attempting to place my awareness on the heretofore mostly ignored goings-on of my pinky toes is what might lead to salvation, I will do as the man says. This guy is a Western Buddhist, a leading practitioner of mindfulness-based stress reduction. The recording is a twenty-nine-minute body scan, homework for the eight-week MBSR course I'd taken a year before this season began.

On the first night we met, at a church in Scottsdale, we introduced ourselves and explained why we were there. One lady couldn't shake the pain from some dental procedure gone wrong; another was having panic attacks in the classroom of the junior high where she had just begun her first year teaching seventh-grade English.

Me? I was Dead Brother Girl.

I see your persistent gum pain, lady, and I raise you a tumor on my brother's sacrum that is killing him slowly. I know it's not a contest, but, hey, "What you are feeling is what you are feeling," as Jon Kabat-Zinn would remind me later; and what I am feeling is something I know to be competitive and trifling: In this cramped room with bad lighting, I win sadness. But I'm also feeling contagious, like nobody wants to look me in the eyes, or their brother might catch cancer, too.

Victoria, the teacher I'd found online, sat cross-legged on the carpet, a thin burgundy shawl around her shoulders, surrounded by notes and books from which index cards sprouted. She gave us a handout with a list of concepts, a paper she wanted us to tape to a mirror or a wall, someplace we'd see the list daily:

**INTEGRATING MINDFULNESS USING ALL
FOUNDATIONS AS A WAY OF LIFE:**

1. Beginner's Mind

2. Patience

3. Non-striving

4. Non-judging

5. Acknowledgment

6. Letting Go

7. Trust/Self-Reliance

"Oh," she said. "Get out your pens and cross out where it says 'Letting go.' I prefer 'Letting be.' Just change that one word."

That's when I fell in love with this curly-haired lady in consistently flouncy pants and with the ubiquitous, chaotic array of paper scraps in a semicircle in front of her when she taught.

She picked up a torn piece of lined paper, deliberately, glacially, and nodded at it, then looked up at us. "If you want to get from point A to point B, you must first be fully at point A."

My entire adult life I couldn't meditate for shit. If there was some peaceful field of poppies, a place of mental nothingness and bliss, I couldn't stay there for longer than thirty seconds without wondering if I should scratch my cheek or give up processed food or pick up the dry cleaning on my way home. But before I leave here, I have to first *be* here.

"Things arise and pass away," she explained. That's the gist of it. I don't have to like point A. I just have to be here. In my closet.

"Become aware of the shins and calf muscles and the sensations in the lower legs," says the voice. My tabby Lolo walks around my head, then settles.

"Let go of the tendency of wanting things to be different from how they are now, and allow things to be exactly as you find them."

The Purple Pinstripes will take the field in a few days for their season opener. My mind is wandering, away from the shins and calves and toward Nate, and how much he'll want to play well, and how many things could go wrong on the diamond. And then I catch myself. I tune back in to my shins.

"Just be right here as you are right now," says the recording. I sense the heaviness of my body on the beige shag carpet.

"Moving your attention now to your fingertips and to both hands together."

He speaks quietly, reminding me that if my mind wanders, I can just bring it back to my body. The scan moves up to the shoulders, the scalp, the muscles in the face. For a moment, I think about the shoebox high on a shelf above me; it contains a red-and-blue-striped thermal shirt that once belonged to my big brother and a plastic bag of ashes that once were my brother, or part of him anyway. After he died, I asked Laura to send me something of his, so she sent the shirt, a blue baseball hat with a Gap logo, and this bag of ashes, some fraction of the total remains.

"We can practice putting out the welcome mat for whatever arises," it said in the book. I highlighted that part, about practice. "Reps," like Daniel said about catching fly balls, fielding grounders clean, and hitting your cutoff man. Practice, like me on the floor of my closet. I'm just running a drill. I'm catching my mind in a whir of unconscious thoughts that are twisting and floating: bad things that happened, bad things that might happen. Time after time, I'm gently redirecting my mind from death, tumors, wheelchairs, coarse white hospital sheets that smell like bleach, unshaven scruff on my brother's face, my dad's hand touching it. Each time I notice the centrifuge of thoughts and elect to release them and put out the welcome mat for what's happening in my toes, in my body, on the carpet, right here, it gets easier. The book says this practice deepens a groove in your brain, a neural pathway. You get better at returning to the home that is your body, the warmth and tingling and aching, over and over. *No substitute for reps.*

I tune back in to the scratch of the shag against my skin, because I'm trying to concentrate on the recording, do what it says.

After the course, I started going to Victoria's weekly dharma talks at a church in Scottsdale. She would lean forward on her meditation cushion, sitting up on the carpeted stage of the sanctuary with her usual array of faded paperback books strewn out in front of her, sipping tea from a metal thermos.

She once broke it down like this: "In Buddhism, it's approach. Don't avoid. We avoid unpleasant feelings because we think life shouldn't be this way, but all sensations change if we let them be."

The big finale of the body scan is a roundup of the entire body, sensing into it all at once, "allowing things to be as they already are." That's so much more doable than anyone telling me to relax, to which my nervous system throws up two middle fingers and says, *No can do*. Sometimes I believe all this is helping. And sometimes I'm just crossing it off a list: stuff you're supposed to do to feel better when your brother died and then your mom died and you're still here.

Lolo meows at the door.

On the recording three bells ring, ending the meditation.

I pull the cheap pillow roll I bought at the airport out from under my knees and tuck it back into the corner, put on my slippers, and leave the sanctity of my closet, heading out into my morning, the tasks to come, the unholy or perhaps ultra-holy shakings of Goldfish crackers into lunch baggies, the searching for lost water bottles and overdue books, the slicing of strawberries for oatmeal.

But at least I'm aware my toes exist, thanks to the body-scan recording.

That's actually a big deal, at least for me.

The visceral sense that blood is pulsing through them, right here, and I'm choosing to notice that, means that *I am also right here*. My toes and shins and eyebrows and elbows are all right here in this moment, *where nothing bad is actually happening*.

Dad pulls his red bandana from his fanny pack and blinks hard, blotting his eyes. He got these eye spasms when my brother first got sick and, despite a few procedures, his eyes aren't great at making tears. It's a malady he's learned to treat only with long, deliberate blinks. And booze. He blinks hard again, against the warm, dry breeze. "Pops, you okay? I got you a fresh bottle of E&J back at home."

"Oh goody! I'll just have a little nip."

The wind twisting through the bleachers smells earthy, the salty perfume of old leather and baked clay. The Purple Pinstripes are taking the field for the last of their ten preseason practice sessions. Dad and I remain those weirdos who watch practice. This is our new routine, together on the sidelines. Powdery dirt is suspended in the air, hovering, a gauzy curtain between us and the diamond.

Daniel's team surrounds him as he stands on the mound, reviewing the mainstay of his defensive strategy: how to hit the cutoff man.

"Like we've been practicing, if a kid hits a bomb, it's probably rolling all the way out to the fence. Most likely, the play is going to be at the plate. But you're all the way out there," he says, gesturing toward the outfield. "It's going to take two of you to get the ball home."

They look up, nodding.

"After you chase that ball down, the shortstop or the second baseman, whatever infielder is closest, he will run toward you, into the shallow outfield. That's your cutoff man. Get the ball to him. He throws it toward the plate. Does everyone understand?" He looks out at his team, scanning their faces for signs of comprehension. "If you don't know where to throw it, just throw it in the general direction of home."

That was Daniel's main defensive focus. When it came to the Pinstripes and hitting, there were a few basic diagnoses made during practice. Some kids were always swinging late. "Be on time," Coach would say. Some players had an uppercut. "Level it out," he'd say, and they mostly would.

And then there was the worst and most common problem, *stepping in the bucket.*

What this means is that instead of striding toward the pitcher, the batter steps back and away, toward third base in the case of a right-handed batter. "It's counterintuitive to step toward the pitcher and the hard object he's flinging at you," Daniel told me when I tried to make him explain why it's called *stepping in the bucket* if there's no bucket. "I don't know why it's called that, but I do know Isaiah has an acute case of bucket stepping. He's the worst offender. I need him to stay in there against a pitch."

Isaiah has an edgy preteen charm, a swagger when he steps into the box. His bat wiggle in the air looks sharp and confident, like this kid is about to hit a nuke. But the second the ball leaves the pitcher's hand, even if it's clearly heading right into the zone, a juicy peach for him to pummel, his hips leak out.

At best, his hips or shoulders would fly open, so that even if he swung his bat, this leakage would make it impossible to drive the ball with any force.

"I'm trash," he'd tell Coach, but Coach kept telling him to stay inside.

As the sun sets on our last practice, he's still stepping in the bucket. "Kid has no chance of getting his bat on the ball if he keeps doing that," Dad mutters.

But if you step backward, you're safe. No bruised rib, no dropping in a heap, no chance of the ball bouncing off the plastic of your helmet. And that's just in batting practice. If you don't swing during a game, you don't swing and miss. You might strike out looking, but you can pass that off like you really thought that last pitch was outside and you were too shrewd to fall for it, and you can shake your head at the ump, incredulous. And if you drew a walk, a sweet, sweet ball four, you could run the bases, come home. You could still get your pants dirty sliding and wear that dirt with honor. You could love baseball without ever letting it hurt you.

"No risk it, no biscuit," Daniel tells Isaiah. I thought about that all season. Stay inside, hang in, or you can't make good contact. I think it's going to be the same with grief as it is with baseball. I can't flinch. If I'm going to learn to live with loss, I'm going to have to feel bad and risk staying with that feeling, riding it out, even when it stings, even when it bruises, even when I hate it. My facile summary: This was *Full Catastrophe Living*, Little League–style. Hang in there against the pitch. Let the pitch hit you if that's what physics has in store and get curious about exactly how and where it stings.

Andrew settles in to sit on his grandfather's lap. Just for a second, though. He never sits still for too long. A scrawny six-year-old, he has the wiry build of a rock climber and the puff-pastry cheeks of a chunky newborn. His shaggy blond hair comes down over his eyes. He studies Nate on the field.

All the fierce focus that Nate uses to track his world, balls and strikes, and who plays what position for which team, Andrew trains only on Nate, studying the way he speaks, dresses, walks, and, of course, stands at the plate or on the mound.

With a few minutes left of practice, Coach calls out to Andrew, "Your turn, kid. You ready to take a few cuts?" Andrew gleefully races to grab a helmet from the dugout and then arranges himself at the plate, trying to get his stance just right.

Nate watches intensely, leaving the dugout to stand on deck along the first-base line.

"FEET APART, Andrew. *Andrew, get your feet apart.*" Andrew's head was always on a swivel for these precious corrections from Nate, and he'd dutifully do whatever his brother said. "More, Andrew."

He moves his feet wider until his brother is satisfied. Nodding his approval, Nate stares, squints, and then adds, "Elbows up." Andrew raises his elbows. Nate takes a step back, hangs his thumb from the back pocket of his white baseball knickers, and watches his little brother hit.

"Not bad for a little dude," Grandpa says, but what he really means is *From where I sit, it wouldn't be any big surprise if both these boys make it to the Show.* Andrew wouldn't dare step in any kind of bucket, not under Nate's watch. After his turn at the plate, he begs for more pitches or permission to shag balls in the outfield, but it's time for the team to do one last base-running drill, then pack up.

Andrew is back in Grandpa's lap. Our left fielder's little brother sidles up. He's handing out candy.

"I love Reese's," Andrew says, greedily accepting the gold-and-orange-wrapped treat.

"Andrew, what do you think Reese's is?" I ask. "It's basically peanut butter. You said you don't like peanut butter."

"Oh, then I hate these. *Yuck*," Andrew announces. He mimics the disgusted expression Nate makes when proximal to any form of peanut butter. He stares at the candy softening in his palm and then hands it to Grandpa. He wrinkles his nose, turns down the corners of his mouth, and adds for the record, "Nate hates peanut butter, too. We both hate it."

Andrew wasn't going to break with the preferences of his big brother, even if it meant releasing a warm Reese's from his grip. At six years old, Andrew had one trusted source, whether it was about nut spreads, music, or the wide world of sports.

Nate would pontificate about basketball to one of his friends at recess: "Michael Jordan is better than LeBron James. He's just more athletic, better on defense—"

"He's better at defense," Andrew would blurt.

"He gets more re—"

"He gets more rebounds," Andrew would interrupt, his voice going high and fast, the words in a race to tumble out because he knew the next part, knew just how it was supposed to go. "MJ only had one all-star teammate but LeBron had SO many and MJ only had ONE and he got more rebounds and he's more athletic."

When Nate watched Andrew's games, played at the smaller field closer to the parking lot, Nate would scram if he saw anyone his own age, a friend or even someone he barely knew, someone with whom to walk around watching games played in parallel, and commenting on who hit a one-hopper, or a dinger, or an inside-the-park home run. But when there was nothing better to do than watch lame Farm A coach-pitch, he would stand behind the fence, directly behind home plate, and coach Andrew on every swing.

Nate wasn't all that interested in Andrew's world, coaches underhanding the ball on bended knee, but after one game later in the season, he lobbed in a compliment for no good reason. Andrew was walking toward the car, his bat sticking up from the side of his baseball bag. Nate sidled along next to him, twice as tall, with his long-legged, loping, heel-toe gait. The older brother said, "I told you to widen your stance. And look what happened. You made hard contact every time and even had a one-hopper to the fence." The younger brother beamed but said nothing, stunned.

"That play you made at short was insane," Nate added. Andrew soaked up his brother like a lizard on a rock soaks up sunshine.

"Hey, Mini Nate!" yelled some older kid walking by, kicking up dust. Andrew waved and Nate tilted his chin up in a quick greeting.

"People call me that," Andrew said, pretending to be annoyed. But he couldn't have been any more pleased if he were Mini Michael Better-Than-LeBron-James Jordan.

"Andrew, you're easily the best infielder your age in the league," concluded Nate matter-of-factly.

Dad and I were walking behind the boys as Nate delivered this blessing unto his brother. We quickened our pace just to see Andrew's face, catching each other's eyes as we did, not wanting to intrude on this moment, this perfect confluence of joyful waters into Andrew's coach-pitch soul, but we weren't going to miss it.

If a compliment could lift and change you, could rearrange your cells and neurotransmitters, heal you like both a drug and a placebo at the same time, we saw that experiment happen in real time. This Little League consecration would be made manifest in future seasons of top-notch play at shortstop. Every ball Andrew dove sideways to stop before it rolled into left field, every hot grounder he stopped with his glove and threw, from his knees, in a succinct and accurate throw to first—those were plays set in motion by his brother years before. The sun makes energy out of plants. It may not be that grand in the scheme of all the galaxies, but here on Earth, it gives us the warmth and light to live. And thus, a big brother's assessment of your baseball skills, a big brother you knew would never go out of his way to flatter you, that made you Mini Chosen.

There is Nate, there is Andrew, and there is a third thing. I study the younger one so hard, how he looks at Nate, and I think about the secret late-night grieving I do. *Morgan is dead*, I say to myself in bed, to see if I can make it sound right.

My mom took us to a family camp in Yosemite for a week every summer. That's when some teenagers taught us a chant, and we practiced it and performed it at the camp's talent show.

You can kiss my acka-backa, my soda cracker,
My B-U-T, my booty whacker
Your mama, your daddy
Your greasy granny got a hole in her panty [pointing to our bchinds]
Got a big behind like Frankenstein
Going beep-beep-beep down Castro Street [car honking motions]
In a car so fine, it blows my mind
All right [clap, clap, clap]
All right [clap, clap, clap]
My belly aches. My back's too tight. My booty shakes from left to right
AAAAAALLLL RIGHT

Everyone cheered, because we said "booty" and "Castro Street" in homage to San Francisco. We did this routine together for relatives, on demand, until we were adults. We did this chant for his kids, my brother in the rented hospice bed in his basement, me sitting in a chair, right up close. He remembered all the words, even when he was dying.

But there wasn't much else in our repertoire. When I was growing up, most people were surprised to find out I even had a brother. We didn't have bunk beds or secret hiding places. We didn't have the same schoolteachers; we never went to the same school. I didn't walk around in the omnipresent glow of my big brother, who would protect me from bullies or teach me cool slang. I always wondered what that would have been like, a whole childhood of clapping in unison, and now, watching my boys, this feels as close as I'll get to knowing.

———

My mom's favorite story about my dad centered on the time she picked me up at the airport when I was five. I'd been flying alone to visit my dad, every month for two years at that point. To put this in perspective, no airline allows a three-year-old to fly alone today. It doesn't happen, ever. Unaccompanied children under five years old aren't allowed to fly on any major airline. From age five to age fifteen, there are restrictions and fees and rules about how one airline employee safely hands a kid off to another. Even accounting for the seventies and for the benignly neglectful parenting style of my mom, who really put the "Me" in "Me Decade," and even factoring in the laissez-faire attitude of inner-city boomer hippies, anyone who has had a toddler, or met a toddler, probably can't fathom shipping one back and forth.

The fuzzy blue coat I'd gotten for my fifth birthday became a matter of grave significance on these flights. "Count your things before you get off the plane, so you don't forget anything," my mom constantly reminded me. But what I was mostly worried about forgetting was my new favorite article of clothing. I figured if I kept my eyes on the coat in my lap, over my seat belt, like a big dead rave cat, I wouldn't forget it. Put it in the overhead bin, you could kiss wearable Grover goodbye.

Back to my mom's story. "Your father put you on a plane, and I picked you up from the airport," she'd begin, arms folded, sitting at our tiny yellow Formica kitchen table. "And when I got you in the car, you were scratching and scratching your head. So, when we got home, I checked. LICE. That's when I noticed red marks on your arm, three little dots on your forearm, then one on your face. I took you to the doctor and you had *chicken pox and lice*. Your father put you on a plane with CHICKEN POX AND LICE," she'd pronounce, still disbelieving. Dozens of retellings of the story weren't enough for her to process his paternal ineptitude. Either my stepmother didn't want to deal with my itchy, infectious conditions, or nobody had noticed. Either scenario was possible.

The airline whose passengers I potentially infected was called PSA, and it went under around the time of my senior year in high school. It was a discount outfit hitting airports throughout California, letting unaccompanied minor passengers fly from LA to SF for around ten dollars. That was my monthly route, and I had a jar of silver plastic pin-on wings to show for it. The airplanes were white with two thick stripes, orange and red, painted around the circumference. Each aircraft had a smile, a black semicircle painted on the nose. The stewardesses, dressed in sleeveless mauve dresses with blue-and-yellow blouses underneath, pinned the plastic wings to unaccompanied minors and sat them in the first row.

My dad was always there at the gate in Los Angeles to pick me up, until the time he wasn't.

That day, the stewardess in charge of the flight's only unaccompanied minor had a stiff, rounded French twist updo with golden highlights and caramel lowlights. She wore what I later came to know was Jean Naté body spray, and when she walked me off the plane, she held my hand and I got close to her and inhaled it. I was overheating in my coat.

She scanned the faces in the crowd, then let go of my hand to wipe mascara flakes from her cheeks, fingernails manicured to mauve points. She straightened the bow at her neck, eyes darting around at reunions, people nervously holding balloons and bouquets. Sparkly white eye shadow under her brow bones glinted in the terminal light as I looked up at her.

"Who's meeting you today?" she asked.

"My dad is meeting me."

"What does he look like? Maybe I can help you find him?"

"He's got brown hair and glasses."

Soon, the rest of the passengers cleared out and all you could hear was the murmur of the airport, a din I knew well, the white noise of a joint-custody airport kid. The stewardess went to the ticket counter, conferred with some colleagues in matching mauve dresses standing close to one another in a circle, speaking quietly. Bright yellow-and-brown flowers bloomed aggressively across my luggage, a groovy rumpus room upholstery fabric that was too loud for me to lose. I placed it on the carpet and used it as a chair, hoisting my elbows onto my knees.

"What's his name? Sweetie, do you know your daddy's name?" I sure did, and it wasn't long before she announced it over a loudspeaker to all of LAX. "Nelson Strasser, to the white courtesy telephone. Nelson Strasser, please get to the white courtesy telephone."

The smell of Jean Naté hit me again. "Sweetheart, do you know your mom's phone number?" I did, but she wasn't home. I'd never seen a sadder stewardess than this most beautiful queen of the terminal when she knelt all the way down beside me, her knees together in shiny panty hose, to tell me her shift was over, that it had actually ended an hour before, and that she had to leave for her hotel. "But you're in good hands, honey. Look, that's Pamela and Ginny. They're going to look after you." She slipped me a couple of extra bags of pretzels from a drawer behind the counter and then strode away, proficiently rolling her carry-on bag, slender ankles above mauve pumps, stride, stride. She looked back and waved, two quick bends of her slender fingers. When she was almost to the escalator heading out to the street, she slowed down for a moment between the water fountain and the phone booth, like maybe she was considering just hanging out for a few more minutes, telling me all about the jets out the window, the lights on the runway. But then she sped up again and I lost her. The sky outside went from dark blue to charcoal gray to black. Passengers formed crowded lines, then boarded and flew away. Janitors pushed vacuums and buffed floors.

"Nelson Strasser. Nelson Strasser. Please get to the white courtesy telephone. Your daughter is at gate 23."

There are two major airports in the Los Angeles area, the other is in Burbank, and as you may have guessed, that's where my dad was waiting for me. Maybe he noticed there wasn't a flight due at the time he'd written down on the back of a pink Delta Battery receipt and maybe he didn't even look up at the board, much like maybe he'd noticed the time I had both head lice and chicken pox and maybe he hadn't.

The terminal was stuffy now, so I took off my coat and draped it over the suitcase, a little girl alone on a blue fur hill.

Finally, I heard feet slapping floor tiles. And there was my dad, jogging like he did every morning, doing his rhythmic breathing, puff, puff, blow, blow, in his Nike sneakers and navy blue uniform. "Can you believe I was at the wrong airport? I'm an idiot! Or your mom told me the wrong place. Doesn't matter." He thanked the

last stewardess on duty that night and gave me a piggyback ride
past the newsstands and duty-free shops, my suitcase in one hand,
the coat in the other.

————————

Dad didn't sweat the details of my whereabouts, but now he worries
about my kids as if that's the way he's always been, Mr. Doting
Family Man.

"Little dude was behind the snack bar playing Wiffle ball with
a pine cone," he reports, standing, shaking out his legs, moving his
fanny pack back around to the front of his body. "I don't like when
I don't have eyes on him."

It's getting dark now, and all the Pinstripes are heading toward
the parking lot. Andrew races toward the car, trying to catch up
with Nate.

Practice is over for the team but it's just starting for my dad and
me, even if we don't know it yet: letting things be because we won't
have a choice, helpless on the sidelines behind a chain-link fence.
Only this time, even if we get destroyed, even if we get mercy-
ruled, all the children will walk off the field alive.

"Well, Dad, if it's a tough first game, it's a learning experience,
right?" I pick up my chair, turn it upside down, and snap the legs
together with a flourish of false cheer.

"I hate learning," he says, throwing his head back, cackling.

"Fuck learning. Let's grind that team into a fine dust."

||||||||||||||||||||||||||||

CHAPTER FOUR

He's Dealing Now

"You can't always get what you want,
but if you try sometimes, you just might find,
you get what you need."

—THE ROLLING STONES

The Riviera Mobilehome Park for seniors is sprawling and quiet, tucked right next door to Green Acres Mortuary and Cemetery. "When I die," joked to my pops when he moved in, "just toss my body over the fence."

RIVIERA, says a white-and-green sign where an American flag and a cactus almost as tall welcome visitors. There are a couple of hundred units inside, on both sides of a winding asphalt thoroughfare.

Palm trees bracket the road on both sides, towering and skinny. Atop each tree, green spiky leaves fan up and out toward the clouds. Underneath are droopy brown fronds alight with golden rays cutting in from the side, at least around dusk.

If you drove by, you might not notice the place, off Hayden Road, across from the Salt Cellar seafood joint, an empty warehouse, and a church with bright green grass and a towering crucifix.

Most folks have small rock gardens outside their front doors, and a potted plant or two, maybe some wind chimes. My dad has an easy chair, a card table, and two metal folding chairs under an awning. From there, you can see the grounds of Green Acres over the low brick fence. Fuchsia flowers in plastic wrappers dot the landscape. Wilted roses poke out of narrow bronze vases mounted to grave markers. There's usually a car driving slowly through the cemetery and a cluster of mourners, two or three, clomping across the grounds, heads down, looking lost.

Dad knows we're coming to visit so he's waiting outside his trailer for us, kicking back in the plush olive green wingback chair the overly made-up lady he met on a free dating app gave him from her storage space. She went away, but the chair remains. The line between indoor and outdoor furniture is blurred around the Riviera. He's been outside on the lookout for us since the minute we called and asked if we could stop by for no good reason other than the kids like the place. "What am I doing that's so important? Of course, come over," he said.

Because his trailer is cramped, I slide into one of the folding chairs outside his single-wide for a spell, as a breeze blows through. It's cool now, toward dusk. "How you doing, Dad?" I ask. A broom and two bicycles are leaning up against a storage shed. His favorite bike, the good one, is protected under the cover of a lime-green fitted bedsheet.

"I'm just as happy as if I had good sense," mutters my dad. I don't know where he got this, but he started saying it after my brother died. I think he just likes the sound of it. He keeps the blue plastic bin with pictures of my brother in the storage shed. The key is on his lanyard, but it's never locked. Still, he mostly stays away from the shed. He's safe in his trailer, away from the pictures and the cracked trophies, but only by a few feet.

On good days, he sees things like this: If you're not underground at Green Acres, under a withering bouquet of tulips picked up from the party aisle at Safeway, you're over here. You're over here with a chin-up bar on your bathroom door that you installed yourself.

You're over here watching your grandkids collect rocks and flip empty water bottles. You're over here, and an entire season of Little League baseball awaits you.

Daniel brought a football, and he throws it to the boys in the road. When the dusk light touches our eyes, it feels soft and comfortably worn, like the matted velveteen seating rescued from a stranger's storage unit.

The long rows of palm trees hug the road, heading out toward nowhere and back, around in a circle.

Dad adjusts his knit beanie, looks at the bag in my lap. "I wish you wouldn't go to this trouble," he grumbles. "Don't spend your money. I'm fine." But when he can see a fresh-baked blueberry muffin from the hipster coffee shop peeking out from the white paper bag, his eyes get huge, but then go back to blinking. He forgets to use the drops the doctor gave him for his eye spasms, "and they don't work anyway. This new genius eye guy, fancy specialist, he said they'd work, but they do bubkes. Waste of a co-pay." He sees what he needs to see, doesn't need the drops. He sees the road on his bike and his grandsons throwing the football back and forth. He can see an at bat pretty well if he's close to the fence behind the plate. He doesn't want my help or a handout or any waste-of-time eye drops, but a baked good is too hard to refuse.

"You got me another muffin," he sings as I hand it over. Then he gets up with a theatrical groan and does a little dance, in his slippers, shuffling in a circle in the middle of the road before returning to his patio post.

"Can I be QB?" asks Nate.

"Why not?" Daniel says, flipping him the ball, changing places.

"Andrew, get open. You're not open," Nate commands his brother. Andrew darts out from behind his dad, arms up, mimicking his brother's ready posture. The football bounces off his tiny hands. "Haul it into your chest, Andrew," says Nate, annoyed. And that's exactly what he does on the next pass, hauling it and holding it for a completion. Andrew spikes the ball, punctuating his trailer-park touchdown.

"Good catch, baby. Way to get there," I call into the evening.

"I can't wait for the game tomorrow," says my dad, speaking only to me, breaking off the top of the muffin. "The first game of the season. Goody!"

I feel the urge to text my brother, to tell him about Nate's season opener, an urge so strong I reach for my phone. Then I remember.

My kids will be out on the field, coached by their dad; Morgan's kids have no dad. That year, my brother's son was forced to make a Father's Day craft at school, to dip his hand in paint and press it onto a tile, a tiny blue handprint on a ceramic square he shoved in his backpack for a father who would never see it.

It doesn't seem fair, and the guilt feels wide and bottomless and ancient. I'd had survivor guilt about my brother before he was even sick.

As a kid, his bedroom in the Santa Rosa house was the utility closet off the kitchen, with a sloping ceiling and a couple of metal poles that went floor to ceiling, emanating heat and making banging noises at unpredictable intervals. Brooms and mops were stored there, pushed up against the corner. A single mattress took up most of the floor space. There was no bed frame or box spring, and just enough room for a lamp, a cassette player, and a couple of *Mad* magazines I'd turned over to him. The house did have an extra bedroom, roomy, with two large windows, but that was Carol's "sewing room." It was where I slept when I visited, on a futon pushed up against the wall. She needed that room, she said, "for my things." It smelled like wet rags and mildew. Still, when I went home to my mom I had a real bedroom, with a flowered bedspread and curtains to match. It was hard to love my bedroom, even the wooden vanity my mom found me at a garage sale with a little mirror attached, because my brother lived in a utility closet. There was always a low-grade sense of dread and worry and sadness for my big brother, growing up far away in a closet.

"Goody!" my dad repeats. "Baseball," he sings. I'm nervous about the game, and I feel stupid worrying about something so petty in front of my dad, but that's just the thing; he cares as much as I do.

"I guess this kid Jackson Gallagher is the best pitcher in the league," I tell my dad. "I wish we weren't facing his team game one. I just don't want their spirits to be crushed. I mean, what if we can't hit him?"

"It's baseball. If you fail six times out of ten—"

"You'll be in the Hall of Fame," I finish his sentence.

A neighbor walks by in long denim shorts, puffing a cigarillo. "That your daughter?" I nod. "Your dad is class with a capital *C*. He helps my buddy Alan who lives up the road. He's in bad shape, Alan. But your dad was over there helping him with something or other."

"Oh, that was nothing. I just changed a bike tire. He leaves that old bike outside and somehow the tire got a cactus needle in it. I just patched it up," my dad said, looking over at the man with the cigarillo, waving off the compliment with his hand. "Easy. No big deal."

"Your dad helps Alan all the time. Class," he repeats, blowing a long drag against the wind. As the neighbor disappears up the road, the smell of the cigarillo wafting behind him, my dad's posture straightens. Not only is he the hero of the trailer park, the guy with the tools, but he's also the man in trailer 78, who gets visitors. He's the guy with the daughter who brings muffins. He's the guy with the grandkids scoring touchdowns for all to see.

"Dad, I thought Alan died."

"Different Alan," he says plainly. "Now, tell me about the lineup."

"I think Daniel is batting Nate third, after Gavin and Leo, but he might bat Finn third, Nate fourth; he's weighing the options."

"Mini Murderers' Row I like our lineup. And our infield is sharp," Dad says.

I agree but hedge. Anticipating a win is bad juju.

"Hope these boys don't get all up in their heads about this Jackson kid."

The last of the gold in the sky is glinting off the mailbox, which rusts and teeters on a wooden post.

The desert darkness lowers slowly over the patio's tin roof, so we pile into the car and Grandpa stands in the road to see us off. Nate rolls down the back window. "Grandpa, you're going to be at my game tomorrow, right?"

"Are you kidding me, Natey? I wouldn't miss it for anything." I look back and see him waving at the boys until he disappears into a wash of indigo.

––––––––

My brother walked with a hitch in his step for years, with lower back pain. When he could still play tennis but no longer sit through an entire movie, his chiropractor said to get an MRI. When the man pulled the film from its envelope and saw the image, his face went pale and he handed it back to my brother, telling him to go immediately to a hospital. That's how my brother described the scene to my mom, who told me, and we'd never known him to exaggerate.

It was a grapefruit-size tumor. The mass was tangled within a web of sacral nerves.

"It could be a few things," my mom told me over the phone. "Bone cancer" is the phrase I remember, but a biopsy confirmed it wasn't that; it was just a thing that wouldn't stop growing and had to be removed from his sacrum before it got even bigger and ate into his bones. It hadn't traveled to his lymph nodes or lungs. This kind of tumor is so rare, there wasn't much information I could find online, with only a couple of hundred cases in the United States each year. I searched until I found what I wanted: Prognosis with total resection had a mean survival time of nineteen years. I could live with that. He was forty at the time, but I decided my brother wasn't just any average guy with a tumor. He was hearty and healthy, barrel-chested and strong. I couldn't even remember him having a cold. So I doubled the nineteen years in my head, and I ignored the part about "total resection."

To remove the tumor would involve a seventeen-hour surgery, teams of neurosurgeons, plastic surgeons, and nurses.

"There's a chance he might go blind," my mom explained solemnly, "because he'll be facedown the entire time, and the pressure might build up in his eyes. Morgan is really worried about that. But you know, there's a lot going on where the tumor is. The surgeon has to untangle the nerves from the tumor, try to save them, and those nerves are big, important nerves, bathroom stuff, walking stuff, so it's going to be complicated. But if they just leave the tumor there, it will grow and grow." She got increasingly quiet. "And it will get bad. Real bad."

Britney Spears was an obsession of the tabloid press, and I was working at a new TV show that covered her every move extensively. In the mornings, I was a radio show sidekick. After we got off the air, I'd drive over to the TV show, on the third floor of 8000 Sunset Strip, a big West Hollywood complex with a boutique gym, a multiplex, and places to get waxed or pick up an order of California rolls.

The job wasn't what I'd expected, and I was disappointed because of the mean-spirited nature of the stories, but it became clear early on that the producers were also disappointed in me, so I was relegated to narrating video stories only. Soon they moved me from the on-air-talent area in the newsroom to a tiny cubicle with the administrative staff. Hidden by some partitions, I spent hours every day looking up myxopapillary ependymoma on the company's desktop: case histories, radiology reports, treatment plans. And that's where I was when my brother came out of surgery. I'd bitten my nails to the quick and traveled down deep into all the internet tumor places. Between running to the voice-over booth to track stories about Lindsay Lohan, I searched and searched, clicked and clicked, and waited.

My only work friend, another sidelined writer, was a dapper guy named Ben. He kept asking how I was doing, and finally he dragged me outside.

"I should be there. My parents said not to go, but I should have gone." The words came out in soggy, slobbering bursts. "My brother is being sliced apart right now and what if something happens and I wasn't there? I won't forgive myself, ever." I mashed my face into the elbow of my sweater.

Tumors and crises can make a best friend out of an acquaintance. "Look, Teresa. First, I'm going to be honest. I don't claim to be a makeup expert, but your makeup looks like real shit. It's a Courtney Love situation and you might want to take care of it because you're already barely on this show and whatever is happening isn't going to help your chances of getting on camera today." I cracked a small smile. "Okay, second. Your brother is at Johns Hopkins. Please, if I need surgery, fly me there, okay? He's not at some understaffed urgent care in Jersey City. He's got the best surgeons working on him. And you told me he's strong. Now, lastly, you're needed here right now more than there. The money that you're making will be a help, whatever his recovery will entail, even if it's just to fly back to help your parents. And if someone gets a photo of Tom Brady with his pregnant ex-wife, and you miss the chance to track that story, how will you live with *that*?"

Now I was laughing. "Good point," I said, trying to mitigate the makeup situation by rubbing my upper cheeks hard with the knuckles of my index fingers. I didn't really smoke except at parties a couple of times a year, but I bummed a strong European cigarette from the British TMZ writer loitering nearby.

"You smoke?" Ben asked. "Not judging. It just doesn't seem like a thing you'd do. Lying about your age is a thing you'd do."

"You're being a real dick to someone who's only twenty-nine," I responded, fudging. Smoking causes cancer, and cancer returns the favor by sometimes causing smoking.

My parents sent updates by text, like **Doctor came out things going well** and **Surgical team happy, plan to close him**, and finally they called from the waiting room when it was all over. I rushed out of the secretarial pool, through the newsroom, back outside, and stood alone in the blinding glare of the Los Angeles afternoon, right in front of TMZ's front doors.

"He's okay. He's okay. Your father was my hero. Morgan woke up and it was like *The Exorcist*. He didn't know where he was and there was a tube in his throat and he shot up and his eyes bugged out . . ." My mom couldn't even finish. She'd seen a horror show and the jump scare was still going. "But your father was calm. He said exactly the right thing."

"I just held his hand," Dad said, picking up the story, "and I told him, 'You're okay, Mugsy. Dad is here.'"

That night, when it was Mom's shift at the ICU, Dad went to find a liquor store, even though the hospital security guard warned him, "You don't want to walk through this neighborhood." Nothing that could happen to him after midnight in East Baltimore was going to rattle him now. A rat jostling a plastic bag barely got his attention. He found a store, slid a ten-spot through a slot in the bulletproof plexiglass, and pointed to a bottle of E&J brandy on a shelf behind the clerk.

THINGS I BELIEVED:

1. My brother would be out playing tennis again in a few months.

2. The recovery would be so miraculous, his surgeon would probably write a paper about it for a medical journal.

3. When I knocked on my head instead of knocking on wood, that was good enough to keep the bad juju away from my brother.

THINGS I HAD ALWAYS BELIEVED WITHOUT EVER ACKNOWLEDGING THEM CONSCIOUSLY:

1. My brother and I would become best friends as adults.

2. My parents would get back together. (This belief had been slowly growing since I was a kid, as secret as a tumor but just as real.)

THINGS I BELIEVED THAT DAY ON THE PHONE, AFTER SURGEONS HAD GRAFTED TISSUE FROM A SOFT AND HEALTHY SPOT ON MY BROTHER'S BACK TO FILL THE HOLE THE TUMOR HAD LEFT:

1. My parents would continue living together like they were doing at Johns Hopkins family housing. It would be like the plot of some movie you'd see on deep cable: "A son's cancer reunites widow and widower for a second chance at love."

2. My mom would forgive my dad for taking her kids and only giving one back.

3. All that would remain of this shitty interlude would be two scars: where the cancer had been, and where the pink flesh of a solution had been found and harvested.

My brother was single and living in Arlington, where he'd moved to work for the Internal Revenue Service, flagging the returns of rich tax cheats. "I'm like Robin Hood," he explained. "I take from the rich and give to the government." Living in Virginia put him in close proximity to Johns Hopkins, to one of the only surgeons in the country experienced at removing sacral tumors. That was so lucky, it had to be a sign, I thought.

Cancer didn't kill Robin Hood. He was one of the good guys. Instead of a sword or a bow and arrow, Morgan used algorithms, which he wrote himself, some still in use even now. I believed he'd even find his Maid Marian, which he did, meeting Laura online two years later. She matched with exactly one suitor on a dating app, and that was my brother. He told her about the cancer and showed her the scars, but she stayed with him anyway, and they managed to have two kids in quick succession, racing against the threat of the disease, moving into a little town house near the Key Bridge, walking distance from Georgetown. Fatherhood was a miracle after surgery and radiation. This was all good fortune, I thought. I squeezed my eyes shut and knocked on wood anytime I mentioned Morgan's health after that first surgery. But a sister's superstitious tics weren't enough to corral a few invisible cancer cells that were left behind.

It's a five fifteen p.m. start for our season opener. Team Gray is the visiting team.

Daniel and Nate arrive an hour before us, for warm-ups with the team.

Dad and I stake out our spots, unfold our chairs just a few feet from the plate. There's a chain-link fence and a million psychic miles between us and home. My stomach is starting to gnash and swirl. A little girl does a cartwheel behind right field. A toddler is looking for his lost shoe. The field looks raked and ready, and I notice umpires, actual umpires in uniforms, are here to call the game. "Dad, this just got real."

The Purple Pinstripes are done warming up on the field. Gavin throws his final warm-up pitch, deliberate and steady. It's go time.

Our ace strikes out the first two batters. "Oh, he's dealing now," says Kai's dad, brushing his fingers against the palm of his other hand, miming a card dealer.

"Two down," whispers my dad.

Then Mighty Jackson comes up to bat. As Gavin gets ready to go into his windup, I see something I've never seen before in Little League. Jackson throws his arm back casually, his wrist flexed. Everything stops. "What the hell is this, Dad?"

"He's calling a time-out."

Jackson steps out of the box at a leisurely pace, adjusts his batting gloves, then returns to face Gavin, having shrewdly interrupted the young pitcher's flow.

The move, confident and wily, has rearranged the atoms in the air, shifted the mood. A new sense of unease ripples through the infield. On the next pitch, Jackson knocks a hot, sharp ground ball to Leo, our lefty shortstop. It goes to his right and then takes a big hop at the last second. Leo reacts quickly. He gets his glove from down low to high over his head on his glove side, grabs it clean. He fires the ball from deep short to first base—the throw comes in a little low, but Nate scoops it—a baseball ice cream on a glove cone, presented in a freeze frame, so the ump can take his full view of it, balanced precariously on the tip of the worn brown leather as Nate's legs are almost in a side split.

"Three outs," says the old man with a theatrical sigh.

"Atta way, Six," yells Leo's dad, calling his kid by his jersey number. "Let's go, boys! Everyone hits!"

"That was a play you'd see in the majors. This is real baseball," blurts my dad. "I knew I loved Daniel," he tells me, laughing a big guffaw at his own joke. "These kids could win all the marbles," he tells me. "Now we need our bats to start popping."

We wait for Jackson to take the mound, but Team Gray has other plans. Their starting pitcher is solid but unremarkable. The top of our lineup hits him.

Someone tries to ask us about the schedule for the next game, or if we have bug spray, or some other bullshit, but that person is insane. Only an insane person makes small talk with a mom and grandpa when their player is walking up to the plate for his first swing in the Minors.

"You got this, Nate. Eye on the ball," I say to myself.

Nate takes an aggressive hack at the very first pitch. I can't look but I'm looking. I'm looking through my fingers. I'm waiting to hear the sound. I'm waiting to hear the sound all Little League parents and grandparents are waiting to hear at this field tonight, at fields throughout Arizona, the Southwest, and every state in the union. A hollow crack fills the air, then the sound of chaos and Nate, clapping his hands twice, is safe at first.

"He didn't hit it square, but that ball had eyes," says my dad, with a mystical explanation of how Nate's underwhelming grounder eluded both the shortstop and the third baseman before ending up in the left-field grass. "One for one with an RBI," announces my dad, to me and me alone. "The Chosen One."

Gavin gets back to work in the second. Kai's dad is standing by the corner of the bleachers now, so I walk over to get his assessment. "He's dealing," says Kai's dad, pacing, miming. "Just like I said."

He deals well enough to allow Team Gray one hit, no runs. The Pinstripes are up again.

Kai lacks mass, but he also lacks quit. On a full count, he makes contact to foul one off. Then another. Then another. His dad drops his head down, props his elbow on the corner of the bleachers. Nine pitches in total yield a pitcher-exhausting walk to first.

"Way to battle," says the crowd.

This became one of my favorite things baseball parents yell, on occasions when a kid might not be drilling the ball, but he isn't giving up, either. He's making the pitcher work for it. The foul tip keeps you alive. You didn't hit a dinger, but you gave yourself a chance. Maybe next pitch the meat of the bat finds the ball. Or maybe you toss aside your bat and stroll to first on a walk you rightfully earned, ready to steal some bases.

Isaiah comes up next. He doesn't swing at a single pitch, but he also gets on base with a full-count walk.

The Purple Pinstripes build a 4–0 lead, but early in the fourth inning of a six-inning game, Gavin gets wobbly. His pitches are slow and wild, hitting everything but the strike zone.

"You have to throw strikes. You can't walk kids. These walks have a nasty habit of coming in for runs," says my dad, irritated.

"So, Dad, let me get this straight. You're saying, based on your many years watching baseball, that the pitcher should or shouldn't walk kids?"

"Should not," he says, refusing to play along. But Gavin walks the bases loaded. Daniel strolls out to the mound and pulls the kid. But Leo doesn't fare much better. They hang three runs on us, on walks, passed balls (pitches our catcher couldn't catch or control, allowing runners to advance), and stolen bases. "*Bad News Bears*," comments the old Jewish Bob Costas with my personal *Inside Baseball*. "Thank God that inning is over."

It's a new inning, a new pitcher for Team Gray. That's when we first see *the* Jackson Gallagher on the mound.

He's a squat, square kid, pigeon-toed, with flat feet. He doesn't look like he could outrun Andrew, but his delivery seems like a miracle. It's a blue rose, lightning in a volcano, a bioluminescent squid, an albino kitten looking you in the face like, *Yeah, I'm real.* How this lightning is coming off the fleshy arm of this child we don't know and we can't know. There's also a new catcher, who squats down to harness Jackson's practice pitches like he's just spent a decade kicking around the MLB. They are the reigning champions, and they carry last year's triumph loosely and easily, an invisible satchel of confidence slung behind their backs, filled with stolen bases and victories.

"This is some battery. That's what you call the pitcher and catcher together, T, the battery. Wow." Jackson's leg lift and stride are easy, his follow-through effortless. Balls hit the catcher's glove with a series of *thwack*s that seem to reverberate through the crowd, each throw crisper and faster than the last. "Balls in, coming down!" yells the Gray catcher. Jackson throws his final warm-up pitch before his catcher fires it down to second to simulate throwing a runner out who is foolish enough to try to steal a base on his watch. The Gray infield tosses the ball around the horn before returning it to Jackson's lofty domain. Team Gray's thick catcher crouches into position behind the plate. Jackson digs his back heel into the white rubber stopper on the mound.

He throws six pitches for six strikes. "Two up, two down," mutters my dad.

Nate's on deck, and he heel-toe walks into the gauntlet. It's my brother's walk. "Even if I could barely see at all, I would know which one is Nate. By his walk," his grandpa says. He's walking out there to face the neighborhood's Little League legend.

Nate suddenly looks small and young, his body undercooked and raw. I want to fling my hand out for a time-out. I want to scream to the ump, *Hey, Blue! Can you call this game on account of I can't have my baby strike out in game one? Look at my dad, Blue. He's an old man. He needs something good because he's all messed up*

about my brother's death even though he somehow manages. He deals,
Blue. He says he's good, but maybe all he does is close the door of his tin
can and cry. Maybe this is all he has to look forward to. So you're with
me, right, Blue?

Nate takes a few practice swings before stepping into the batter's
box. We study his swings like tea leaves, wondering if they spell out
the future. They look level; level is good. This could be okay. But
maybe he's going to try too hard—the swings are on the edge of
looking reckless. Who knows what the practice swings foretell?

"Why do we have to face him the first game? Fucking Jackson
Fucking Gallagher. Fuck him," I murmur, careful to modulate my
volume. I'm cursing a child, but he's not a child to me now. He's a
flame-throwing mythological beast about to crush our dreams and
make us remember that everything is shit.

At night, every night now, there's the same monologue in my
head. *Morgan is dead*, says the voice. It's my voice. But I don't know
how I'm making the words. *Morgan is dead*. It's like I'm giving
myself little shocks. *My big brother is dead*. I roll to my other side.
My neck and the base of my skull ache. I don't know if I'm hearing
myself say the words or making myself say them. *He died. He was*
in a wheelchair. He wore a diaper. He died. His body was burned up.
The secret bruise I press at night is too deep and too tender and too
old. Every night I worry I can't come back from this simpleton's
Hamlet, this dead man's float in the black night of the bedroom.

"Emotional Rescue" isn't the best Rolling Stones song. It might
be the worst. But when the video premiered on *Solid Gold*, the
pop music countdown show hosted by Dionne Warwick and featur-
ing an in-house crew of deeply emotive dancers, I couldn't believe
what I was seeing. I was watching the small black-and-white TV
propped up on my mom's nightstand. It was next to her vintage
ceramic panther lamp with the tiered red lampshade. "*I'll be your*
savior, steadfast and true. I'll come to your emotional rescue," sang

Mick Jagger, whom I was seeing for the first time. He moved his face close to the camera's lens. First he stared me down, a look both complete and unapologetic. Then he twirled away. He was dancing around a red room in white pants, and everything was effortless and light, his moves, his falsetto, and the way the wind machine blew back his hair. He jumped around with his bandmates. He was in control and absolutely uninhibited all at the same time. There were freeze frames and what seemed to be an improvised spoken-word section toward the end. I had to tell my brother about this immediately. Morgan was watching the other TV, the bigger one in the living room. That morning, we'd separated so he could watch the Dodgers play the Giants (a matchup that posed an internal struggle for my brother that I don't think he ever resolved, having one parent in each city until he was almost out of elementary school). Meanwhile, I had just wanted to sit in the lotus position on my mom's bed and watch the *Solid Gold* dancers interpret the subtext of Air Supply songs, using only leather metallic gloves and the majesty of dance.

When I got to the doorway, my brother was already heading toward me. He'd flipped channels during a commercial. He'd seen what I'd seen: the force that is the Rolling Stones.

Hyperventilating and giddy, I said we should pool our money. We walked right down to Aquarius Records on Twenty-Fourth Street to buy the single with all the spare change we could find, including a few quarters from a ceramic ashtray where someone had left a half-smoked joint.

We dropped the needle on the vinyl. Our flat in Noe Valley had big bay windows with a view of the fire station across Church Street. In the movie version of the "Emotional Rescue" scene, we dance and sing along, two siblings in the warm glow of a San Francisco afternoon, beams of sun slicing in through the bay windows. In reality, we listened to the song once or twice before the whole thing fizzled. There was still time to catch the rest of the baseball game, so that was that. And within a few weeks, Morgan was embarrassed to have ever liked the song at all. He made me promise never to mention it to anyone. I'm only breaking that promise now.

Because I had so few childhood memories with my brother, I've always cherished this one, which wasn't anything cinematic or grand, but he'd elected to hang out with me. And we both liked the exact same thing—until he went back to Hendrix and Iron Maiden and Rush and Reggie Smith and Steve Garvey and Ron Cey. I wish it was a better story about a better song.

"T, I think he can hit this kid. Nate loves fastballs. I've seen it. Just like Mugsy."

The old man is playing it cool, but I see his fingers are splotchy pink, clutching his Diet Pepsi. "Sodas are poison but I'm just going to have this one today. They're so good," he said, sending Andrew off to the snack bar with a dollar and his poisonous beverage order. Wind blows the red dirt up from the ground, but my dad is a statue holding a soda in a mist of rusty salt, silt, and clay. "Righty pitcher to lefty hitter. Advantage, lefty," he adds, bolstering his own confidence in the odds his grandson can make this happen for us.

Nate swings hard at the first pitch, spins himself around with the power of it, the fearlessness and the longing. Strike one.

He looks at his dad for guidance. Coach keeps it succinct. "You're late," Daniel says. "Swing sooner."

The next pitch comes in just as hot, Nate swings on time, having internalized the correction quickly, but the cut misses. The next throw comes in as high as his chin. Nate lets it go.

"Good eye," chirps a smattering of parents, myself the loudest. My cheeks flush. I meant to remind myself only to root audibly for other people's kids. That's the classy move, but it came out, an off-key note into the wind. "Good eye," I repeat, giving myself a softer do-over.

The meaning of "good eye," became more nuanced to me in that moment, during that non-swing. It's a chorus of parents saying, *Listen, little child up there all alone, you had to make a decision in a second, in front of everyone: the cool kids from fifth grade who came out to watch the game, clutching their phones; the gruff ump that yells "HUH" after every strike; the girl you had a crush on in first grade; your neighbors and cousins and teachers; your whole world. We want you to know that we are cheering for you doing nothing, because doing nothing isn't easy. It isn't easy to be so discerning in front of everyone, for all the marbles. Our hearts are in our throats for you, kiddo. You're doing great. Good eye.*

"What's the count, Dad?"

"One and two," he answers, squeezing the life out of his plastic soda bottle.

Then Jackson fires one low and outside. Nate checks his swing. "Good eye," screams the chorus in the bleachers.

"Two and two," says my dad.

From the dugout, the Gray kids chant, "Two and two, whatcha gonna do?" and it's all I can do not to bum-rush those turds. The diamond should be golf-gallery-in-a-black-hole quiet because any little distraction could blow this whole thing up into smithereens, a strikeout in game one, all because these kids have *no* sportsmanship with their bratty rude chanting. I hate all of them.

Nate swings at the next pitch on time. He makes contact, taps the ball, which makes two big, juicy, fat hops to short. Nate runs hard to first, head down, but he's out.

"Damn it," I say.

"But he made contact. I told you."

The rest of our lineup doesn't get their bats on the ball.

"We still have a one-run lead, right?" Gavin's mom asks us, leaning over from her canopied canvas seat. We agree, it's 4–3.

Now it's the top of the sixth and final inning. We're clinging to our one-run lead. Leo's pitches start to float and rainbow over Finn's head; little butterflies that mean you no harm, they flit about with no never mind about where to land. His motion is becoming floppy and disjointed. He strikes out a couple of kids at the bottom of the Gray lineup but then walks the bases loaded. I see Daniel heading out to the mound and I know Leo is done, cooked, and that the next best option in our bullpen is Nate, about to make his minor-league pitching debut. The towering stadium lights have been switched on with a thud. The mountain has disappeared into the evening. There are just the lights of the houses sprinkled up around Camelback and puffs of cotton-ball clouds in the sky. Andrew wants something or other but I shoo him away. Why have the baseball gods done this to me, game one?

Nate's very first pitch is low. It craters right in the dirt. Finn can't catch it off the bounce, so it rolls to the backstop as a runner trots home. The sound of the Gray fans cheering is garish and echoing as they rise from the bleachers, applauding. Nate looks so alone out there. His face is stoic, his eyes downcast. He gave up the tying run. That's not what he wanted to do, beneath the buzzing glare of the lights.

"The go-ahead run is on third, T. We can't have any more wild pitches." Nate doesn't hear his grandpa, not literally, but he takes a deep breath, gathers himself, and throws two strikes in a row, right down the middle. "One strike away. My kingdom for a strike!"

Nate summons all the velocity he can, cocks his left arm back, and wheels it around, unleashing a pitch that blows in, high and tight, sending the batter spinning out of the box. He falls momentarily into the dirt. He brushes off the side of his pants, unhit and unhurt, but he's skittish now.

He doesn't know if a pitch is going to hit him, the dirt in front of him, the backstop, Camelback Mountain, or the catcher's mitt. "This little dude ain't swinging. Nate has to throw a strike."

Overcorrecting, Nate throws the next one way wide. Finn can't grab it. It ricochets off the backstop, then pinballs around as the go-ahead run is racing toward home. Nate leaps off the mound to cover the plate, but by the time Finn corrals the ball, it's too late. The ump crosses his arms, then flings them open. "SAFE!"

"He's going to settle down now. I think that was nerves. He's better than this." And my dad wills Nate to find the zone with his next pitch. Strike three. Inning over.

We have one more chance, but Jackson returns, mowing down three batters in ten pitches.

The Pinstripes lose their first game. Dad and I sit in silence.

"Let me fold the chairs, T. Don't do it. I don't want you to get your fingers stuck."

"All right," I concede as he starts bending the chairs, clicking the straps to keep them together until next game.

"One for two with an RBI," notes my dad. "Not a bad day at the office."

He loads the chairs and the bucket of balls onto our red wagon. Andrew perches himself atop the cargo for a free ride.

We recalibrate what it will take for us to be happy now. The calculation is swift and decisive and mutual and silent. This was the best team in the league. We held our own, 5–4. No shame in it.

"Nice scoop," says the mom who had been a catcher as she passes by Nate leaving the dugout. Vicki Kanner is one of the neighborhood Alpha Moms. They give me a headache in my eyeballs when I try to interact with them, so desperate am I to sound and act normal so my kids will be invited to their kids' sleepovers and birthday parties. In her Lululemon leggings and dangling earrings, she has stopped to regally dole out this compliment. A statuesque presence of a woman, she bends down to look Nate right in the face. "That one was right on the tip of your glove, but you weren't gonna drop it," she coos. He wasn't. And he didn't cry up there, or argue any calls, or get shook. And he had a strikeout, an actual strikeout in a real minor-league game with umps and everything. And he got aluminum on one of Jackson's pitches, the fastest in the league.

As we leave, players and siblings and parents are all crowding through the corridor between fields, highlights of games spreading fast among the kids. "Jack hit a one-hopper," some classmate of Nate's said as they passed each other, both carrying baseball bags, bats in the side pockets sticking up toward the sky. A few yards later, Nate spread the word to Gavin, walking by us. "You know that kid Jack? He hit a one-hopper to the fence."

Andrew skips toward a crowd of little brothers anxious to town-crier this important news. "Jack hit a one-hopper. To the fence." He doesn't know what this means. He doesn't have to. It's a message he can decode later, in the only language that counts, the dialect he's been studying since birth: the argot of his brother. He phonetically repeats Nate—ABBA singing lyrics in a foreign tongue—never once doubting the significance of the song's mysterious meaning.

As Grandpa pulls the wagon over clods of grass, I see Jackson Gallagher up close. I try not to stare, but I want to take in his entire deal. It looks like he's used a full crayon of eye black, smeared it in two reverse pyramids under his eyes. It's now streaked down to the bottom of his baby face. The most fearsome flamethrower in all of Arcadia is eating a Bomb Pop, walking knock-kneed, his mommy a few paces behind.

That night, I call my dad to review all the highlights and low-lights. We talk for almost half an hour, about the position players, our pitcher meltdowns, and bullpen issues. "Gavin hit the wall at fifty pitches," he said. "So did Leo. We are going to need *arms*, T. I hope some of these low-draft-round kids can throw, absorb at least a few innings. We need arms. And once Nate gets command, look out. He's all over the place and his delivery has a glitch, but he'll figure it out and he throws hard. Maybe he takes some velocity off of it for more accuracy. He'll figure it out."

I still don't smoke but I'm smoking along the trash-can side of our house, on a busted Adirondack chair with peeling paint. Dad wouldn't understand about me smoking at night. He'd freak out about cancer. I mute as I inhale.

Before biking home from our house, he had "taken a little nip" of the brandy we keep for him. Maybe he added another swig when he got back to the Riviera to calm his nerves, and the warmth of it going down had smoothed the game's edges, brought the good moments into relief. "I keep seeing that last swing of Nate's in my mind's eye. I could tell from the sound it wasn't exactly right, but I just keep seeing that swing. It was beautiful. Next time we face that kid—what's his name? Carter? Connor?"

"Jackson, Dad."

"Whatever. He's going to hit that kid next time," he says. "Trust me. I'm telling you, I'm right. Nate eats up fastballs. Just like Mugsy."

He knew Nate and my brother weren't just both lefties, born on the same day of the year. There was something else familiar about my son's temperament, how competitive he'd always been. It was another way Nate reminded me of my brother. And it wasn't just about baseball. Morgan's cheeks would flush when we played gin with our mom. She had the kind of mind that could count cards. She always knew exactly what was left in the deck, and it was impossible to beat her. My brother would get dark and dejected when she called out "Gin!" time after time. There was fierceness to the way he was wired.

Nate was the same. Once I had to pull him out of the class party on Valentine's Day when the candy-heart-stacking competition got too intense for him. He had stacked way more than any of the other kindergartners, and the teacher was writing down the numbers on a chart. Nate sat on the floor, focused on the candies like they were actual hearts and he was performing cardiac surgery, the patient anesthetized on the table; two little girls bumped into him and his stack toppled. Frustrated, he started again, stacking the hearts. Same thing happened with this new stack, kids jostling around, making him knock over the hearts.

"I was about to win, Mom." He was incredulous at the injustice of these thoughtless kids horsing around when winning was at stake. He struggled to keep from crying.

"I know, honey." I knew he'd be embarrassed to cry, so I escorted him outside the classroom, into the hallway. I knelt down and put my hands on his shoulders. "I know you're competitive. But there's a time and place." He stared at his shoes, despondent. His cheeks were flushed, like Morgan's used to get.

"You and I know you stacked the most hearts, okay?"

He returned to class, but in no mood for red-doily crafts. What was the point of Valentine's Day if you couldn't win it?

With my brother, time rounded the jagged parts of his nature. He even laughed off losing at tennis on one of his first dates with Laura, and I figured Nate would eventually soften in the same way. So I didn't try to serve up any slosh about how winning isn't important. I didn't do it about candy hearts, and I didn't do it about baseball.

Even before I lost my brother, all his similarities to Nate were comforting, the genetic spillovers you couldn't exactly explain, the way they both looked off with a distant stare when they were thinking about a problem, the bouncy heel-toe walk. My brother was mine, whether or not we'd been separated for most of our lives, and all I had to do was look at Nate to know it.

Nate was going to hit those fastballs someday, like my brother had. I pray my dad was right about that. I see my son's swing as I try to sleep that night, and it is beautiful, even if it didn't connect just right. *Not a bad day at the office*, I hear my dad's voice say. And the words interject my usual nightly, silent monologue about Morgan. *My big brother is dead. He died. His body is burned up.* I can't stop the thoughts. I can only dilute them. With baseball. I hear my dad again. *You can fail six times out of ten and be in the Hall of Fame.* I see the blue-paint handprints of my brother's son on the Father's Day tile. The smeared blue handprints are too much for me. I wish them away. I see the beautiful swing again. *Eye on the ball.* I see the candy hearts toppling. And I see Nate bending over to pick them back up, one by one.

Grief doesn't go away, but other things come around to dim the glare. Baseball is one of those things, because it's an excuse to be together, because it's generational and nostalgic and timeless, and because baseball itself provides guidance for living with grief, because failure is baked into it, and because you can start over, a fresh at bat, three more chances to hit the ball. Game after game, season after season, you just begin again.

||||||||||||||||||||||||||||

CHAPTER FIVE

On the Side of the Santa Monica Angels

"For the parents of a Little Leaguer,
a baseball game is simply a nervous
breakdown divided into nine innings."

—EARL WILSON

The old man walks toward the shed behind his trailer. The sliding metal door is off the tracks, which are rusty and brittle. He can get it open only about a foot, so he picks up the entire rectangle of corroding metal and moves it halfway over.

He's handy, and good at fixing things, but he never does fix the door. It's always at least partially open.

He ducks his head under the shed's low doorframe and steps inside, next to a vacuum cleaner covered with dust. He hears the sound of his sneakers, the soles scuffing the unfolded cardboard box covering the wooden slats on the floor.

Near the vacuum is a large gray bin with a lid. A paint can is perched on top of the lid. *Nocturnal gray.* Something left by the previous owner. A plastic watering can is on the ground, tipped sideways. Most of what's in the shed was there when he moved into the trailer, and it's now mixed with what remains of his old life, the items that didn't fly out of the back of his truck en route to Arizona.

The old man stands there not moving. *What do I need in here? A towel? A light bulb?* He can't remember now.

He feels a mosquito bite his leg, just above his knee, and swats it, then looks over at a white plastic chair teetering on top of two yellow throw pillows and a bike pump.

A rolled-up carpet stretches horizontally over the top of a bright blue bin with no lid. Despite the carpet, he can see down into the bin as he leans over it. The faded gold cover of a photo album peeks out.

The old man just stands there. He hears the sound of a neighbor's television from across the road, a muted laugh track. The neighbor's trailer door must be open. He scratches at the bite on his leg.

It's dim in the shed, even with the door half-open.

He looks again at the gold album; he doesn't have to open it to know that the first three pages contain newspaper clippings preserved under clear plastic overlays, box scores telling the story of M. Strasser of Rincon Valley Little League helping his team defeat Sonoma Valley in the All-Star Tournament. The corners of the old man's mouth curl up just thinking about it. *Most reliable hitter they had, even if he was the youngest.*

In the bin, loose and in albums, there are dozens of photos of Morgan, including one of him as a little kid, standing with his feet in sand, swinging an imaginary baseball bat. But most of the photos are of father and son: near some boulders, an ocean in the background; standing in front of a submarine at the Museum of Science and Industry. There are pictures with his son across decades: wearing bathing suits beside a river or fancy clothes at a table set with wineglasses, or hoisting backpacks, arms around each other's shoulders on a hiking trail.

Tucked into the back of the album, underneath a few photos of his daughter at a ballet recital, are a couple more newspaper articles.

One headline reads, STUDENTS REFUSE TO DISPERSE. He was one of those students protesting the war in Vietnam, captured in the photo sitting cross-legged, a row of armed National Guardsmen in the background. DEMONSTRATORS ARRESTED. *Yep. Spent two days in the slammer.*

There are pictures of his ex-wife with him and the kids. *Tammy was crazy, never cut out to be a mom*, he thinks, *but it was sad how fast she died after Morgan went.* She was just done. He blinks his eyes and shakes his head. Somewhere in that box is his only photo of Carol, sitting on a log in a denim skirt, shoulder-length hair blunt cut and fluffy, only one photo after all those years, a blurry image from somewhere scenic, but he can't place it and doesn't care to. She helped him for a time, but he doesn't give her much thought now.

Chunks of broken glass from an old frame jut out along the side of the bin.

Near the glass, he sees a thick white envelope, a holiday card from Morgan.

Penguins holding candy canes dance on the front.

> *Thanks for being a wonderful father.*
> *We probably could not have made it without*
> *all your love and support.*
> *Take care,*
> *M*

That card wasn't like Morgan. Too sentimental. He knew he was dying.

Take care.

In another stack of loose pictures, there's a shot of Nate swinging a plastic bat. He's maybe two. *Already had a sweet swing, that kid.* The thought of it makes the corners of his mouth curl up again.

What did I want in the shed, anyway?

His legs feel heavy now and it's stuffy and he doesn't care anymore to remember what he needed in the first place.

He squeezes his skinny body out through the metal door and tries to slide it shut, but it won't close. He jiggles the door around a bit but can close it only three-quarters of the way. That's good enough.

The canned laughter of a television audience wafts over from across the road. He grabs the railing to his staircase, feeling shaky, and climbs the two stairs from the patio into his kitchen, where he pours a generous dose of E&J brandy into a tall glass. *Should I be looking at the pictures of Morgan more?* He can't. But he hasn't thrown away the pictures, either. Everything that remains of his dead son is close to home, but not so close it could destroy him. He kicks up his feet and sips his drink.

The blackness outside engulfs the shed. A starry evening breeze blows dust out through the opening of the sliding metal door, dust from now and dust from before, particles from his old home, from all his old homes, and from this one, his tin can in Arizona, where he rinses the brandy glass, places it gently in the sink, and shuffles off to bed, thinking only about baseball, his son's imaginary bat, Nate's plastic one, and all those he'd see swinging at Ingleside Middle School when the sun rose again, when he'd sit with his daughter along the sidelines.

Somewhere between the Pinstripes warming up and Nate taking the mound for his first start of the season, a clean-cut dad with a 1950s haircut hovers near us, making small talk. It's a Saturday morning and the Pinstripes are winless.

Our loss has released a pressure valve. Sure, it stinks. But is has also rearranged us. The stomach butterflies feel different. They've been inoculated by defeat and now they aren't as brightly colored or blinding. I recall a section of the biology textbook I sold for cash back in high school and then bought back before finals. It was in the chapter about heredity, this whole thing about peppered moths during the Industrial Revolution. Almost overnight, the moths evolved, turning from white to black. They took cover in a newly soot-filled world, turning dark to survive.

"You know what Cameron has started doing?" says the dad, whom we'd gotten to know the previous season when his kid was on Daniel's Farm AAA team. "Calling me by my first name. I don't think I like it. It just sounds weird. Don't you think it should be Daddy or Dad?" He clutches his commuter mug of coffee and watches the warm-ups on the field.

It's true, we both agree, looking up from our low beach chairs. Nobody wants to hear a fourth grader saying, "Frank, can I have a dollar for the snack bar?" or "Craig, have you seen my water bottle?"

Craning my head up to engage with the towering dad, who brushes his hand over the top of his military haircut, I know what my pops is thinking without even needing to register his expression. He shifts his Nikes in the dirt, forward and back. His forearms are draped over plastic armrests, until he unzips his fanny pack to pull out his blue bandana. It's dusty this spring and the Arizona air is thick with irritants—Bermuda grass, ragweed, cottonwood and juniper trees—and there's no telling in these parts who has allergies and who has eye spasms and who has a dead kid.

"My son always called me Dad," states the old man. "Always." He dabs at his eyes. Then he fixes his gaze on Nate, whose practice throws are looking effortless this morning. He's not chucking the ball with a crazed first-game desire to set the Arcadia Little League on fire; he's delivering it safely across home plate. The boy has taken a little juice off the velocity, but now he's commanding the ball's placement, his left arm gliding back and riding a low, arched pathway, the ball thudding cleanly into Finn's mitt.

My dad's words hang in the air between us, with the pollen and the dust and the citrus scent of bug spray.

We have our own private and terrible memories of Morgan's

prolonged cancer death, but I also know exactly what my dad is thinking, because on the rare occasions he talks about Mugsy, it's often to describe the last time he saw him, the last trip back East, when it was close to the end. "His cheeks were scruffy," he always said, his boy's scratchy face being a pivotal detail in this ghost story, a haunting by some savage, visceral memory stored in his fingers. "I touched his cheek, and then I held his hand. And I told him I loved him.

"He just let me hold his hand. Then he said, 'I love you, too, Dad.'"

Dad.

I'm sitting in denim cutoffs, a water bottle in the armrest cup holder, and what's left of my lukewarm coffee in a paper to-go cup by my feet. I'm seeing the scruffy cheek, sensing the unwanted re-play of the moment in my dad's head, until I catch Nate's freshly washed pin-striped jersey glowing in the morning light, tucked into his purple belt. It's a known fact that washing a jersey after a loss rinses away whatever residue of unseen life forces contributed to the shoddy kismet that only your black laundry arts can undo.

There are only a few minutes left before game time. Hovering Dad will need to shuffle over to the other field for his kid's game, but he can sense that the small talk he endeavored to make has somehow gotten big. "Mr. Strasser, I'm real sorry to hear about what happened and what you've been through." Stupid, well-meaning High-and-Tight-Haircut Guy and his innocent conversation starter.

My dad stuffs the bandana back into his fanny pack. "Well." He sighs. "The day you have your kids is the same day you're signing their death certificate."

The sounds of the Little League stands are now on mute. There's just static, the low hum of an echo in a tunnel.

"Okay, Dad. Maybe we let Mr. Pereira finish his coffee before we remind him that we're all gonna die. Sorry," I say, tilting my head up. "Grandpa doesn't always read the room."

"Hey, it's okay, man. I lost both my parents before I was nineteen. It's hard."

"It is. But my dad is doing great. Thanks for the kind words."

The catcher yells, "Balls in, coming down." Then the ump gives us clearance to move on with a cleansing recitation of "Play ball!"

"Okay, well, Mr. Strasser, I love seeing you out here. Good luck to the Purple Pinstripes," he adds cordially, wandering away to watch his kid on the neighboring field.

Nate is standing up on the mound, a heap of reddish brown soil. He digs in, nestling his left foot against the long white rectangular pitching slab.

The Black Pinstripes settle into their dugout as their leadoff hitter trots to the batter's box. He's the coach's son, a reliable player with a good eye. And while Nate's pitches aren't atomic, they're precise and cold-blooded. Three pitches, three strikes.

"One down, T."

"Nate is dealing this morning," says Kai's dad from the corner of the bleachers. "*Dealing*," he emphasizes, doing the hand motion.

Nate keeps dealing, strikes out the side.

"Three up, three down, baby," mutters my dad out of the corner of his mouth.

We hang a few runs on the Black Pinstripes. Nate pops out on a lazy fly ball to center, but it's okay because we are on the board. When he returns to the mound, it will be with a soft cushion of runs: three for us, none for them.

I figure nothing as good as his first inning could ever happen two innings in a row, but when Nate returns to the mound, the next batter hits an infield fly. Nate jumps off the mound to catch it. "YES!" we scream.

"Did you see that? That was a major-league play. That's tough when you're focused on pitching, and then you have to make a play like that without warning out of nowhere. Wow. One out," notes Grandpa. "Outs are precious. *We need outs.*" The next batter fouls off two pitches, then a swing and a miss to strike out.

"Two down," says my dad as the slain batter hangs his head and shuffles away.

"Plenty can still go sideways with one out left," I chime in to appease the baseball gods. I'm wearing a jade pendant on a gold chain for this game. It used to belong to my mom, who said jade was lucky and kept it hidden in the pocket of an old winter coat in her closet. I squeeze it hard.

The smallest kid on the Black Pinstripes ambles out; his strike zone is impossibly tight. Shoulders to knees on a waif of a kid doesn't give a young pitcher much room for error. The first pitch is way outside. And then Nate overcorrects, taking it near the batter's tiny chin. The kid is small, but he's also one of the oldest kids in the league, shrewd. He's not swinging at bad pitches and has no intention of giving it away. If Nate wants to take him out, he'll have to throw strikes. It's all coming unglued now, I figure. The black moths flutter a bit. Nate gets the kid to a full count. Pausing with his cleat pressed hard against the pitching rubber, he motions the catcher to move over a bit, takes a big inhale, squints. My dad and I are breathing in sync, or actually not breathing. We are holding our breath. And then Nate strikes that kid out. Inning over.

As soon as the ball leaves his hand, he knows it's right down the middle. He jumps off the mound, allowing himself a modest celebratory fist pump. And by the time the ump yells, "STRIKE," it's old news. Skip-walking, Nate is halfway back to the dugout.

"That was worth the price of admission," says my dad, inches from my ear, all memory of the scruffy cheek erased by the beauty of these shutout innings, the almost imperceptible fist pump we've now both etched into our minds. "And I didn't even pay to get in here!"

"Just another day at the office." I shrug.

We are careful to speak in low tones and monitor our body language, because overt Little League bragging is not a good look, and who knows if High-and-Tight-Haircut Dad will wander back over toward us? One must appear modest and almost insouciant about a perfectly thrown fastball on a full count to shut it down. (Privately, though, we are tamping down an interior enthusiasm that can be described only as "Lifetime Cubs fan in 2016 meets Sally Field finally winning an Oscar meets Brandi Chastain in her sports bra meets you just came up with a unified field theory to explain the relationship between all fundamental forces." That's pretty much where we are.)

After the Purple Pinstripes' first game, Daniel rethought his bullpen strategy. He's pitching three kids two innings each so they don't get worn down and ineffective. That means the hard part is over for us. "It's all gravy from here," according to my dad.

On my way to the restroom between innings, I can't miss Coach Bennett getting ready to skipper Team Chartreuse. He notices me holding my hand up to my heart as I lurch by him and he stops me. "You have Pitcher's Mom Syndrome," says the man in neon yellow. "My mom used to call it PMS." He laughs heartily, punching me lightly on the biceps. "My mom hated the games when I pitched. She still talks about it. Hang in there." I wish him good luck. Go, Team Chartreuse.

Our bats are still popping, though Nate gets on base only with a walk. "He just didn't get anything good to swing at," my dad insists. We score a couple more runs, though, and, hardened by our first defeat, we aren't cocky about our lead. Leads can be fleeting.

Finn is pitching now, a beacon of fortitude no matter how many kids he walks. "In the car on the way to the game, I told him to

visualize strikes. C'mon, kiddo!" trills Jen, his birdlike mom, looking at the field. "You got this, Finn!"

He's allowed four runs in his second inning. One more and the
team runs up against the five-runs-per-inning Little League mercy
rule. The spiritual cost of getting run-ruled is too high. I just can't
have this for Finn, the jujitsu kid with the already low voice who
visualizes with his mom in the car.

Because Finn is pitching, our backup catcher, Caleb, is behind
the dish. I root for Caleb from afar because I see his grandfather is
usually at the games, too. He's a fancy grandpa, with a sweater vest
and loafers, but he sweats every play just the same as we do, and
played catcher himself back in the day, and now Caleb has strapped
on the "tools of ignorance" (a nickname for catchers' equipment)
and has been trusted to keep his team in the game. On an outside
pitch, Caleb misses the grab, and the ball bounces away from
him. In a swift move, he prevents the ball from rolling to the backstop, but by this time, the runner on first has taken off to steal
second. Caleb fires the ball to our shortstop, Gavin, who is covering second. The runner is now in a no-man's-land between bases.
He turns around to scramble back to first base, Gavin chasing him
with the ball for the tag out.

"PICKLE!" blurts my dad, and I learn this is baseball slang for
when a runner is stranded between two bases, in jeopardy of being
tagged out or forced out by either one.

"We got ourselves a rundown!" Dad scooches all the way to the
edge of his chair, his baggy Dickies shorts folding over his knees.
"Gavin, throw to first!" he intones. Nate catches the ball at first
base, sending the runner back toward second. Nate tries to touch
the runner's back with the ball, but he's run too far away. With
Gavin out of position, Easton is supposed to cover second base, but
he's ten feet behind it, unsure of what to do. Until you're in the
middle of one, nothing quite prepares you for your first pickle.

"EASTON, COVER COVER COVER SECOND BASE! EASTON!!" Coach Daniel screams, taking his hat off his head, waving it. Easton blinks and his large, slow body seems to come to.

"E, cover!" echoes Nate, waiting to throw the ball until he knows the kid is ready. Easton gets his foot on second.

We rise from our chairs, screaming, "THROW IT!" The Black Pinstripes coaches are yelling, "RUN," and "DO NOT RUN," and the kids are on their feet in the dugout shouting instructions into the din and the players on the field are screeching and confused and there's an overall chaos only a Little League rundown can create.

The odds of last-round-pick Easton making a catch under this kind of pressure aren't great. If you're wondering what he's doing in the infield, Little League requires every kid to spend at least one inning playing an infield position, and this is Easton's. He's in a pickle, right in the middle of the action, where he never intended to be. He tries to look around the base runner toward Nate, his eyes behind dark corrective lenses. Easton's arms dangle and dance without purpose or intention, but somehow his foot does remain on the bag.

Gently, Nate tosses the ball to Easton, the way he might to Andrew, a soft toss, more like a cornhole throw than anything you might see on a baseball field. Easton, shocked, raises the ball in his glove, where it has miraculously landed. The runner slides under the tag. He was probably safe. But the ump calls him out.

Easton is a hero. Daniel is the genius who drafted him. Caleb made a "helluva throw to short," as my dad declared to his grand-father. Finn dodged getting mercy-ruled, and we somehow got out of a pickle.

Squeezing the jade pendant between my fingertips, I ask the baseball gods, who have already bestowed upon us a very generous strike zone, for one more thing. I know it's greedy. Since Nate popped out at his first at bat and walked the second, it would probably be too much to ask for even a single hit this game. We already got two shutout innings on the mound. *Just maybe do me this one favor*, I speak quietly in my mind and I honestly don't know to whom, and it feels like to nobody but it can't hurt.

During his final at bat, Nate taps a ground ball that eludes the third baseman. When he reaches first, we turn in our chairs and double high-five, then collect ourselves like we didn't just do that. "Was that an error or a hit, Dad?"

"Fielder didn't get his glove on it, so that was a hit." (I don't know if I buy that and later I'll ask Daniel. "Well, the infielder should've gotten to it. It was a routine play. But let your dad have it. Nate got on base.")

"Put the ball into play and good things happen, right, Dad?" I say, like I know anything.

Zander comes in to close. He's long-armed and semi-coordinated. His mom teaches art at a local magnet school. She wears a quirky flowered dress, black with pops of pink. She doesn't know much about baseball, but I can see from how she stands and smooths her dress and sits again that she has PMS. Zander walks a few kids, but he does what he has to do for the Purple Pinstripes. His team backs him up in the field on defense, clicking and confident. Isaiah vacuums up a blooper to third for the last out. He is all swagger, tossing the ball back to Zander with a flourish. *Game over.* The kids line up along the white-chalk third-base line to shake hands.

We beat the Black Pinstripes 8–5.

I washed the jersey. I wore the pendant.

I can control the universe.

In the glow of this feeling, safe and warm like being tucked under a heavy down comforter, but also electric and high, jittery on the stimulant of winning, I keep seeing the way my baby looked up there on the mound.

The look on Nate's face when he threw that last strike in the second inning, resolute and good mean, it was the same look I'd recently seen on my brother's face, in a photo attached to an email.

> It was a total shock to see several links to obituaries when I Googled Morgan. I lived in Santa Monica from 1975–1982 and coached Morgan in Little League. You can deal with a parent passing, but not someone much younger. Please tell Nelson that I would love to hear from him. I kept all the team photos from Santa Monica and this one is my favorite because this team unexpectedly won a City Championship.

It was only when I got this email from Coach Walter that I realized he never did have a kid on the Angels. None of the kids were his, and all of the kids were his. I sat on the email and the photo for some weeks, unsure whether the picture of the Angels, taken indoors like a school photo, would be too much for my dad. Photos of my brother were for the bin inside the shed. But there was something about Morgan's coach of a thousand years ago still clocking the whereabouts of his clutch first baseman, something about the picture, Walter beaming, hands behind his back, in flared gray trousers. There's the heavy curtain of a school auditorium's stage behind the players as they pose in white jerseys with yellow sleeves. The Santa Monica Angels wore yellow hats with stiff brims. My brother is ten in the picture, a year older than Nate is now.

"Dad, do you remember Walter, Morgan's coach from Santa Monica?"

"Walter? Yeah. Of course. He was a CPA. He didn't have a kid on the team; he just loved baseball. And he loved Morgan. We had a kid, Teddy, who played shortstop. It was Teddy to Morgan at first base, and Morgan never missed a single play. It was automatic. Boom, to Teddy, BOOM to Morgan. I never saw anything like it."

"Walter sent me a note and a picture of the Santa Monica Angels. You're in the picture, too. You must have been assistant coaching that year."

"No, I didn't really do much. I don't know why I'm in the picture. Walter wrote to you?" He kind of trails off and I don't chase it.

My brother, stern-faced, glowers at me from the afterlife. He is right in the middle of the photo, his dark hair splaying out from under his yellow hat. He has a baby face, rounded cheeks, but his eyes are black and his expression is all business. Put kids out. Make pitchers pay. This kid, chin tilted forward, was living under the auspices of our evil stepmother, and you can see in the photo that he's absorbing something, almost too much of something, this scrawny kid who got to shine only a few hours a week. Coach Walter's gritty little assassin.

Santa Monica was the home not only of the Angels, but also of Synanon, the rehab facility turned group therapy center where my dad met Carol. This photo of him—fluffy hair, plaid shirt, look of confusion—takes me back to the Dad from those days, to that apartment in Santa Monica where he moved in with Carol and her teenage kids. "They taught this thing called 'attack therapy,'" he told me recently of Synanon. My dad and I got along okay after Carol died, but eventually something would trigger me, and I'd almost always start grilling him about Carol, and he'd clam up, and things would go sideways. It was only after he moved to Phoenix that he offered any details about the unsavory group therapy joint where they met. "Someone would criticize you for being a selfish loser or an egomaniac or a fat slob, and then everyone would pile on, you know, sitting in a circle. They thought that would help you, this group assault, people just calling you out. Everyone would be screaming over each other. Maybe it worked for junkies," said my dad. They hadn't stuck around very long, fortunately; the place later became a full-blown cult. When I looked it up, I discovered several members were convicted of violent crimes. "I thought it would help me because I didn't have my shit together, but it didn't."

Looking back on an afternoon when Carol cornered me and I ran away from home, I wonder if she was just doing what she'd been taught to do at Synanon, a one-way dose of attack therapy. It goes without saying this aggressive truth-telling barrage wasn't cathartic for me at age seven.

"Your dad loves me more than you," she spat as I stood against a doorframe, her hand pressing into the wall above. She shouted into my face, her skin crinkly and golden tan around her eyes, a red scarf in her hair. She was the Great Santini in a denim wrap skirt, terrifyingly free of subtext and gleefully sadistic. "There are two kinds of love. The kind your dad has for me is more important. DO YOU UNDERSTAND?"

"Yes," I squeaked. I'm sad for that girl because she probably cried and believed everything Carol said, including that she was fat and dirty and uncivilized.

Carol carried herself like a misplaced royal forced to live in the servants' quarters with us, a lower class of people. She always made fun of my dad's hands because of the grease under his nails from rebuilding car parts, and she made sure she was never seen with him in his Delta Battery uniform.

"You can't wear *that*," she would say with a snicker. Then she'd throw her head back and laugh theatrically at the thought of being seen with him in his grease-monkey suit. He'd apologize and good-naturedly rush off to change. But first he'd say to my brother and me, in a big, funny Valley girl voice, "Yuck, like, I am *SO gross*," and we'd laugh, but I didn't want that for my dad, for him to be subjected to this scorn, to be living with this person who didn't seem to love him or even like him. There were never any niceties between them, at least when I was around, and maybe that can't be right, but that's how I remember it. She was always on him about his dirty uniform; the "shithole" house he bought her in Santa Rosa; that he forgot to do the composting or some other chore; her dissatisfaction with their sex life, which she yelled about loud enough for us to hear. She was always angry when he spent time with us, because she was a mental health expert, in the middle of logging the hours of supervised clinical counseling work she needed to get the therapy license she never got, and she knew what was what, and she said he was spoiling us, and that's why she mostly referred to us as the Prince and the Princess. All of it was jarring, and I couldn't ever figure out what he saw in Carol.

At least my dad knew how to fix things. All she did was break them.

One Saturday, after my dad got home from work and changed out of his uniform, we were heading out together, even if Carol didn't like it.

"Do not take her to the GODDAMN movies," she yelled. My brother was with my mom that weekend, so I'd spent the day by myself collecting blackberries in a bucket from thorny bushes across the road, because I didn't know how to make any of the fancy health food in Carol's kitchen, rows of mysterious dry goods in mason jars. Carol had already banned my dad from taking me to the library to rent poetry records, like we used to do, and now she didn't think it was right to take me anywhere at all, even though I was there only once a month, and it was a four-hour round trip on the Golden Gate Transit bus to get there. But he already had his fleece sweater over his arm, and he was really leaving, and she couldn't stand it. "The Princess doesn't need your attention every single second. She should entertain herself, Nelson. WHAT HAVE I BEEN TELLING YOU?"

On that drizzly afternoon, the vein in Carol's neck bulged as her volume rose. My dad stepped away from the front door, unsure what to do. I looked at him, then at the door, then downward, frozen. When he made no other move, Carol grabbed the round base of a glass lamp and threw it at my head. It grazed my hair and then smashed against the front door.

Calmly, like an action hero, Dad said, "You better pack up and get out. Be gone by the time we get back." We stepped over shards of glass and left for the movies and didn't discuss the lamp. In the cool darkness of the theater, I sat next to my dad eating Jujyfruits in a state of rapture, picking out the licorice ones to eat first. It was like when people called my dad at Delta Battery and said, "My car is making a sound. It's going EHHH-CH-CH-EHH." But then when they brought it in, the car wouldn't make the sound, and the problem couldn't be diagnosed. For years Dad had defended Carol and said she meant well and was a good stepmother. But now he'd witnessed the malady in the machinery for himself, loud and clanging, so it couldn't be ignored. He'd heard it and seen it and he wasn't going to stand for it.

But when we got home, Carol was there, same as ever. The glass was swept up. Nobody mentioned it again.

———

After the game, our shoes still dusted with rust-colored Little League dirt, my dad offers to tag along with me to Costco. Daniel and the boys stay to watch the next game.

We stroll by kids eating Drumsticks from the snack bar as they process wins and losses. In the parking lot, trunks open and shut. My dad and I have to keep expressions on our faces that say, *We understand this is Little League, and we don't take it too seriously, because these are children. We are not crazy. We are normal, well-adjusted people.*

No biggie.

I've been invited to some sort of "moms' night" and asked to bring "finger food." Neither of us knows exactly what that is, but we have a clear mission: We are a father-and-daughter team who don't understand finger food, brought together for a purpose and in no particular hurry. And now we can freely discuss the Little League victory with no need to contain our joy. We traipse through the aisles of Costco powered by ebullience so intense that even we understand that our euphoria is well out of proportion to a third grader striking out five kids.

"Dad, feel how cold it is in here. Seriously. Just see if you can stand it. This is the coldest place in Arizona." I hold open the door to the refrigerated produce room and he follows me. Pallets of berries and boxes of bagged greens line the outskirts of the room. We stand in the middle, holding out our arms to take in the full arctic chill, bracing ourselves, daring ourselves to stay put. "I think I can outlast you, if my nose doesn't freeze off."

"Don't pull a—

"Beck Weathers!" we shout into the chard and carrots. Beck was the doctor who survived a disaster on Mount Everest and returned safely, albeit having lost his nose and a few other appendages to frostbite. We dash out through the heavy doors and shake ourselves warm. Now, down to business.

"Are these finger food?" I ask my dad, holding up a tray of turkey and Swiss pinwheels. He owns one set of sheets, and only because I bought them. I know he doesn't use the fitted sheet on his bed, because it's in use as his bicycle cover. He doesn't know from classy shit like finger foods, and neither do I, but together we have cracked the code of hostess gifts, because we have each other, because we can do anything, because Nate. Throws. Strikes.

"BINGO!" he shouts. His grandchild is not only possibly definitely the greatest lefty third-grade Little League player out there, but now his daughter has found the absolute perfect item to bring to moms' night.

We confer with some others in our midst, our new best friends in the aisles. We have so much room now in our hearts to love everyone. Costco has no strangers. All the sorcery of the universe has gone our way. We love the retired couple buying coffee pods, the single guy picking up a twelve-pack of hamburger buns, and the mom with her baby in the front of the cart. "Isn't that the cutest baby? Look at her, T, with her little pink Binky!" All humanity is righteous and good and chubby-cheeked and healthy. The retired couple confirms this tray of pinwheels is absolutely finger food. They're happy to help. Everybody loves us and we love everybody.

"Should I bring a second thing?"

Normally, my dad's trailer-park parsimony dictates never spending an extra dime. He's done making it rain with crazy schemes. He lets Daniel hold his extra cash in a bank account, maybe a grand or so, and the old man doesn't believe in frivolities. But that was before. Not today.

"Yes. You can't just show up with one finger food," he says, a twinkle in his twitchy eye. We turn a corner toward an island of refrigerated crudités. It's post-Little-League-victory, Costco afternoon nirvana, the intoxication of a thousand guzzled bottles of Kirkland bourbon, a high that only we can understand, in this moment, in this store, which happens to be sprinkled with Little League players of various ages in red and turquoise jerseys, with dirt-caked white pants. Everyone in this neighborhood plays ball, and here we are, doing our errands like everyone else, but *we've* survived a pickle and seen a (questionable) hit and watched our lefty dealing and pumping his fist, and I knew when my dad suggested another $13.99 purchase that was wholly unnecessary that he just didn't want this Costco trip to end. "Get the veggies. You need to get the veggies."

As stupid and meaningless as the pitching performance of a nine-year-old boy may be in the world, we award ourselves a special grief dispensation. We are recused from reasonable human behavior.

My dad leaned over a hospice bed to touch the cheek of his son, knowing it was for the last time.

"I love you, too, Dad."

We were allowed to celebrate a stupid fucking baseball game.

———————

So much happens to your body when you have a cancerous tumor that it's not clear to me why my brother had a stroke, maybe something about blood thinners or not walking around enough. But one day he called my dad from the hospital, and though he'd managed to dial his cell phone, he was saying nonsense like "Dad, the people are here outside the window to get me. The police people."

My dad called me, finally undone by the cancer and the return of the cancer.

Five years after Morgan got out of the hospital, after surviving the first long and perilous surgery, a spinal fluid leak, two additional surgeries to cut out infection, and then weeks of radiation, something was wrong again. He'd spent more than a month in the hospital that first go-round but had managed to live a pretty normal life after that. He had to empty his bladder with catheters he took to work, hidden in a messenger bag, and he sometimes had terrible fatigue, but we figured that was a small price to pay for being alive. Then one day he was playing tennis with Laura and felt a sharp pain. The rod surgeons had placed in his back had snapped. When they went in to replace it they saw the tumor was growing back. At that point, Laura and Morgan were living in Arlington, and they had two little kids. My dad was living in the woods way up in Northern California. I had already moved to Phoenix with Daniel and the kids to take a television job. My mom was a widow in Vegas. My parents dropped everything to help Morgan's family when he went in for surgery, but that procedure led to infections, more surgeries to carve away at the tumor, more surgeries to cut away more infections, the wound that got so big it wouldn't close, and now the stroke.

My dad sobbed, "This is it. It's over. He's not Morgan anymore. He's not my son and I can't go back this time. I can't go back." It was the first time I had heard him cry about my brother. He didn't like to burden me; he liked to keep things sunny, the news about whatever procedure upbeat. And, of course, there was his lifelong tendency to bury his head in the sand. "You know Morgan. He's tough as an ox. He's already asking for chocolate cake," he'd say.

"No, Dad. It isn't over," I said now, stern. "And if it is over, you're going to want to say goodbye. I know this is awful. I mean, I can't know how awful. But listen to me. You are going to get to the airport. Daniel is going to buy you a ticket and send the boarding pass to your phone. Take a taxi from the airport to the hospital. You're going to pack right now." He couldn't stop crying. "Dad, you can do this," I pronounced as confidently as I could. "*You're* tough as an ox." And he did.

When I landed at Dulles International Airport, as I had so many times before the stroke, I knew I didn't even have time to stop for water at a kiosk. If I missed seeing my brother alive for a Dasani, that just wasn't going to be okay. I sprinted through the airport in mismatched sweats, thirsty.

But the brain is resilient. Morgan was only a bit off by the time we got there, and Laura played me her favorite Argentine pop song on her phone and we danced around the ICU room, Morgan kind of out of it, but I like to think amused by the apocalyptic dance party. A few weeks later, he was almost back to normal. I wish this was a story about the miraculous ability of the human brain to bounce back, but the dying is the headline and the rest gets buried.

"What do you want to do when you get out of here?" I asked my brother, in a faded green hospital gown and a dying man's beard.

He said he wanted to see one of his son's soccer games—but he didn't survive until soccer season—and "I want to go to a movie," so on my next visit, I spent hours calling every car service I could until I found a random guy with a wheelchair van. It was pouring rain as we all traipsed out to see *Trainwreck*. I gave the driver a hundred in cash to be there waiting for us after the movie at exactly 2:35 p.m. We left the theater and stood waiting on the corner for twenty-five minutes under an awning, sheltering from sheets of rain, my brother looking nervous, until the man came to take us home.

My brother had laughed repeatedly at a running joke in the movie about LeBron James being rich but also a cheap bastard. He sipped his big movie fountain drink and laughed, and I gave myself the assist for that laugh, which was almost his normal laughing-at-a-funny-movie laugh. He watched the movie and I watched him. In the dim theater, watching him sip a Dr Pepper like he used to do, it seemed like the old days, like when I pretended to love *The Jerk* so I could love the same movie as my brother. Except this time he was in a wheelchair space, wearing the white nylon pressure socks, the wide Velcro-strapped shoes. "There's going to be a time when I don't leave this room anymore," he said later, lying on his hospice bed in the basement as I sat on the red couch near the wall, a desk covered with IVs and medications and Desitin between us. We sat in silence with our dad, watching the 49ers lose.

"Dad" was the last word my father heard his son speak. But that wasn't the last thing my brother said. His last words were to his wife: "Will I return home?"

It's like he knew he was going somewhere, but he didn't know where. Home was where his kids lived, where he read them *Goodnight Moon* before bed. Home was where he kept the Nikon camera he'd bought on eBay, and all the special lenses he had collected for

it. Home was where he parked his car, a Toyota Camry he'd managed to keep for almost three hundred thousand miles ("If you
change the timing belt on those things regularly, you can drive
them into the ground," my dad had said. "That car is a work-
horse."). He wasn't coming back home to *that* place. Did he mean
Earth? Was that the home he meant? Was he talking about reincar-
nation, wondering if he would return as a baby or a potted fern or
a mountain lion? I was never sure what he was asking but, for my
part, I wondered if his consciousness would return to preside over
life like an ump, watching closely but not playing and not coaching. I didn't know, but I knew what I wanted to believe. I wanted
to believe my brother had walked to the edge of a cliff, turned to
face all of us, and leaned backward, a trust fall he was forced to take
into nowhere. I wanted to believe that, after a moment airborne,
he'd been received, flying into a cloud of eternal contentment, free
from his suffering. But if you put a gun to my head, I'd probably
have to admit that I thought about things more like my dad did. I
could pretend I didn't, when it was time to pray to birds flying
across center field, as if my brother had sent them, like he was a
Santa Monica Angel and he had nothing but time for all my anxious Little League wishes. I could rub my jade necklace and talk to
him and ask, "Can you believe this kid? A lefty who loves baseball,
just like you." I could find a penny and pretend Morgan had placed
it on the sidewalk to tell me he was still my big brother and that he
was okay, and that finally, finally, he was in a better place than I
was. I didn't have to feel guilty anymore.

Ashes to ashes, my dad always says. Dust to dust.

At least I can fake it long enough to allow for the possibility that
Morgan has made it to someplace that feels like home, some eternal, galactic resting place, an easy chair in heaven where you're so
at peace kicking back that you don't even remember the wounds or
scars you used to have.

My dad can't sign off on any kind of afterlife bullshit. His home is a tin can, and his son only ashes.

"**How did the pinwheels go over?**" texted my dad that night. And I didn't care that he wouldn't know a crudité from a Camry. And it was okay that he'd record-scratched the pregame niceties at Little League. I should have overridden my knee-jerk impulse to correct him, to tell him not to embarrass me in front of Arcadia people, the perfect, polite Range Rover crowd. It was true that normal people made light conversation at youth sports events without publicly acknowledging the existential truth that all the children would one day die. But I wasn't going to bust his balls anymore, not about chewing with his mouth full, not about banging his spoon on his bowl when he ate, not about going full circle of life on some unsuspecting dad before the first pitch was even thrown on a Saturday morning.

He's got very few teeth and gives very few fucks. His ears are hairy and his eyes are twitchy and his hat is sweaty and he has no pension to spend on a time-share or a speedboat and he owns no pants. All he has is a tin can and a bicycle and a storage shed. And maybe, if you believe in all that—and he most certainly does not—he's got himself one left-handed, all-star angel, right out of Santa Monica, who may or may not show up someday, take hold of his hand and his soul, and shepherd him somewhere nice, to a wide gap, way out in deep center.

CHAPTER SIX

Hello, Goodbye, Shalom, and Play Ball

"Baseball is like church.
Many attend, but few understand."

—WES WESTRUM

Dad arrived in Phoenix with nothing left. He'd failed to secure his possessions.

He threw his belongings into the back of his pickup truck a few weeks after my brother's funeral. He didn't tether anything down, so by the time he arrived in the desert, most of the stuff belonging to his old self, the self who *hadn't* been shot out of a cannon into the grief-o-sphere, was littered on freeways and byways from California to Arizona. He hadn't bothered with bungee cords because gravity was just another force he couldn't control.

The blue plastic bin filled with pictures of my brother survived the journey, along with the trophy they had won together in a paddle tennis tournament decades earlier. "You know how we won? You know how a klutzy old man like me got the only trophy I've ever won in my whole stupid life? Your brother told me, 'If anything is even close to the line, stay out of my way and let me make the shot.' And he never missed one. No one could believe a shlep like me, five foot nothing, produced an offspring like that." MORGAN AND NELSON

STRASSER, said the engraving on the award, MEN'S DIVISION, CHAM-
PIONS.

It was my idea for him to move to Arizona. His place in Northern California was remote. It was so far north of wine country that
it was more like meth country. It was hours from the nearest airport
and far from any decent hospital. And now we both knew what it
looked like if you got really sick, how you'd need people. "Dad,
you're not getting any younger," I'd told him on the phone. "What's
the point of being out there when you can be here? With us."

When he arrived in Arizona, he didn't have much more than his
thick head of hair, which he promptly shaved. "Haircuts are a waste
of money," he grumbled, but I knew he had shaved it to recast
himself. The guy with thick salt-and-pepper hair had spent a couple
of years caring for his sick child, watching him die. This bald guy
was different; he'd walked through a crucible, and now there wasn't
much left to singe.

He looked like a monk, but he hadn't formally renounced all his
possessions; he'd just let them fly away. "I didn't need any of that
stuff," he said a few months after he'd settled in Arizona. He insisted he hadn't even noticed losing it, but Daniel and I agreed he
must have heard or seen the boxes tumbling onto the road, seen
sheets and towels and moth-eaten sweaters aloft in his rearview
mirror. We figured he simply had no desire to cling to things from
his old life. Who cared? If the forces of wind and propulsion and
torque and momentum had encouraged the release of some meaningless possessions, he wasn't going to put up a fight. "I love my
little trailer. I use everything I have." He gestured grandly toward
a foot and a half of grimy counter space in his kitchenette, where
he fixed his standard dinner of canned black beans, quinoa, and
tofu. The place was furnished with odds and ends like a dinged-up
secondhand end table. "You want to talk small carbon footprint? I
don't even use my air-conditioning unit. In *Phoenix*!"

"Plus, not many people get to rotate the tires on their house, Dad."

"Very funny. It's just called a mobile home; it's not actually mobile."

His house didn't have wheels, but he wasn't going anywhere anyway. "I loved the desert right away, right when I moved here. I'm a Semite, T. I'm built for heat," he always tells me. The first time we visited him in the hot tin can off Hayden Road, I realized I hadn't lived in the same city as my dad since I was four years old. Now he was ten minutes away. That year, we watched our first season of Little League together, coed T-ball. No outs, no score, but we had already started getting way too into it, even back then, when nothing counted. My kids were thrilled when their cheering section expanded, and Grandpa was always around. Even I couldn't believe this guy who stored orange-slice candies in his fanny pack for his grandkids was the same guy who hadn't noticed if I'd had chicken pox or lice or both. "These are two for three bucks at the 99 Cents Only Store. They shouldn't even allow that. Or change the name of the store. But it's worth it for these orange candies. Look at the back of the package, kids. Zero fat!"

My dad seemed to worship Daniel, praising the detailed weekend sports schedule he texted to us every Thursday, gushing about his coaching, how calm he was with the kids, how attentive.

"The best thing you ever did was telling me I wasn't getting any younger, that I should be closer to family. You were right. Moving here was like a do-over," he announced the week he arrived in Arizona. "Being a grandparent is a do-over."

———

Three months before the start of Little League season, I dragged my dad to a Jewish memorial service held next door to his trailer, at Green Acres Mortuary and Cemetery. Three local synagogues held the service jointly, before the High Holy Days, for anyone looking for a communal grieving ritual. We weren't members of any of the temples, but I saw the flyer and figured nobody would be checking. My brother, my mother, and hopefully God would forgive the trespass and appreciate the effort, even if I didn't really believe in a Talmud kind of God, and even if nobody in my family was very religious.

It seemed like a good excuse to spend an afternoon with my dad, do something healing and ancient and ritualized. And I'd been worried about the old man. He almost never said Morgan's name out loud.

Under a temporary canopy, the middle-aged rabbi tucked his prayer shawl around himself against the warm afternoon breeze. "The Mourner's Kaddish doesn't even mention death or dying," he explained. "The prayer only sanctifies and glorifies the greatness of God, so that even in our darkest times, when our faith is tested, we affirm our belief in the divine." We looked down at our printouts, the swirly Hebrew letters on one side, the English translation on the other.

"We say it as a community, as a reminder that in grief none of us is alone." The group then delivered an out-of-sync and hesitant recitation of the prayer, after saying all our dead loved ones' names, as is the Jewish custom. All the names went from our mouths into the breeze, in our makeshift open-air house of worship across from the Salt Cellar seafood restaurant, where every night an oblong sign illuminates a painted lobster. *"Yitgadal v'yitkadash sh'mei raba b'alma di v'ra chir'utei . . ."*

Dad crossed and uncrossed his legs, then planted his sneakers in the grass. His jaw twitched a little. I looked down at the translation. "May there be abundant peace from heaven, with life's goodness for us and for all thy people Israel. And let us say: Amen."

"Amen," Dad mumbled, a beat late.

"As Jews, we don't say 'goodbye' when someone dies. We say 'shalom,' because 'shalom' means hello and goodbye. It's a word with many definitions," said the slender rabbi, his auburn beard tightly groomed, his voice rising to compete with sniffles and nose blows, the sound of a plane cruising toward Sky Harbor Airport. "It also means wholeness, peace, and contentment."

Pops can take religion only in small doses. He seemed ready to go the second he sat in his folding chair. "Jews really know what they're doing with death stuff," I'd promised him. "I'm telling you, other than challah, our baked goods are for shit, but we've got mourning rituals down."

Sensing his restlessness, I felt selfish for making him come with me, even if everyone says communal grieving is good, even if I was worried about my dad and thought this might be helpful to him somehow.

Dad looked fragile staring into his prayer book, his cheeks gaunt, his lower eyelids puffy under his green eyes, all the specks of lint on his long, baggy shorts glaring in the daylight. He'd just gotten them at Walmart, he'd told me, for eleven dollars. The long workman's shorts and his threadbare gym socks looked out of place among the khakis and loafers. He didn't want to be there, even if he could wear shorts, because he didn't care about kaddish, and all this just reminded him how much he didn't want his son to be dead.

And now I was ready to go, too.

"You want to say shalom to this service?" I whispered as my dad shifted in his chair.

"Let's blow this Hebrew Popsicle stand," he responded. We lifted ourselves from our metal folding chairs. Dad dropped his borrowed white satin yarmulke back into a bowl and we slipped away quietly as the rabbi read Psalm 23 into the wind. "The Lord is my shepherd; I shall not want . . ."

"I shall not want to stay," said Dad as we walked out of earshot and into Green Acres. I punched him in the arm.

"That was nice, though, right?" He nodded with half-assed enthusiasm to remind me that religion was bullshit and that he wasn't falling for it, not even now, when it would have been nice for God to explain his son dying.

We walked around with the dead people.

Stone benches and bronze grave markers blanketed the grass on either side of us as we traversed the winding paved road back out toward Hayden. I stared at a bench, slowing down, my dad next to me. TAYLOR was engraved on the side. IN OUR HEARTS FOREVER.

A few feet away a Taylor grave was marked by a slim rectangular slab in the grass, blue plastic flowers on one side, a ceramic pink flamingo on the other. A few yards behind it, a round fountain sprayed water into a small pond. **NO DOGS ALLOWED**, warned a sign stuck in the grass.

We kept walking, not rushing to get back to the Riviera. A ball of used Kleenex was stuck between the grass and the pavement. You could hear the wind get louder, and the sound of the fountain water hitting the surface of the pond.

"What are the odds that in any dimension we will ever see Morgan again?" I asked.

"Dust to dust," said Dad. "There's just nothingness."

We strode by a white pickup truck parked haphazardly by the side of the road. A middle-aged couple had left it there to walk to a grave off in the distance. They stared down toward the grass. The man put his hands on his hips. The woman took a sip from a bottle of water. How far had they come? Had they driven for miles, or did they live right down the road?

"There's a famous story in Buddhism called 'The Parable of the Mustard Seed,'" Victoria had told us one Monday night at a dharma talk. That story came back to me as I stared at the couple, unable to look away. "It revolves around a woman whose only child died. She carried the baby from neighbor to neighbor, just distraught, begging for medicine to bring him back to life. An old man told her to go to the Buddha for help. The Buddha instructed her to go back to her village and gather mustard seeds, but only from households that had never been touched by death. From those mustard seeds, Buddha promised he would create a medicine to bring her son back to life. She went back to her village and tried to find the mustard seeds, knocking on every door. I think you all know what happened, right?" She looked at us in the pews, her weekly dharma group of maybe a dozen at the church in the desert. She pulled the shawl from around her shoulders and placed it across her knees, took a sip of tea from her thermos; then she spoke deliberately, leaving air between all the words. "The woman couldn't find any of those death-free mustard seeds, because *there is no home free of mortality*." When I looked down at my hands in my lap, I envisioned the bereaved mother running around with her dead baby, knocking on door after door, and I had to squeeze my hands together hard so I wouldn't cry. *But what happened to the mom?* I wanted to ask, but I got real shy at these dharma talks and never raised my hand. As if Victoria could hear me thinking, she continued. "That day, according to the parable, the mother understood the universality of death. She later became enlightened." *Did Victoria just give this tearjerker some kind of happy ending?* Enlightenment. I could now meditate for a whole twenty minutes instead of just two, but I was a hundred lifetimes away from enlightenment.

There are no resuscitating do-over mustard seeds, I thought to myself, peering over at the white-truck couple. But I liked the cemetery, because it was a place you knew for sure that you could cry and knock on doors until your fingers bled, and nobody had the seeds to bring the cold baby in your arms back to life, but at least everybody there had bloody knuckles, too, the kind you couldn't miss, fresh from knocking.

The faraway man stood very still, neck craned down. The woman wore a bright yellow T-shirt. She leaned over to give a bouquet of orange flowers one last rearranging, her fingers lingering over the petals. As they headed back toward the shiny white truck, I caught her eye; then I looked away, embarrassed. *I'm not a death tourist*, I wanted to say. *I'm one of you. I live here, too.* By the time I glanced back over at them, they were already in the pickup truck. It was sparkling clean. *Did they get it washed for this visit? Or are they just clean-car people?*

The names of four more Taylors were etched into another bench. NOW WITH OUR LORD AND SAVIOR JESUS CHRIST. Must be nice to believe, to believe so hard you'd etch it in stone. The truck drove away slowly.

"Dad, there's so much we don't know. I mean, you can't totally discount all the near-death experiences, people flatlining and then coming back to life, reporting that they were floating in some otherworldly wash of light and peace." I stopped to peer down at a weed-covered granite stone told me that the being buried below me had been born and had died the same year. "I'm with you, Dad. Most of what humans cling to about the afterlife is just a salve. But the images are so consistent."

Ahead of us, two bronze plaques were attached to a large rectangular brick pillar. One explained about the rules.

FLOWER INFORMATION

ALL DECORATIONS WILL BE REMOVED

THE WEEKS OF MAY 15 & DECEMBER 1

FLOWERS MUST BE IN CEMETERY

REGULATION VASES

ALL OTHERS WILL BE REMOVED

Above that was another plaque. We stopped to read it.

THIS IS A CEMETERY

Lives are commemorated—deaths recorded—
families are reunited—memories are made tangible—
and love is undisguised. This is a cemetery.

"Deep stuff for a Green Acres plaque that's long on flower in-structions, right, Dad?"

"Uh-huh," he said softly, distracted.

We passed the Keller bench. TOGETHER FOREVER. Two colorful windmills on wooden sticks twirled in the wind. How long had the windmills been there? The colors looked bright and fresh, unmuted by the elements.

NGUY, I read on a dark gray bench, and there was some writing in Vietnamese. Next to Nguy, there was FOWLER. BELOVED SON, BROTHER AND FRIEND.

Beloved son.

An old-fashioned toy truck, robin's-egg blue, was tucked under-neath the Halliday bench.

Over the cemetery's brick fence, you could see tall palm tree tops far in the distance, and miles away, the giant rock formations of Papago Park populated the horizon, between the clouds and the city below. Those are the same rocks you can see from the south ball field at Ingleside Middle School; from Green Acres, you're just see-ing the other side of those same red rocks.

All you could hear now was our steps slapping the pavement, Dad's little puff, puff breaths, birds chirping, wind whipping through the air. I knew the old man didn't want to talk, but I did.

"Everyone says when you're dying, you actually see other dead people—you know, all your loved ones, they just appear. If it's just some brain chemicals, a neurological response to trauma, or maybe some anesthesia thing, a trick of the mind, you still get to see your dead loved ones again," I said as we headed toward the exit. "I'm not saying they're angels—they may just be hallucinations—but it must be comforting."

"I hope so," he replied. "I'd like to see my baby boy one more time." My legs got heavy, and I wanted to stop walking, freeze mid-stride, but I played it cool and didn't even slow my pace. *His baby boy.* Morgan had been my brother, but first, Morgan had been his baby boy. Grief wasn't a competition, but he won.

"Maybe we can't rule it out completely," I said.

MILLER, said a bench, the name carved between a pair of Jewish stars. A little bird landed on it. I approached, crossing the squishy grass. The bird stayed. On top of the bench was a black-and-white photo of a couple. STEWART AND LEEANN. FATHER AND MOTHER. She wore a stiff 1960s bouffant.

"Dad, do you want me to put you in here?"

"No. Waste of money. Burn me up and throw me in a card-board box." He wasn't kidding. He'd put Carol in a Chupa Chups gourmet lollipop tin. The day I saw the tin was the first time I'd been to his gloomy Santa Rosa house since I was seventeen, the day Carol accused me of stealing a brooch shaped like a bumblebee. It later turned up under the couch, and she blamed the dog, but I announced that if my dad ever wanted to see me again, he could come to me, and from that day forward that's what he did. After Carol died years later, the coast was clear. When I went to look inside Carol's sewing room, the lollipop tin was propping open the door. How he had acquired this lollipop tin I didn't know—she never would've had candy in the house—but the pieces were com-ing together. "Dad, do I not want to know what's in there?"

"Don't ask."

"Just so I'm sure: Those aren't lollipops. *Those are stepmommy pops, right?*"

This exchange ended up in a story I wrote about Carol for a Los Angeles newspaper; it was about the relief associated with her death and whether, spiritually speaking, it was okay. *Ding-dong, the witch is dead* went through my head all day for weeks. My editor put the story on the cover, with an illustration of a witch under a house, nothing left but striped socks and ruby slippers. The first few months of post-Carol happiness exploded into a single moment of euphoria one night after the story had been published.

I was at the Biltmore Hotel for the Los Angeles Press Club Awards; the story about Carol had been nominated. My editor was sitting next to me, his hair a floppy mess, but he still looked dashing. He'd encouraged me to write about Carol's death, to explore how complicated it was. When my name was announced, "Teresa Strasser, Best Feature Story for 'The Evil Stepmother Dies,'" I stood up in the dark ballroom, and a spotlight found me. As I walked up to the podium to get the award, my editor was clapping hard and standing, and then everyone stood, and a couple of prerecorded lines from the article played from speakers all around the periphery of the room, and from overhead: "What do you do when you lose someone? Someone you really hated? It's a little awkward. I'll tell you that much. Last month, my stepmother of more than twenty-five years died at age sixty-seven of lung cancer. It was a terrible death, one I wouldn't wish on my worst enemy, which, incidentally, she was."

My words came out of the speakers, but what I heard was Carol's voice saying, "Nelson, she's a kleptomaniac; she steals things in this house." She said I'd never amount to anything, and here I was, amounting to something. I didn't forgive her in some mature, Yom Kippur kind of way. And I didn't let her be, in some kind of Buddhist way. She always said I was a loser, but in that moment she'd made me a winner. How much she would've hated me winning any kind of award on account of her made me fuzzy and light-headed with glee.

No religion would celebrate this reaction. I knew that. I was dancing on her grave in a pink dress. She was riding out eternity in a lollipop tin.

Near the Miller bench, Dad said, "Don't spend any money on me, T."

"Should I just put you in the mobile home with your bicycle and set the whole thing on fire like a trailer-trash Viking funeral?"

"Fine with me. I'll be gone. Don't bother with anything on my account."

Windmills turned. American flags fluttered. A gust of dry air blew across the big green lawn. We passed an overfilled trash bin. A dried bouquet of red roses was coming out of the top, along with a clear plastic iced coffee cup. A patch of dried gum was hardening on the can's opening.

GATE OPENS AUTOMATICALLY, said a sign on the way out of Green Acres. We crossed the driveway onto the sidewalk, turned right, passed a bus stop where you could catch the 81 Hayden/McClintock, then a few feet later we came to the entrance of the Riviera. Cacti at least a story tall stood guard along with a couple of old-fashioned streetlamps.

NO TRESPASSING, said a sign.

We walked past the giant ivory-and-green cement Riviera sign, welcoming all to this fifty-five-plus community. We passed the always empty pool behind an iron gate and headed toward Dad's trailer.

We sat on the low, rickety steps covered in charcoal gray carpet that went from his porch to the door, bolstered by a decaying wooden railing. He dabbed at his eyes with his bandana and then put it back in his fanny pack.

"Baseball starts up in January," he said, after we'd sat there wordlessly for a few minutes, hearing nothing but the sound of the neighbor's wind chimes. "The Minors, T. Kids don't just pitch the first two innings. They pitch the entire game." He'd had enough of ashes and angels and the afterlife. He was trying to change the subject. And I was going to help the old man.

"Remember last year in Farm AAA?" I said. "Nate was throwing pretty hard, and now he's a year older. He could be throwing gas out there come January.

"And his hitting last season was pretty good. When he hit the ball square, he absolutely crushed it," I added, peering over the wall toward Green Acres.

"Crushed it," Dad said, nodding in agreement. "And we should've won that AAA elimination game, but our defense was porous."

Dad shook his head, attempting to rid himself of all the mistakes he'd seen in that game, all those numb-nut children who stole from him a chance to see his grandson play one more game. "It was a comedy of errors. I still have a grudge against that Ellis kid," said Dad, joking and not. "He had no business at short. Every ball, right through the wickets. His parents made him play. Baseball isn't for kids who don't love it. They should have let him take guitar lessons or something."

And we talked about baseball until it got dark, just a couple of trailer-park Jews who had logged half a grief service. *Amen.*

For now, heaven isn't a white light that pulls you toward some wordless, holy oneness. Heaven is a Little League game we can win, right here on the terra firma of Ingleside Middle School.

It's dusk, and Dr. Coach Patel's Team Black is warming up, their pitcher tossing accurate but juicy meatballs from the mound to his catcher. Team Black is winless so far. "Don't count out Patel,"

Daniel tells me the morning of our game, about the quietly competitive anesthesiologist who coaches his twins every year. "He takes the draft almost as seriously as I do. *Almost.* But I don't think he puts his foot on the accelerator until midseason. Honestly, his team could win it all, but I think we have a chance tonight."

This is the game overview I report to the old man as Andrew skips off to jostle for position at the snack bar, barely seeing over the counter. "Balls in, coming down!" yells Team Black's catcher, ending warm-ups. "Goody," squeals my dad, settling into his beach chair. And everything in the atmosphere changes when we hear the words "Play ball!"

Team Black's starting pitcher isn't a disaster by any means. All his throws are right around the strike zone. But he's hittable, and Leo leads off with a single.

Nate is batting second today, with Gavin arriving late because of a Boy Scout meeting. "Boy Scouts," mutters my dad. "He'd rather tie some knots? This is *baseball.*"

Nate lets the first pitch go, which plops at his toes, skittering toward the backstop. "Good eye!" we all yell as Leo advances to second.

"ATTAWAY, Six!" yells Leo's dad.

Then, before we can fret about this change in the lineup screwing up Nate's mojo, he lines a double to the left-field corner, bringing Leo home. "Let's go, Natey!" yells my dad, clapping his hands in fingerless knit gloves before melting back into his seat.

"Did you hear the sound of that one?" he asks, pausing to hear it again inside his head. "Double with an RBI." Dr. Coach Patel heads toward the mound to have a chat with his struggling starter. The kid could still turn things around, having only given up a couple of hits, but he's already lost his stuff emotionally, and it doesn't look like he can get it back.

Even from behind the first-base line, we can see the kid's wiping away tears with the back of his hand. Taking a couple of steps off the mound, he nods vigorously, then glumly drops the ball into his coach's hand. And Dr. Coach has no choice but to bring in little Eddie Lawrence, his best hitter and oldest player, but a slight kid without much of an arm.

Eddie's first pitch goes into the dirt, takes a tough hop, and the catcher misses it. On the next pitch, Finn hits a single to score Nate, and I walk over to high-five his mom. I love her. I love her even though I'm pretty sure she sells multi-level-marketing skin care on-line. She's just got an entrepreneurial spirit, this petite sprite with a perfect elfish nose! I love her kid. I love her lucky white jeans, which she wore to make this happen, thank God. I love how Nate looks crossing the plate, navy cleats stomping against the slab of white rubber in the ground. I can't even look at Eddie's dad in the bleachers, holding a thermos, not moving a muscle, still worn-out from his shift at the fire station.

Team Black's starting pitcher is out in center field. As dusk turns violet in the sky, he never does stop crying. His eye black is smeared to high hell.

The top of the first inning ends with five runs and the enactment of the mercy rule.

I can't think about the symmetry of baseball now, how that kid crying in center has a mom and how she must feel, or about the fireman, a single dad who never misses a game. I can't think about how every one of our hits or walks counts against one of their pitchers. I can't consider that every action in the score book has an equal and opposite reaction. Newton's Third Law of Little League Emotions.

There's no way for us to open ourselves to some Newtonian explosion of empathy, forces and counterforces, other parents and grandparents needing good things, by which this law of baseball and nature would dictate bad things for our kids on the other side of the equation.

Once, I got to know the wife of a flag-football coach. Three months after my brother's funeral, Nate had caught a pass to win a game in double overtime. My dad and I were euphoric. I think we both cried. That wife later shared that her mom had died of cancer a few months before that big game. And I knew that she'd probably imbued that exact same play with lots of feelings and wishes and emotions. Her kid was guarding my kid; her family had just endured a loss and desperately needed this big win. And I saw it from the other side. It was a pretty cosmic but fleeting understanding of the oneness of all parents. Yet, not long after learning the backstory of the kid guarding Nate that day, I returned to my previous state of aggressive, boisterous, chauvinistic pride in my own kid, and all I could see was Nate catching that pass in double overtime, then running off the field to hug his grandpa.

"In case you were wondering . . . ," sing-talks Kai's dad, wandering over to our chairs.

"Of course I was," I answer immediately.

"Leo is dealing tonight." He tucks the score book between his hip and his elbow, makes one swift card-dealing gesture, then turns sharply and walks away.

The boy, tan and handsome, with big, dark eyes, deals. And when we are back on offense, Ethan gets a single, Zander gets on base thanks to an error, and Isaiah, for the third game in a row, never swings his bat. Still, nobody looks cockier throwing it aside at ball four and taking first.

Between innings, Daniel walks by and turns to talk to us through the fence. "Forget my new bullpen strategy. I'm riding Leo as long as I can." We are insiders, trusted confidants of management.

Innings go by under the lights, and just before Six gets to his pitch count, the seventy-five pitches he's allowed to throw according to his age and Little League rules, he gets us the W.

The Pinstripes take it, 7–3. We are 2 and 1, with a winning record for the first time.

"Life goes on," I hear Dr. Coach Patel tell his team as they gather around him outside the dugout after the handshake line. Leave it to an anesthesiologist to put things in perspective. I hadn't heard that phrase since I'd *really* heard it, as if for the first time, from a cloying, verbose widow at my first grief group.

Since I had double the grief—my brother died in January, and my mom died four months later—I also took two shots at grief grouping. The first was at a hospice in Central Phoenix.

"There is no chew, bite, swallow, no timeline," said the short-haired woman running the group. She couldn't help herself. She had to bite into the dry chocolate chip cookie baked by one of the elderly widows. "People think we should be over it, but it takes an indeterminate amount of time," she told us, nibbling another delicate bite of widow cookie.

Under the table, Bonnet, the white, fluffy dog of a different widow, began to growl and tug, also unable to resist the cookies.

"Does your dog need something?" the leader blurted. "Maybe he needs some water?"

The dog lady shook her head but took the opportunity to launch into her tale of lonely nights and meals eaten alone without her Harry. The monologue continued, cutting into everyone else's grief-group share time. There was another dead-brother girl there, wearing scrubs, sitting at the other end of a long table, but she never did get a chance to say much. I stewed about the cookies and the widows and the dog and the leader who couldn't wrangle the whole thing. She did have a craft project for us, handing out leaf-shaped pieces of paper where we could write a special memory for a grief tree. I searched my purse, but I didn't have a pen.

After the session came to a close, I went to introduce myself to the lady in scrubs as she headed toward the mammoth carved wood door. But before I could get to her, the talky widow and Bonnet buttonholed me and it wasn't long before she was vigorously wiping her phone screen with her argyle sweater vest so she could show me photos of Harry. "Here he is in Hawaii. This is from our wedding day. And this is his elementary school picture. Would you look at that bow tie?"

"Adorable," I said, staring down. "I'm so sorry for your loss. I'm sure he's still with you in your heart and watching over you." I strung together the clichés I thought sounded most right. I glanced behind me out the window and saw a leg wearing scrubs swinging into a car in the parking lot. The other grief-group sister drove away as it started to drizzle.

"Life goes on," retorted sweater-vest widow, in a game of dueling death clichés.

I handed her back her phone. Then I threw my blank leaf in the trash and left.

As I drove home through the soggy bleakness of a rainy night, I couldn't help seeing her face as she said those words. Life goes on.

It was as if she'd invented the aphorism just for me, just because of how much I wanted to fling my arm behind me and call for a time-out, so I could get my shit together, figure out life and death. I worried grief was making me distracted as a mom, because I was feeling so guilty all the time for living. It was hard to focus on Uno when I was mostly thinking about where we go when we die. And I was constantly concerned about everyone dying, and I worried about myself dying, mostly because the kids wouldn't have a mom. I told Daniel that he shouldn't feel bad about getting remarried. And to please make sure if I died that the boys had pants that fit: "Make sure they aren't too short. You know, don't send them to school in 'We don't have a mom' floods." My thoughts were ghoulish. I felt stunned all the time, like I'd been smacked with a frying pan in the forehead, even after I thought I shouldn't feel that way anymore. I was always getting colds and rashes, sties on my eyelids, aches and pains. I got woozy if I saw a man in a wheelchair on the sidewalk. I missed my mom so much, it hurt, even if she always worked my nerves when she walked the earth. I just wanted a do-over with her, because her dying cracked the code, that all I had to do was let her *be*. She loved me and I was haunted by how much I'd snubbed her and resented her and all the imaginary fun we could've had. Also, I needed to figure out exactly how to stop sweating every little thing, how to stop getting headaches when I spoke to other moms who made me nervous, how to finish projects I started, how to stop being phony so people would like me and think I was normal, which never worked. I wanted to figure out how to make the kids' lives more magical, take them to Morocco or at least Yosemite, or, okay, maybe just camp out in tents in the yard. But we didn't have tents. How was I going to get tents and carpe the parenthood diem? I needed to understand the whole point of everything so I could stop waking up in the middle of the night worried that maybe if my brother had never had the surgery to fix the broken rod in his spine, he'd still be alive. That's what my mom had said once, and she was the smartest person I ever knew. It was a hushed thing, mentioned once and only in passing, but she thought that surgery was what had triggered the recurrence, a surgical trauma that threw gasoline on the cancer fire. Maybe that was part of Mom's grief, paranoid and delusional, but maybe it was real. I needed to figure all that out, and why he got a rare cancer and how to be a good aunt to his kids, even though they lived far away and their little faces looked like his, like mine, and broke me. But life goes on while the whole thing is a mess. That's how the widow cookie crumbles.

And having eked all the usefulness out of that grief group by absorbing the most profound of all death clichés, I was done. That is, until I gave grief groups one more chance. I saw a flyer for one at a woodsy Franciscan retreat center where I'd gone for a full day of meditation with Victoria, kind of a continuation of the mindfulness course. I figured I'd give grief grouping one more go, since the retreat center was beautiful and close to home. I showed up and found the room, cramped and round, far from the dorms and cathedral. The leader had choppy gray hair and ankle tattoos.

There was a dead-brother girl in the circle there, too. "I'm Elena. I'm here because my brother died eight months ago," she said, introducing herself to the rest of us. "He was young and healthy. He actually helped me move just a few days before he died," but he'd had a heart thing nobody knew about, fallen off a ladder at work, and died instantly. "One day he was moving big, heavy boxes of books and dishes into my new apartment, and we were eating pizza and drinking beer. And now he's not here. I guess I'm still in shock, which I know is normal, but I'm just grateful for all the time I had with him." She readjusted the elastic on her ponytail. "We were best friends."

And as I listened, I could think only about the fading receipt for flying lessons I'd found between two of my brother's eight-by-ten photographs, pictures of Yosemite he'd taken and developed himself. I didn't know where he'd found a darkroom, and I never even knew he'd taken flying lessons. I could tell from the amount on the receipt that it would have been a big splurge, what with his law school loans to repay every month. It probably cost too much to continue taking lessons, get his license. Why hadn't I asked about his hobbies? We spoke on the phone only once every few months, and it seemed I always jumped in just when he was about to talk. He was much more soft-spoken. "No, you go. I interrupted." "No, you." Silence. We'd start talking at the same time again. "Go ahead," he'd say. I never yielded. I should have shut up and listened and asked more questions. Later, we had some vague talks in hospital rooms about things he wanted to do; by then he wasn't feeling well enough to leave the ground. He and Laura got decent seats to the musical *Avenue Q*, which was the only musical playing in town. I never even knew he wanted to see a musical or that he'd never seen one before. When I was growing up, my mom took me to see every kind of live performance. She carted me along to *Richard II* at the American Conservatory Theater, every touring musical that made a stop at the grand old Curran Theatre near Union Square, mime troops performing in city parks, folk music concerts at Stern Grove. Every December, we got dressed up and stayed up late on a school night to see *The Nutcracker* at San Francisco Ballet, and *A Christmas Carol* with the haunting Ghost of Christmas Yet to Come on stilts and covered in a long black cloak. We sat in the cheap seats wherever we went, the performers tiny people far away, but my brother hadn't gone at all. Maybe when we'd been in the balcony, my heart swelling as Annie sang about her hard-knock life, he'd been staring at the ceiling of a utility closet, listening to the bang of the water heater. A few times over the years my mom had taken my brother to see the Giants play at Candlestick Park. He'd bring his mitt, just in case a foul ball came his way, and Mom would let him eat all the hot dogs and junk food he wanted.

Before he died, he also got to see an NBA game, and because he was terminal, Laura had been able to arrange for them to meet one of the players after the game. It ended late, and Morgan and Laura were taken into some dark office to wait. It took so long for the NBA shooting guard to shower and do press, Morgan's pain pills wore off and he was so tired they almost went home, but they stayed. Laura texted a photo, and I stared at it on my phone in the middle of the night. Morgan's face was puffy and pale. He was wearing flannel pajama pants. The wound vacuum was on his lap. I wanted him to fly, not roll his wheelchair through a tunnel at a regular-season basketball game for a lousy photo taken in a gloomy

office. And then there was Ethan Hawke. The only other live performance in the area during the two months when my brother
knew he was dying but was still well enough to leave the house was
a one-night-only event, the actor discussing a novel he'd written at
a nearby synagogue. Morgan wasn't necessarily a huge fan of the
actor, though he liked him well enough, and he hadn't read the
novel. He just wanted to see a live performance, something I never
imagined would be a dying wish, and the synagogue was wheelchair accessible.

"He was a real nice guy," texted my brother along with a picture, Ethan Hawke in a tweed hat, leaning down next to my brother,
smiling.

That was all. No more wishes fulfilled and no more flight simu-
lators and no more sitting in the magical atmosphere of a dark
theater, watching singing puppets or orphans or ghosts or kings.
No more cheering a fast break in a stadium with a big crowd, or
getting to meet someone famous. There's no way Ethan Hawke
remembers meeting my dying brother, but I still have a soft spot for
him, though I can never watch anything he's in ever again because
I see only the photo of him and my dying brother in a makeshift
grown-up Make-A-Wish scenario. I wanted to give him flying lessons and an entire helicopter, front-row tickets to every musical
until forever. I'd take his wound and he'd take flight. I wanted to
give him every single thing I ever had, but I couldn't, and life was
going on without him, an empty seat on the aisle.

The only person I could deal with in my grief group was hairy-
eared and wore a knobby knit beanie over his scabby scalp. That
person had known my brother every second of his life. He had
known my brother when he wasn't a patient we were helpless to
save, when he was a phenomenon eating up fastballs and always
playing the bounce, never letting the bounce play him. We didn't
know shit about physics or Hebrew. We knew only that life, death,

baseball, and gravity were forces we couldn't control, forces that pulled things apart and brought them together.

———

"Another day at the office," says Dad, sunny-voiced, as he hauls the wagon of baseball gear across Ingleside's grassy field through the night. "Do you want me to babysit again this Sunday?"

"Thanks, Dad."

"Stop it. Don't thank me. They're my grandkids," he says. He's been coming over every Sunday, and when Daniel and I return from the movies, when they hear the garage door open, there's a scramble. The kids hide the electronics Grandpa lets them use against the rules. They throw away the wrappers from the candy Grandpa smuggles into the house. They take their positions on the couch, pretending to read. I never bust the old man, the little boys.

"Next game is Thursday, right?" asks my dad as he yanks the wagon, doing his rhythmic jogger breaths, puff, puff.

"Right. Late game. Bike to our house and I'll drive you. Let's take Osborn Road again. It's the luckiest route."

"Like we'd go any other way. Duh, T!" He throws his head back, grabbing his beanie, cackling.

There would be no more kaddish, and no more grief groups. But baseball would meet again on Thursday night, hello, goodbye, shalom, and play ball. Amen.

CHAPTER SEVEN

IIIIIIIIIIIIIIIIIIIIIIIIIIIIIII

Play the Bounce

"There's no crying in baseball."

—JIMMY DUGAN, *A LEAGUE OF THEIR OWN*

A rake leans up against the fence near the dugout. Warm air whips my hair in front of my face. It's dark in the desert when the late game gets started, except for on the diamond, where the moon and the field lights illuminate every particle in the air. Team Teal bats first.

Ethan is our third-string pitcher. He's wide-cheeked and sweet-faced, with a throwing style to match. His throws are like rainbows dipped in sugar, with a pot of gold at the end for even a half-decent hitter. Coach hoped to use him for two innings but has to pull him in the first.

"Time to stop the bleeding," my dad announces.

Nate comes in to relieve Ethan, but the bleeding only continues.

"He's all over the place," says Dad. "He doesn't have his release point."

In the ten feet of uninhabited wasteland between home plate and where the backstop meets the fence, errant balls jitterbug in the dirt while Finn scrambles to chase them down, lumbering and lunging in chunky black leg guards as runners advance. Pitches continue to whoosh by him outside, or sail above him, or hit the dirt in front of the plate, bouncing up unpredictably, hitting his chest plate, his face mask.

"These walks have a way of coming in," mutters Dad, "and biting us in the ass."

Kai's dad ambles over with a very generous assessment. "The ump is calling it tight tonight."

Nate drops his head back in frustration after throwing another outside pitch, and adds a few extra fidget motions before his windup. And despite every single thing I know to be true about parenting, sports, and the human condition, I need my baby to throw strikes. You could back up a Brink's truck full of beta-blockers, but there is no tamping down the physical reaction to a crisis that isn't happening. I mean, it *is* happening, but it isn't a real crisis. My body can't tell the difference anymore. Grief and baseball have crossed my wires; I can no longer tell what's urgent. A couple of slouchy fifth graders shuffle up behind the fence. "Oh, that's Nate," one says. "I heard he's good." But after a low pitch nails the batter's foot, they wander away toward the other game, where the crowd is cheering about something or other. I fight the urge to move the rake, open the latched gate to the field, and rush the mound to grab my son by the shoulders. *You got this, kiddo.* I want to speak into his very soul. I understand I can't keep my kid from painful situations, from failing, from coming apart at the seams, out there in the Little League spotlight, but I can't *accept* it.

"Dad, I'm freaking out."

"He just doesn't have his stuff tonight," says Dad testily. He blinks away dust. Looking over at him, I'm irritated at the old man, his blinking, his wrinkled old bandana held up to his eyes, his lack of anything comforting to say. He's given up on Nate, and his taking it too hard is making me ashamed of how *I'm* taking it too hard.

"I'll be right back." I get up and hide behind the bathroom, ducking my head out from behind the gray cinder-block wall to watch between my fingers.

"Are you waiting for the bathroom?" asks a little girl, the denim strap of her overalls falling off her shoulder.

"Oh, no. Sorry. Just making a call." *Mind your business, girlie.* I fake-fiddle with my phone. The feeling of helplessness tightens the muscles across the tops of my shoulders. When I look back toward our game, I see the infield on the mound, the catcher's face mask flipped up. They surround Nate, who says nothing. He just nods grimly, his purple hat casting a shadow on his pale cheeks in the night.

"I hope this meeting on the mound helps hit the reset," I say quietly, sliding back into my chair. "*We need outs, Dad.*"

"My kingdom for a strike," Dad mutters back.

Blood is pulsing at the base of my neck as everyone returns to position. Nate digs his heel against the pitcher's rubber.

I don't know what the infield said to him before they left him on the world's loneliest hill of dirt, but it's as if the pause itself hit the refresh button on Nate's motion. He's smoothed it out. He strikes out the next two batters.

"*Please* strike this next kid out and let's be done with this hellscape of an inning," I whisper to Dad, poking his biceps. Nate hurls one right down the middle, but the batter gets ahold of it, sending a ground ball toward third, where Easton makes little attempt to field the ball and it rolls toward the grass out in left field.

"Why is that poor putz out there? You need reflexes at the hot corner."

"Because Little League rules state that every player must play at least one infield inning. This is his."

"Well, that rule is idiotic. It's like the ball knew where to find him." Dad groans and mumbles something about the left fielder taking too long to find his cutoff man to get the ball back to the infield.

Finally, Team Teal hits a lazy pop fly, caught by Gavin at short. Top of the first inning is over, and we are already losing 4–0.

Team Teal's pitcher takes the hill to warm up. We study his throws and, yes, we know we are terrible people, but this kid is definitely not looking like their ace and we hope warm-ups don't make him any more accurate. He's guiding the ball instead of hurling it and, even so, he's missing the catcher's glove, throwing way outside. He can't find the zone much better than Nate, and by the time the ump calls, "Balls in!" he hasn't gained command.

He walks the first two batters.

Nate could bust this thing wide open with a clutch hit. Here's the thing about watching Little League baseball: There's always a sliver of hope in our hearts, and not because we're foolish. Good things happen out of nowhere. Even the mercy rule is relinquished in the bottom of the last inning, so the Little League truth is that almost any damage is reversible, and any wound can close.

His first swing looks jerky and disjointed, but he connects on a low pitch, firing the ball almost to the bulbs in the stadium lights. The right fielder has all night long to get under it, which he does, catching it clean.

"Can of corn." My dad shrugs. "He's trying too hard. Not waiting for his pitch."

The Pinstripes get a few runs on the board, and when it's time for the top of the second inning, I see Nate return to the mound. "*Oh, damn*" is what comes out of my mouth. It was then that I remembered *Full Catastrophe Living*, the mindfulness book Victoria had assigned us in her meditation workshop.

"To move to greater levels of health and well-being, we have to start from where we actually are today, now, in this moment, not from where we would like to be." That's what the book said, and I *want* to be in this moment, I deeply believe in that whole thing: that life is just waves; they don't stop coming but you get better at surfing them; you get better only by being present, welcoming everything that already is, right now, in this eternal moment. But I don't like what is. My surfing is shit and I'm terrified of the ocean. I'm failing Buddhism so hard. I'm resisting and hating this baseball game, the tightness in my ribs, the amorphous blob of anxiety I'm becoming. I can't find any chill.

And Nate still can't find home.

"Danny needs to give him the hook. He doesn't have it today, T. This is a debacle." But Daniel isn't going to panic and give Nate the hook. Coach grabs a few sunflower seeds from his pocket, stuffs them in his mouth, adjusts his hat. Then he crosses his lanky arms, stands with his feet out wide, sneakers covered in red dirt, watching, face placid. He isn't living and dying by every pitch, like we are.

Andrew comes looking for snacks and I hand him a baggie of Goldfish crackers. "That's not even food," my dad points out, shaking his head.

Health food was Carol's obsession, so it became my dad's. They proselytized about it constantly, and anything Dad says about what people should or shouldn't eat still hits a raw place. The kitchen was Carol's domain, the mysterious dry goods in glass jars lined up on wooden shelves. Nobody else had any idea how to turn what was in those jars into a meal: chickpea flour, dried mushrooms, bulgur, barley, kidney beans, and potato starch. We didn't understand most of the items in the refrigerator, either, like kefir and miso. There were certainly no ready-made snack foods. She said nobody should snack at all, or eat butter or eggs or any other kind of fat. My brother and I weren't starving, but we were always hungry when Dad was gone, scrounging for Carol's baking chocolate hidden on the top shelf of a cabinet, bitter and crumbling, or cutting off a piece of the special jack cheese we weren't allowed to have, slicing off rectangular hunks with a butter knife, hoping she wouldn't notice, slathering them in mustard.

Dad never cooked one thing, or went grocery shopping, or thought at all about what we might be eating when he was at work. He lived in a sort of la-la land where food appeared and he just cracked opened his beer and ate it. He allowed himself to be demeaned and shamed, exposed his kids to perpetual disdain, all for some ratatouille, I thought to myself, infuriated by the memory of those jars, of Carol lording her power over us, him letting her. *The old man should shut up about Goldfish crackers*, I thought. *He should really keep his thoughts to himself as they pertain to my kids, who eat plenty healthy, because there is a thing called balance, you stubborn coot who refuses to update his thoughts on nutrition since Carol told you what to eat and think.* The base of my skull hardens and something in me just wants to punch and kick and yell at my father for being a bystander in his own life. It's a flash flood of feelings, out of nowhere, about nothing and everything. *Get it together*, I think. *Goldfish crackers* are *processed crap. He's right.*

The next kid who steps into the batter's box is Ollie Reed, son of Team Teal's assistant coach. Everyone knows Coach Reed. He's a screamer, and he's not afraid to tell you he played a little minor-league ball.

"Keep your head on it, Ollie. Elbows up. Hands higher," barks Reed in a baritone that reverberates in the now-quiet bleachers. The little boy, his face all sharp, angled features, looks over at his dad for approval. "Feet apart more. Get your back foot back. Now, watch it in, all the way." Aware now of the parents in the stands watching him, Reed removes his hat, runs his hands through his hair, yells a cheerful, "Give it a ride," and replaces his hat, tucking it tight to his head.

"That coach is too intense and he needs boundaries. Stop living

through your kid," my dad moans. "He's making that kid crazy." If
I had a mirror I would shove it in the old man's face. He never really
got over my brother's baseball yips. He's out here judging Coach
Reed? At least he didn't give one kid away and leave the other alone
at home with a lit fuse of a step-monster who loved to starve us out.
Dad is very lucky I've started meditating, I think, feeling my heartbeat in my eyeballs, because he's sure got GALL and BALLS to
open his yap.

Ollie steps out of the box, takes a practice swing. The kid is
focused, the swing looks easy, and he glances over at his dad, who
gives a thumbs-up on his stance, wider now, his elbows perched
higher in the air.

"Jeez, Dad. Maybe he's intense, but he thinks he's helping. This
Reed guy just takes it seriously. He used to coach last year in Farm
AAA, and I talked to him a couple times. He seems like a really
good guy, not some kind of hypercompetitive baseball douche. He
played second base for a semipro team in Mexico City. I don't think
he's reliving his glory days or anything. I think he just loves baseball and he's trying to help his kid."

"He's not helping. Big deal, he had a cup of coffee in the minors.
He can't accept his kid being mediocre so he's going to pick, pick,
pick at everything. Shoulder down, elbow up. This Coach Reed
needs counseling. I can tell you that. And his coaching is ridicu-
lous. He's so desperate for his kid to be great that he's out here giving a thousand stupid corrections, as if that scared little kid can fix
ten things at once while he's being barked at by his dad, the big
shot. Well, you have to be exceptional to make it in baseball, and
his kid isn't. Deal with it. Stop with this nonstop bullshit correct-
ing. None of it matters. Kid can't hit."

But he can and he does. The sound of it travels into my dad's
ears and ripples out across his face in a rolling twitch. Dad blinks

hard. His jaw juts forward and back. Daniel steps toward the mound wordlessly and just reaches out for the ball. Nate drops it slowly into his father's hand.

Gavin now comes in to relieve Nate for the Pinstripes, and we still have a chance, because at least one member of our bullpen is dealing.

Nate is at first base now. My dad grimaces as he misjudges a tough bounce on a hard-hit ball. "Morgan would've gotten that." The batter rounds first toward second as Nate deftly sweeps up the ball that got by him and throws it to second. It is a perfect throw, confident and instinctive, but the runner beats the throw to the bag. "Mugs never missed a grounder. You have to play the bounce. Don't let the bounce play you."

I feel defensive about my kid, and proud of my dead brother, and mad at my dad, and mad at baseball all at the same time. I'm proud of Daniel for being sane enough to know he can't protect Nate from life, and yet I wish with everything I have that he could.

"This game has gone to shit," the old man says, never looking in my direction. I notice the dark shadows of his ear hair, black and white, a patchy fur, his head like a stuffed animal you'd win at an arcade.

I don't want it to bother me, but it does. I just want him to be *normal*, a normal adult who takes care of himself, who understands how to get by in the world, who doesn't divvy up his kids for no good reason, or let one kid live in a utility closet, who doesn't show up at the wrong airport, or default on his mortgage, or park his bicycle right where everyone can see it, everyone I know, and cover it with a hideous green fitted sheet. I don't want my dad to be a doofus who can't figure out what's right, can't even see clearly to deal with his own ear hair, even though I've asked him to.

I've even talked about it with a professional. Ruth, a Scottsdale psychologist who was about eighty, was recommended by a T-ball mom, and ended up on Daniel's "Grief Counselor Options Spreadsheet." I started seeing her to wrap my head around my brother's terminal diagnosis and continued to see her sporadically over the years, even after my dad moved to Arizona. Ear hair isn't really under the purview of grief counselors, but she always said loss brings up all kinds of things in a family.

"How's it going, living in the same city as your dad?" asked Ruth. The tiny woman fluffed up her short, reddish brown box-dyed hair.

In a corner, on a small, upholstered cube, were two stuffed turtles, one wearing a plastic gold crown.

"It's mostly good. But I'm annoyed with all these petty things about him," I confessed. "With all he's been through, I should be more tolerant."

"Like what?" she asked. I swiveled back and forth in an off-white pleather chair. Then I stared at a chart on the wall filled with rows of cartoon faces with different expressions. HOW DO YOU FEEL? asked the chart.

"He has these eye spasms, and I know he can't help it, but sometimes the spasms go from his eyes and take hold of his face, down to the teeth, which, by the way, he doesn't have a couple, right here." I gesture to my incisor on the right side. "Doesn't like the bridge I had made for him because he says it's uncomfortable. There's hair coming out of his ears, his nose, hair out to here on his eyebrows." I'm gesturing, doing a whole dance. "Sometimes he wears Lycra bike shorts with nothing over them, skinny old man in tight bike shorts, everyone looking at his old-man balls. The hat he wears is saturated with old sweat and yesteryear's sunscreen. He's rail thin but he thinks he's fat; he's obsessed with health food but drinks bottom-shelf booze every night." She leaned forward, looking up from her clipboard. She seemed so interested, I reviewed it all for her. "Greasy hat, nose hair, ear hair, eyes twitching, entire face doing this." I mash my features together, then jutted my jaw out a few times in succession.

"And you can't look away, because there's so much going on, and then *bam*, only a thin layer of man-made fiber between you and the outline of his actual testicles."

She gripped her pencil, her hand over her face. Then a laugh escaped, which she tried to stifle. "Sorry," she said. "You paint a vivid picture."

"Thanks."

"You know, why not offer to take him to one of those fancy barbershops? He'll love the pampering. If he's spending time with your family, it's okay for you to request basic grooming. You aren't asking him to wear a tuxedo, just to be presentable."

We took him to a real barbershop with a red-and-white-striped pole. Leaning back with a hot towel wrapped around his face, he said, "I'm just as happy as if I had good sense." Then he moved the towel away from his eyes. "Don't waste your money again, though. This is too much." He never went back, even though he said he would, even though we were always offering to take him. But he did put away the Lycra. "I didn't know it wasn't appropriate. I won't do that again," he said, contrite.

"Goody! Natey's up next," he says. "He gets a hit here and he's one for two."

In the crowd, a voice admonishes, "Wait for your pitch!" but he can't do that. Not tonight.

"He's chasing pitches. Just wants to hit the ball," Dad says, eyes blinking shut. Nate strikes out trying to dig up a bad pitch from the outside corner.

Helpless is how I feel, and I don't need a cartoon-face feelings chart to figure that out. I've felt it since the day I found out my brother had six months to live. That was the reason I went to see

Ruth in the first place. My brother was going to die, and all I could do was sit on the sidelines.

"**I can't use my right foot anymore,**" Morgan texted me. "**But I'm hoping the tumor is stable.**" It wasn't.

There was a spot on Morgan's hip bone the doctor didn't like. But there was no way to keep cutting away at the tumor, because there just wasn't enough flesh to replace what kept getting taken away, tissue and more tissue, tissue and tumor. The hole on his lower back was gaping, along with two other smaller holes where they'd harvested material to fill the first, the way you'd stuff decorative paper tissue in a designer handbag to hold the shape. "He never complains," my dad had said. "Stoic. That's how he is." But the spot grew. Laura sent me a text: **Dr says terminal. Six months.** She added a sad-face emoji, because what the hell else was she supposed to do?

"Where do we go when we die?" I asked, settling into Ruth's swivel chair.

"That's easy," she said, her fragile bones in a tidy heap. "I've died before, so I know. I drowned when I was a little girl, and that's why I'm not afraid of death. Can I tell you what it was like?" I nodded, incredulous and eager. Daniel's spreadsheet didn't have a category for therapists who had died and come back to life. I moved all the way forward to the edge of my chair, balancing a box of tissues on my lap. "It was so beautiful," she explained. "There was a white light, and Jesus was there. I could feel his presence, and I wanted to go with him but he told me it was too soon, it wasn't my time. I'm happy I didn't die then, but I'm looking forward to dying, because I know what's on the other side. Just love." Her eyes got big and innocent and in her face and voice I could see the little-girl version of her, the one who had almost drowned.

This was not at all what I expected from her. A framed degree from Columbia University hung on her wall, and yet here she was, delivering airy-fairy reportage from God's waiting room, her one-on-one with Jesus. "Ruth told me she died and went to a white light and there was Jesus and it was glorious and she can't wait to die for realsies," I told Daniel on the phone, driving home.

"The lady who went to Columbia?"

"Yeah. I didn't expect the white light, but I like it. I'm just going to be this person now. I'm just going to believe in the white light." I could hear the microwave ding as Daniel finished defrosting frozen tamales for the kids. "Ruthie is weird, but good weird."

"I'll make you another appointment," he said, then called her receptionist as the kids ate dinner.

The following week when I returned to her office, in a low brown building in Paradise Valley, she reprised the drowning story. She had forgotten she'd already told me, so I pretended I hadn't heard it before. And on my third visit, I cut her off early, before Jesus even got there.

"Do I say anything to my brother? About him dying? He's very private and we don't really have that kind of relationship—like, talking about feelings."

"Well, let's not make him uncomfortable by forcing him into a conversation he may not want to have. That wouldn't be right. If you wouldn't have this kind of talk normally, don't force it. But I would write a letter. Because there are things you won't be able to say later, and you can't go back."

He never responded to the letter I wrote. Laura says he read it, and his eyes welled up, but still, on the precipice, days and weeks stuck in the basement, in all that time, he never wrote me back.

You were a great sister, he could have written, or *I'm proud of you*. But at least we watched sports and movies together, and we made fun of Dad, the way we'd always done.

"Oh, it was the worst!" Morgan exclaimed. "Dad got hold of a French roll, and he was making *so many* mouth sounds. I couldn't exactly go anywhere, so I turned up the TV, but he didn't get the hint. I finally told him to eat in the other room."

"Oh, no way! You? You're so patient."

"He finally broke me. Then he finished his roll upstairs, came back, and went on and on about some Herbert Hoover biography he's been reading. Good thing these pain pills make me drowsy. I slept through Hoover's reelection campaign."

Ruth was right. I'm glad I sent the letter. But I still can't believe he left me hanging. I like to think responding was just too hard, that it was too hard to say goodbye to me because it would prove he was really dying, leaving Laura and his beloved kids. I like to believe it the way I like to believe in Jesus wrapping his arms of light around little-girl Ruth, who drowned and came back to life.

He was my mother's son. I knew that for sure when she died four months after he did, and with no more intimacy.

"People act weird when they're dying," said a tall nurse named Bob with a gray Mohawk and icy blue eyes.

He leaned back in the hallway, propping a black clog against the wall.

"We all have coping mechanisms to deal with living, and dying is no different. I've seen it a thousand times," he explained. So I hugged him and wept on his shoulder in the hall of the palliative care wing of UCSF.

When you've seen as many buckets kicked as Bob has, nothing throws you, I guess.

"She wanted me to come," I moaned. "Why won't she *talk* to me?"

"Was she good at emotional things before?" he asked, raising his eyebrows, knowing the answer.

Just a day earlier, the hospital had called and told me to get on a plane, that my mom's antibiotic-resistant infection was probably going to be fatal. They said she was asking for me. They knew my brother had just died and that she'd probably been physically weakened by the trauma. She didn't want to talk about him, they said, but she wanted to see me. After I'd rushed there from Phoenix, I told her I loved her and she told me the same. I said, "I hope you're proud." I stopped myself from saying "proud of us," because I didn't want to bring up my brother.

She said, "I have been and I am."

She said, "It hurts."

I said, "I know. It will be over soon."

My mom's last act on planet Earth was to binge-watch *Portlandia*, which for her was better than nothing—that is, the nothingness of sitting with me, making sense of her last few conscious hours on Earth. Sometimes I offered her a lick of the See's chocolate lollipop I'd bought, but mostly I sat and waited. I waited for her to take me on a morphine-fueled walk down memory lane—the ballet recital where I elbowed a girl who was getting out of line, the birthday parties in Dolores Park, our cat Ginger and her "senior feline howling syndrome."

My mom didn't howl. She didn't even much talk. My entire adult life I'd been watering my grudge garden over all the ways she'd been negligent, from putting me on Greyhound buses alone to visit my dad or my grandparents, to, worst of all, deciding to bow out of my brother's final months because it was too much for her to watch him die. I didn't think she should have been allowed to do that, and I had told her then that I never wanted to see her again.

But Bob wasn't going to let me hold it against her. She'd never been good with big, sad feelings and was never forthcoming or warm, and you can't expect dying to change a lifelong personality. So I went back into her room, staring briefly out the window at students rushing to class, life going on in San Francisco, the city my mom had chosen for herself. I plopped back down in a vinyl chair.

It wasn't the most moving death scene, a daughter reading the sports section while a mother watches a cable series about life in the Pacific Northwest.

"I'm going to stay here tonight, Mom. I'm just going to stay here until you go to sleep," I told her.

She looked at me with terror, not about death, but about having to converse. "But I don't have anything to say," she said, her lower lip quivering.

"Don't worry. You don't have to talk. I'll just sit here."

I think that was the single most loving thing I ever did for my mom. And the best night I ever spent with her. Letting her be how I didn't like, letting her fail to deliver a monologue on the thrill ride of being my mother. Forgiveness was a Koufax curveball I just couldn't hit, but I could focus on what kind of daughter I wanted to be instead of what kind of mother I wished she'd been. I want to do that for my dad, too, here at the ballpark.

"Too many black holes in this lineup," moans my dad. He sips his diet soda, Mr. King of All Healthy People clutching a plastic bottle filled with chemicals. *What a hypocrite.* I fixate on his black T-shirt covered with lint. Everyone knows diet soda isn't good for you, because it's not 1982, but this old dummy can't update his own software or buy a lint roller. And now he can't let the kids be kids, imperfect and inconsistent.

Dad takes another sip, dripping a few droplets of soda onto his lap, clueless. "And these umps are usually good, but this guy is terrible," he whines, quietly gesturing toward the home plate ump. "He's out to lunch. His dipstick isn't touching any oil, that's for sure. And he's fat."

"Dad, let's not fat-shame the ump. These guys make almost no money, and they're out here covered in pads and gear in this heat."

He rolls his eyes. I sigh loudly, irritated.

"Dad, what's the count?"

"Don't know. This ump doesn't hold up his fingers long enough like the other ones. My eyes aren't good."

Our batter strikes out looking. "Terrible call," Dad grouses. "That pitch was at his ankles."

Nate is up to bat again.

We are down only one run. It's 9–8, Team Teal. The tying run is on third. *Please get a hit. Please. Get on base, kid, and you're the winning run.*

Nate grounds out on a weak tapper.

Team Teal wins. "Oh for three," says Dad, standing and snapping his chair shut. His voice has a quality both wistful and brittle. "Chosen One, my ass."

All the kids clear out of the dugout, but one kid remains in the corner, his face streaked with red dirt, his glove in his lap. He's stalling so he can collect himself. He picks up his water bottle by the handle and stuffs his bat into the side of his bag. His eyes are red-rimmed and heavy. There *is* crying in baseball. Any Little League parent knows this fundamental truth.

On the way to the car, Andrew and Nate walk way ahead of us, out of earshot, and my dad grumbles, "That game took forever."

"No it didn't. All games are ninety minutes until playoffs. Sucking just stretches time."

"No, it was longer."

"It wasn't."

"Terrible."

"You don't have to be so negative, Dad. It's baseball. Nobody wins all the time." I'm faking this Zen so hard. This is how I want to feel, how I want us to feel, how I want Nate to think we feel.

Picking up my pace, I sidle up to Nate, struggling to recall anything positive. "You kept your composure out there," I tell him.

"I did awful, Mom."

Okay.

I drop back next to my dad. Cold and agitated, I snap my puffy vest closed. I know I should play the bounce, but it's playing me. Before I can remember to let things be, then pass, and then change.

"Nate doesn't want to talk to you right now," Dad says. "It's obvious. Stop intruding. Leave him be."

I snap at the old man, "Aren't you lucky? You don't have to know what to say or when to say nothing." His chin tucks in, but he keeps tugging the wagon, walking harder and faster toward the parking lot gate.

Andrew is rushing to keep step with Nate. He didn't pay much attention to the game, mostly running around collecting pine cones. "Nate, did you hit any nukes?"

"No, Andrew. Go away."

Everything is gushing up, how Dad insulted my snacks and my pep talk, how he criticized Coach Reed and his lack of baseball boundaries, how he just sat there, covered with lint and diet soda, a bigmouth know-it-all, the man who gave away his kid, making pronouncements, throwing stones from a glass house that he couldn't even afford. *I cosigned on his glass house and he ruined my credit, and now he lives in a glass trailer looking out over a cemetery and he's telling me what's what?*

"You've got your nerve, Dad, insulting other people's parenting, like you're an expert. You're B. F. Fucking Skinner. I mean, say what you want about some overbearing baseball dad; at least he didn't give his kid away."

Dad is pulling the wagon ahead of me, but I catch up, swinging my arms, marching across the grass. He now wishes to rewrite the whole tale, how he knows all about parenting, when he was working all the time and Carol raised us and did it very poorly, and hated us, and he pretended not to notice. *This guy is going to ride his high horse? Not today, you old bag of bones.*

"You don't know what it's like to be there all the time, for all the tiny, tough moments. You just did what you wanted. You worked six days a week and barely saw your kids on the seventh. You didn't have to take us to the dentist, or buy us socks, or make dioramas and other boring parent shit. It must've been nice to be you." I think about Ollie looking over at his dad, searching for the answers, finding them. "You don't know shit about parenting."

Then, casually, and without breaking stride or looking at me, he counters, "You don't know what it's like to watch your son die of cancer and not be able to stop it."

Touché, old man.

———

That night, I don't think about Tom Hanks unsettled by the crying in baseball. I think about my favorite scene in that movie.

> **JIMMY DUGAN:** "Baseball is what gets inside you. It's what lights you up. You can't deny that."
> **DOTTIE:** "It just got too hard."
> **JIMMY DUGAN:** "It's supposed to be hard. If it wasn't hard, everyone would do it. The hard is what makes it great."

It's hard being in a fight with my dad. It's hard being a good daughter. It's hard losing. I don't know what makes anything great, or what makes us great at anything, but I know from watching baseball practice that reps can't hurt, at least when it comes to playing the bounce. The next game is in a few days, and I want to be with my dad. I want to sit in our beach chairs and let every play, every off-balance hack and every missed grounder, ripple through our central nervous systems at the same time.

"Dad, I just didn't know what to say to Nate," I admit, calling him when the kids are in bed. "And I took it out on you."

"You're the best mom there is. The best," he says. I feel myself soften.

There's quiet on the phone. "Dad? You still there?"

"I get scared it will happen to Nate," he confesses, lowering his voice. "The yips."

"Yeah," I agree.

"What if he just loses it one day, the way Morgan did?" And I know the old man was surly and impatient and judgmental at the ballpark because the yips could come for you, unexplained, and he knew it as well as anyone. "He loved baseball more than anything. It was all he had."

"I know, Dad. But he was okay. He lived a good life."

"I'm being stupid. It's just baseball."

"Who is this, and what have you done with my dad?"

He laughs, one hollow "HA" echoing through his tin can. He sips his brandy.

"Sorry for getting mad at you about my childhood, Dad. I should stop doing that. And it's good for Nate to fail. I know that, but parenting is too hard," I say, regret flooding me instantly, chilly and nauseating. My hurts don't involve tumors, or wounds that won't close. But still, I repeat it, because I know he understands. "It's too hard."

The hard is what makes it great. At least, that's what Jimmy Dugan said to Dottie, right before their team lost game seven of the World Series.

CHAPTER EIGHT

IIIIIIIIIIIIIIIIIIIIIIIIIIII

Hitting for the Cycle

"The fundamental truth: a baseball game is nothing but a great slow contraption for getting you to pay attention to the cadence of a summer day."

—MICHAEL CHABON, *SUMMERLAND*

The old man picks up his pace, cycling shoes clipped into his pedals, flying down the sidewalk until he gets to the overpass just before Hayden Road, a square chunk of cement in the ground reading, **FLOOD CONTROL DISTRICT OF MARICOPA COUNTY.**

He turns onto the Indian Bend Wash Path, a bike trail winding through a city park. It's dark now, and he can barely see the palm trees and pagodas, the faded blue plastic dome-top trash cans. The parking lot behind the CVS, and the red and white lights of the Circle K—they stretch farther behind him now, just some dim lights down Thomas, across from a sleepy La Quinta Inn.

He pedals as hard as he can, then lifts off the seat, coasting along the yellow painted stripe on the path, to the place where a bridge takes him over a creek bed, the bottom only stones and browning leaves and broken glass. Yellow letters painted across the path spell out **SLOW**, but he doesn't heed the words as he heads into a sharp left turn at full speed. He's taken this turn a hundred times before. He straightens out, seated again, passing the outdoor patio of a closed sports bar on his left, then a sprawling beige apartment complex, the

El Dorado Hermosa. A thick steel chain connects wooden posts the entire length of the path on his right.

It's quiet now, deep in the park, just his heart beating and the babble of faraway city sounds. He lets out a tentative shriek. Nobody can hear him. He's not bothering anybody, he figures. So he opens his mouth wider, pushing out a fuller tone. Now he's screaming, full out, into the dry desert wind.

He gets to an intersection, crosses the road into El Dorado Park, where the bike path picks up again, and he catches himself as he passes the shoddily manicured flowering bushes behind the Continental Villas apartments, **NOW LEASING**, and the neighborhood watch sign. He still yells, but he tamps down his volume until he's back in the thick of the woods, whizzing by empty gazebos, picnic tables with benches attached, a volleyball net sagging over a rectangular patch of dirt and sand. Now when he screams, it's from deeper down, with all the force in his bony old body.

Moans from the vast maw of fatherly loss travel through the air, undulating vibrations of unspeakably shitty times—long lists of medications on dry-erase boards in hospital rooms, late-night trips to the pharmacy for pain pills and cans of Ensure—and, worse, the happy times, when he was so stupid, he didn't even know to take note of them: talking about the 49ers' offensive line; eating burritos at the taqueria on Mission Street; laughing so hard when his grown son pinned him, his big grown bear of a child, wrestling on the carpet in front of the couch, that it was only haltingly he could spit out the words, "Don't . . . hurt . . . me. I'm brittle."

You don't know when you're done screaming about your dead son until you're done. He lets out another wail.

He passes the man-made fishing pond, ducks floating, asleep. The air is salty now, a brine that carries the sound, which is nothing more, really, than a disturbance of the particles in the air, a disturbance that sets off the transportation of energy from one place to

another, moving through solid surfaces and water, the pond and the
ducks; a transmission as invisible and mysterious to me as the whereabouts of my brother. It turns out, a cold night is a good time for a
father to scream: Sound waves are louder and travel farther when
there's a chill in the air. I looked it up, the physics of it, how the speed
of sound isn't a constant, how it changes depending on the environ-
ment. The cold slows the molecules, saps their energy, so they're too
still on an Arizona night in early spring to vibrate as much as they
do in the warm light of day. The old man's cries take longer to ripple
out than they did in summer, but they travel farther in the cool air,
through crisp, sparse leaves, birds' nests, the fence along the edge of
the bike trail; to the Sonic Drive-In in a nearby strip mall, to the
Asian market and the gas station, to the beings going about their
business in cars, whooshing toward home, windows up.

He'd be done screaming if my brother's kid hadn't just gone to
grief camp somewhere in the woods of Virginia, a weekend away
with other kids who had lost parents to cancer. They made paper
boats to put on a river. Say the name of your dead dad and drop the
boat in the water with the warm support of a trained facilitator in
khaki shorts and a ball cap. The kids stood with their boats, dropping them in the water, one at a time.

But my brother's kid is just standing there, and all the dead-
parent kids are looking at him, and he's holding the white paper
boat between two fingers, but he can't deliver this vessel to the
water because he can't remember his dad's name, because he's only
seven years old, and the only name he can remember calling the
man who died on a winter night in his basement is Dad. He stands
there frozen. It's one thing to be the odd man out on Father's Day
in your classroom, when all the kids paint ceramic tiles for their
dads and yours is blank, but it's another to flop out here with your
own kind, who might think you didn't even love your dad, because
you can't say his name, because you can't remember it now.

"It's okay," says the counselor. "Just say 'Dad.'"

If it weren't for the goddamn ceremonial paper boat at grief camp, the thought of it; the child's face, embarrassed, and him wiping his long bangs to the side; his pants too short—because nobody noticed or replaced them in the year everyone was paying attention only to the business of his dad's slow death—if it weren't for the IDIOTS who should have known better running a grief camp, my dad would be done shouting. But though he wishes he didn't know this fact, he does, and now the picture of the child on the edge of the river with his white paper grief boat is right in front of his handlebars, and even at his fastest the old man can't outride it. He lets loose a howl, sending out a million paper boats of rasp, a diaspora, floating through the air from the old man's throat until they run out of energy, sputter out into the darkness, and it's back to silence, and the din of faraway traffic, and the hum of the wheels beneath him.

When he arrives home at the Riviera Mobilehome Park, he doesn't even glance at Green Acres Mortuary and Cemetery. He's already paid his respects. He left flowers all across the bike path, a secret bouquet of yells through the desert.

I know about the biking and screaming only because he admitted it to me, and I still don't know why, except grief needs a witness, according to one of the grief books in a stack on my nightstand.

"Sometimes, I just start screaming. I'm not bothering anybody. So I just scream when I'm riding home," he confessed sheepishly, between innings, a couple of games back.

I sent Andrew away with a crumpled dollar from my purse to buy grandpa a Diet Pepsi. I needed to know everything about this.

Does he scream my brother's name?

And which name? He was named Morgan after a character in a 1966 British comedy that nobody has ever heard of, but my dad and I called him Mugs.

"What do you scream?" I don't know if that's an appropriate question. Do you scream the name of your dead son on your bike ride home, or do you just kind of scat?

"I don't know," he answered shyly, looking away at Camelback Mountain in the distance, way beyond the outfield. "I just yell," he answered with a shrug.

I wanted to know more, but the game was starting, and I knew that was all I was going to get. If I wanted to talk loss with my dad, it would have to be about Little League baseball.

———

Now it's on my mind, Grandpa flying through the darkness, and I try to redirect, rerouting my thoughts to my feet.

"Just sense into your toes," says the voice.

I'm on the floor in my closet again, feeling my toes, the lights out. There's no right way to feel in my toes, says the soothing man coming from my phone.

"Become aware of the shins and calf muscles and the sensations in the lower legs," says the familiar voice, avuncular and soft. My tabby Lolo walks around my feet, then settles.

"Let go of the tendency of wanting things to be different from how they are now, and allow things to be exactly as you find them."

The recording says, "Just be right here as you are right now," and the thought of the ride fades, my dad's Tour de Grief replaced by the heaviness of my body on the beige shag carpet.

———

Nate's been pitching in the yard before school. Along the side of our house, a wooden fence separates us from our neighbor, leaving a narrow lane between the house and the fence. My husband measures out the correct distance—forty-six feet for Little League Minors—puts down a plastic mat for a makeshift home plate, another for the pitcher's mound, and then he squats behind the plate to receive each pitch as it comes down the pike, calling balls or strikes against an imaginary batter.

This morning, Nate stops. "Hey, Dad? When I look at you the whole time during my delivery, I throw more strikes."

"What *have* you been looking at?" asks his dad, who has missed this one small detail in the bevy of body movements that make up a pitch.

Nate slows down his motion, reenacting it.

A left-hander's body faces first base—in this case, the side of our house—before initiating delivery. He holds the ball in his left hand, cradling it like a baby held low. He turns his head to look at his dad, his body still facing imaginary first base. He cranks up his right knee. His hands separate, the gloved hand going toward his target, his dad's catcher's mitt. His ball hand stretches back as his body weight moves forward. He draws his elbow back, like an archer, and then flashes the ball to the batter as his front foot lands. His throwing arm comes forward, trailing his leg by just a fraction of a second, flinging the ball toward the strike zone, arcing forward in a rainbow. After the ball is released, his left leg comes all the way around, parallel to the other, so his hips, shoulders, head, everything, are facing forward, squared off, ready to field a ball.

"I've been looking at first."

"Oh no," says his dad. "You should always be looking at the catcher. Keep your eyes on the target no matter what your body is doing."

Coach says that's pretty much an ironclad rule when it comes to Little League pitching. Maybe it's even true for major leaguers.

Fernando Valenzuela was a notable exception. He would look up for a moment during his windup, a very unorthodox delivery that somehow worked for him. I only know this because my brother had a poster of Valenzuela Scotch-taped to his bedroom wall. The left-handed Dodger from Mexico looked pudgy and jovial, his lead leg lifted all the way to his elbow, gathering himself to hurl his other-worldly screwball toward the plate, eyes lifted toward the heavens.

Nate holds his gaze steady toward his dad's glove.

They go through a few more counts against invisible opponents, some balls, but mostly strikes.

"You just struck out two batters," Daniel says, in the measured tone of a guy temperamentally suited to being a Little League dad.

Things are looking up for Nate in the bullpen that is the narrow patch of dirt along our fence, but irrational exuberance is not his coach's style, nor is taking his eye off the ticking clock on a school day.

"One more, Dad. One more," Nate begs. But it's time for breakfast, and Coach rises from his squat, removes his glove.

"My arm feels good today," Nate tells me over oatmeal, in a rare tell-Mom-a-thing-I-feel moment. My breath catches in my sternum for a second.

I look sidelong at Daniel, who is rinsing a dish at the sink. He raises his eyebrows, tilts his head to the side, but doesn't look up. "Yup," he says, nodding and rinsing. "Looking good."

When I get to the field in the late afternoon, I see the lime-green sheet my dad uses as a bike cover, which has become a flag he's planted into the earth wherever he goes. *I'm here. My bike shorts are tight (but now covered with Dickies work shorts, thank you very much), my teeth are gone or crooked, I spent months of my life watching my only son die in various hospitals and rehab facilities throughout the Northeast, and if you think I care about the conventions of polite society, tell it to the green sheet.*

The green sheet is paper napkins, and forks on the wrong side, and elbows on the table, and the last trailer for sale in the trailer park, the cheapest tin can available in the state of Arizona the day it was purchased, empty and decaying save for a brown pleather recliner with a footrest that's almost an appliance, so long has it resided by the broken window in the tiny living room. The green sheet calls attention to itself, ill fitting and gauche, pulling focus with the unpleasantness of its tint. Somewhere in the distance, just beyond the outfield, near the outdoor basketball court where he chains his bike to a rack, the fitted sheet is a beacon of bargain, the hue and shade of a guy who may once have cared about appearances but now cares only about sheltering his ride from the elements.

As I approach the field from the car, I can tell by the way he's taken his usual seat, two feet behind the plate, and is already deep into a game of Scrabble on his phone, that he arrived his customary thirty to forty-five minutes early. If he doesn't drive over with us to one of the boys' sporting events, whether it's flag football, rec basketball, T-ball, or baseball, he rides alone on his bike and usually gets there before the refs and coaches and umps. "I wasn't doing anything, T. Wanted to make sure we got our seats." I unfold my chair beside his. The big overhead lights will come on at any moment, spotlighting a zillion tiny specks of red earth swirling in the air, which smells like musky leather sports gear and bug spray.

A gaggle of younger siblings, joined by Andrew, tosses a football around in something resembling a game of sharks and minnows, crashing into the moms in line for the bathroom; that line is always the longest just before the first pitch is thrown.

Isaiah did not want to pitch, not this night, not any night in the Purple Pinstripes' season, not ever.

"*No*, I'm TERRIBLE. I'm not pitching," he told Coach, every game.

Unfortunately for him, Coach Daniel is a math guy, and he's run the numbers on pitch counts, days of rest, innings needed through a potential four playoff games. "Some kids are going to have to step up so we can save the more reliable arms to close out crucial victories. Ethan didn't pan out, but he could have. I need to see what I've got."

Isaiah knows he's pitching until he either gets three outs or gives up five runs.

His mom, the overnight nurse, has gotten her shift covered to see the game. His dad, a tall, quiet Black man, runs the zipper of his sweatshirt up and down, pacing. You can hear Gatorade caps twist open, Fritos bags crinkle.

"Balls in!" yells Finn, with raspy hints of his future man voice. Isaiah takes a deep breath, adjusts his purple jersey.

And he walks the first two batters.

His mom holds up her phone, trying to get video, intermittently running her fingers through her long red ponytail, looking toward the heavens like Fernando, telling her younger kids to scram.

And then he sprinkles in a few strikes. Dad and I cheer, overzealous, every time he hits the zone. "Great pitch, kid! Way to fire it!"

But mostly there are wild pitches. We hold our breath, silent, except for a few mutters of "Darn it" and "Shit."

With a runner on third, as there is now, the pitcher should cover the plate if the catcher has to scurry around for a wild pitch, but Isaiah doesn't know this, has never been in this position. He stands paralyzed somewhere between the mound and home.

The opposing coach is yelling, "GO," to his runners, and Coach Daniel is yelling, "COVER HOME," to his pitcher. A run comes in, and Isaiah puts his head in his hands. You wonder how a kid will recover from this chaos, of which he is reluctantly the cause, but he has no choice. The only way out is through.

Then, miraculously, Isaiah strikes a kid out to end the inning. His mom squeezes her eyes shut, looks toward her husband, who raises his eyebrows, his hands shoved in his pockets. "I got the video," she mouths, pointing to her phone. The struggle that had come before it is gone now. There's just the final strikeout, glorious, captured forever.

"Kid actually recorded a strikeout," Dad says, beaming, but also way too loud. I shush him and he lowers his voice. "All's well that ends well," he adds.

"I'm way too happy about this," I confess.

"Same," he says. "Especially since we're losing."

The Pinstripes are down four. Again.

Nate isn't a leadoff hitter, doesn't quite have the wheels, but tonight Coach is mixing things up. Despite his recent mishaps at the plate, Nate is just as likely to put the ball in play as anyone else.

Before stepping into the box, he takes a practice swing, and I know he's working to keep the bat nice and level, like his dad taught him. He steps into his stance, taps the bat on the plate, swings the bat all the way around, toward the pitcher and over his head in a circle, taps the plate with the bat again, and then rocks back and forth until his weight is centered, his cleats parallel. The first pitch is a ball. He doesn't swing. *Good eye.*

On the second pitch, he gets under it, makes contact, and launches the ball into the air toward center field. There's a very particular sound when the sweet spot of an aluminum bat hits the leather, cork, and rubber that make up a baseball. "You hear that?" my dad says when Nate hits it square. "I love that sound." It's a sharp *thwack*, something you take in more like echolocation than hearing, the bat flexing and vibrating, the acoustics of two solid objects connecting in exactly the right place.

But this isn't that sound. It's dull and flat. It's a hollow, three-quarter echo of that sound.

"DROP. DROP. DROP." We can *will* the ball to drop; if we chant, in unison, *the ball will drop.* Maybe we shouldn't, because it's embarrassing, but we can't help ourselves. I clutch my jade necklace for luck, because I know I can help this weak hit somehow land where a fielder isn't. The moment I hear the sound, the aluminum hitting the ball, sending it out, I know that I control how fast and how far it travels and whether it finds a spot to drop. In that fraction of a second, when I clutch the pendant hanging on a chain around my neck, I believe in God, I believe in angels, I believe dead people are angels looking out for me, I believe in the indescribable embrace of Jesus and his love-light, I believe my dead mom, who never cared about baseball, is taking a pause from some heavenly game of bridge to see to it that this goes right for me. Forget letting be. Forget the here and now, my toes, the dirt, the earth. Forget meditating in my closet, letting life unfold, accepting and being present. I'm as far away as I can be, in the phony afterlife of cheap figurines and basic-cable mediums, chugging a bottomless cup of crave. In that slice of time, between contact and landing, I set aside all the things I secretly know to be true: that when you're dead, you're dead; maybe when people think of you there's some sort of momentary reawakening of your essential being in the atmosphere, but basically you're gone, nighty night and shalom; and angels are just nice people who are repairing cleft palates in war-torn countries or working at food banks here on Earth, not prancing around looking like Stevie Nicks in the afterlife, wearing feathers and wings. But for this pause in the space-time continuum, angels are dead ancestors on puffy clouds listening to actual harp music. My mom is peering down over her bridge hand, through the clouds, aware that Nathaniel James has just made contact with a baseball and things might not go his way, so of course she has the power to bend the wind, or the Earth, or the left fielder's arm. My brother is up there, hearty and whole. He doesn't have cancer and he doesn't have the yips, but he does have divine superpowers. For the thin sliver of time when the outcome is up in the air, I'd swear angels exist. I'd pay to have my aura photographed and my palm read. When it's time to control the world for my kid, *I'm one hundred percent that bitch.*

DAMN.

Caught by the third baseman, who smugly returns it to the pitcher. I knew heaven was bullshit.

"Oh for one," I whisper to my dad.

"What was that?" he says to me out of the side of his mouth. We both keep facing the game, faking it, acting like we actually care about the next batter.

"This is a disaster, Dad. His timing is way off. Still."

"Disaster," Dad repeats, talking like a trailer-park ventriloquist, mouth barely moving. He takes off his knit cap, holds it gently in his lap, looks at the traffic on Camelback Road, swigs his Diet Pepsi.

We are holding out hope for his next at bat.

But first, Kai Lee-Baker must face his time in the barrel. This is another kid who has never pitched before in his life. But unlike Isaiah, he doesn't protest.

Kai, fierce and fast of leg but unpracticed in the art of maneuvering his torso and arms to hurl a baseball, throws some strikes but mostly misses the zone. We've already been through Isaiah's inning, Dad and I, so we're taking it better.

Finally, he is run-ruled, but I sense a feeling in my body that I can only file under PLEASANT. He threw some strikes in a Little League game. Nobody can ever take that away from him. As Kai trots back toward the dugout, I see his dad hop off the bleacher and hustle toward the fence. With one hand, he wraps his fingers through the metal triangles, and with the other, he gives his kid a thumbs-up. Kai wasn't dealing tonight, but he was dealing enough for his dad.

The Purple Pinstripes are down nine. But I'm not that down, because my heart is happy for Isaiah and Kai, for their parents.

The first two innings were so painfully slow, they ate up most of the time. By our calculations, Nate will get only one more turn at bat.

When Nate steps up to the plate, he takes an overeager big hack at the first pitch, which is so high, it's at his eyeline. He swings so hard he turns himself around, like a screw going into the ground. He collects himself, looks toward his coach. "Wait for your pitch.

Lay off the high stuff," says Coach Daniel casually, spitting sunflower seeds into the dirt. On the next pitch, Nate is way out in
front. Down two strikes in the count, he keeps his eye on the ball
and doesn't swing at a high one. But the ump calls it a strike, and
he goes down looking.

"Oh for two," mutters my dad. We shake our heads, roll our
eyes. We sit in silence. And more silence.

"I lost my son to cancer, but this is the worst thing that's ever happened," he murmurs. This is a green-sheet joke, dark and wrong and
something only we could understand as not true and absolutely true.
He lets out a huge guffaw when he sees the words register on my face,
dabs his eyes with his blue bandana. Then the reality hits us. It's just
not fucking funny. No majestic line drive to discuss the next day. No
clever base running where Nate comes out the victor. No sweet sound
of a shot coming off Nate's red aluminum USA Baseball–sanctioned
bat for us to hear in our heads as our heads hit our pillows, for us to
parse the next day on the phone as we review the game. Nothing good.

Fortunately I can cheer my dad up by sharing my inside information, conspiratorially, as Nate hits the dugout, registering no
emotion on his young face but hanging his head low as he removes
his helmet, shakes out his hair, and checks his outfield assignment
on a clipboard hanging from a nail by the door.

"Dad, Coach promised Nate an inning on the mound tonight,
because friends from his school are on Team Turquoise." My dad's
eyes get wide. Then he remembers. I see him blink away the specter
of the yips. "Danny worked with him, Pops."

"He did?"

"Yup. And this morning, Nate told me his arm felt good. And
he never says anything like that."

"He did?"

I say, "Look," as Nate heads toward the mound purposefully,
with his bouncy, flat-footed heel-toe swagger.

"Even with my bad eyes, even with everyone in their uniforms, I can always tell when it's Natey. He has that shuffle." I can hear him add, *Same as Mugsy*, in the silent conversation we're having and not having as Nate throws a few practice pitches.

"Balls in," yells the catcher. And all I want is to get the fuck out. UNPLEASANT.

Get ahold of yourself; it's one inning. These are children. The out-come doesn't matter. Be present. Enjoy the process. Just like Victoria said, "All sensations change if we let them be." Isn't it a beautiful night to be watching Little League?

UNPLEASANT.

I chew my thumbnail. I have a searing feeling between my lower ribs, like I just ate a thousand Flamin' Hot Cheetos and then swallowed one of those novelty punching-nun toys, which is sock-ing it to my solar plexus from the inside.

Victoria would be pissed if I missed the fundamental point she made in the drafty auxiliary chapel of that giant church in Scottsdale. The only thing to do is rip open a bag of sunflower seeds with your teeth and make yourself uncomfortable, because there's nowhere to run when you're a pitcher's mom. You can't escape it hiding behind the snack bar or watching between your fingers, and maybe you shouldn't even try. After the six-week course ended, I continued spo-radically attending her weekly dharma talks at the church, sermons on karma, suffering, attachment. "Approach, don't avoid," she'd say.

That's the reason I'm glad I heard the sound of my brother's rattling breaths on the day he died, the thick respiratory boots beat-ing a path from a pair of congested lungs, through some secretions in a relaxed throat, to the Great Beyond.

Laura taped my brother, using her iPhone so she could send the video to the hospice nurse for advice on what to do.

How long do you think he has left based on this? she texted the nurse, copying me, attaching the file. By the time the nurse responded, he was gone.

That might sound creepy, to know that I've seen and heard images of my brother in the last hour of his life. All I can tell you is that death is pretty mysterious if you haven't been around it much, and frankly even if you have. The recorded evidence just says, *You don't have to wonder exactly what it was like. It was like this.*

The strangest thing is that I could sooner listen to an iPhone recording of my dying brother than watch my son pitch. There's ancient Buddhist wisdom; then there's the anxiety of a grieving Little League mom and her broken-down old dad, and the two of us can't handle any more wild pitches.

I slap a placid look on my face like *No big deal, my kid's got this, and if he doesn't, so what?*

When Nate throws his first pitch, he has his eyes on the catcher's glove all the way, start to finish, the hitch in his windup having been ironed out by these school-day mornings in our makeshift bullpen.

Nate throws fourteen pitches in that inning. There are no base runners. There are no walks or hits. He throws nine strikes, five balls. And on the third strike of the third batter, he allows himself one subtle fist pump and half a smile.

Game over.

We pack up and Grandpa heads toward his meditation cushion, a molded plastic saddle beneath the green sheet. It may not be pretty or proper, but the old man is keeping the rust at bay. A roof is a roof is a cover is a home is a tin can next door to a mortuary is a place to be until the next inning, the next night rolling home, a toothless poem shooting through a sketchy neighborhood, rounded over his handlebars. He's a kind of poem to me now, because the cyclist pedaling through the blackness is happy and sad at the same time, seeing two boys. One lefty slugger is just ashes, a Ziploc baggie of dust shoved in a shoebox in the closet where I meditate on the magnitude of his loss, and the other slugger—the image the old man also now holds in his mind, holds tight, knuckles fully flexed—has freckles across his nose and allows himself one restrained pump of his fist, and Grandpa sees that fist as he turns onto the bike path from Thomas Road, heading downhill, rising from his seat, coasting, past the fishing pond where the salty air fills his nose, and the Continental Villas, and the back of Oscar's Taco Shop, closed for the night, the sombrero over the *O* barely visible.

If you hear the sound of my dad's screams bouncing off some trees in the desert, it's okay. He's getting from point A to point B through the park on a path he can barely see.

As we head home, singing along to "Old Town Road" on the radio, I wonder if my dad will scream out into this night or laugh maniacally. Will two of his favorite sluggers be sitting next to each other in the dusty, dark dugout that is the no-man's-land of a grieving grandpa in the afterglow of a lights-out pitching performance by the lefty who lives?

I don't know about his ride home, but when I check my phone later, I have a text from my dad.

As I read it, I know his feet are crossed, kicked up in thick gray socks, resting on the pleather recliner that came with the place. He's wearing his navy knit cap, sipping a reasonably sized shot of cheap tequila he picked up at Circle K on the way home, and I know he doesn't even need his little space heater to keep him warm tonight as he taps out a text with his pinky.

Struck out the side.

CHAPTER NINE

Leave It There

"Grief helps us to relinquish the illusion that
the past could be different from what it was."

—SHARON SALZBERG, *REAL LOVE:
THE ART OF MINDFUL CONNECTION*

The sky is a confection this time of day in early spring, between school and dinnertime. It looks like a slice of cake on the horizon, cotton-candy blue on the bottom, pale pink on top. From the doorless bathroom of the Arcadia Little League, hot air blows in bursts from the hand dryer, trumpeting into the bleachers, blending with the steady sound of faraway cars racing around Indian School Road.

Nate is up to bat. Mighty Team Orange is in the field.

"Leave it there," yells Daniel, after Nate lets a ball go by him, into the catcher's mitt.

"BALL ONE," shouts the ump.

Team Orange is up a few runs by the third, but that's no surprise because they are the best team in the league, undefeated.

Nate lets another pitch go. "STEEEE-RIIIIKE," hollers the ump.

"That's okay," says Daniel coolly, standing by first base in his purple joggers. "Wait for your pitch."

I turn to my dad. "How can you know if it's your pitch in a fraction of a second when a ball is hurtling toward you?"

"That's just what good hitters do."

Then he turns toward me, a trailer-park mystic in a beanie. "*They slow down time.*"

On the next pitch, Nate checks his swing as the ball whizzes over the plate just above his knees. He changes his mind about whether it was his, stops his hips and shoulders cold. This decision is conceived and deployed somewhere tucked inside of a momentarily lengthening millisecond. It wasn't his pitch, but it is strike two. Gavin's mom shouts through the fence and into the batter's box, "Now you've seen it."

This I interpret as a standard therapeutic reframe. *You didn't get had because you stood there and let a perfectly good pitch fly into your strike zone, untouched. No. You left it there because it wasn't your pitch. It wasn't the one you knew you could crush. And in the process of leaving it, you saw it up close, clocked all 108 bloodred double stitches. And because you've seen it, you're one pitch closer to hitting a nuke.*

Isaiah is on third, waltzing on and off the bag, keeping Team Orange's pitcher on edge. "Bring me in, Nate Dog! C'MON!" he shouts from the infield toward the batter's box. He got on base on a walk, a sweet, sweet ball four.

"Is it just me, or has that kid not taken a single swing in five games?" my dad had wondered aloud during Isaiah's at bat. I shushed him.

"Inside voice, Dad."

"But we're outside."

"A walk is as good as a hit, Dad. Did you not see *Moneyball*? *On-base percentage*, old man. And we need base runners."

As Team Orange's pitcher gets himself set, Isaiah calls out again to the batter's box, "Don't leave me stranded!"

Nate connects on a two-strike count, lining it to right.

We are on our feet, rudely blocking the view of everyone behind us, but we don't care. My dad yells, "GO, NATEY, GO!" and Daniel windmills his right arm, signaling his son to keep running to second, and then third, where the ump calls Nate safe. We ease back down into our low chairs, watching Nate as he bends his legs into ready position, left foot on the bag. All he's thinking about is making it home, his dark eyes shooting down the third-base line.

Dad elbows me. "A triple. He pulled it. Did you see that? Because that's his pitch. That's just how he likes them, a little high in the zone." He leans back, stretches out his legs toward the fence, one sneakered foot holding down the other. "That was a SHOT."

"And an RBI," I add, just to see the curves of my dad's mouth smile harder.

"Worth the price of admission," brags my dad.

"And you didn't even pay to get in here."

Still, even with the run, Team Orange has already hung eight on the Pinstripes, and they haven't even put their ace on the mound yet. Deacon, the coach's kid, is behind the dish. He's the best catcher we've seen so far, and the best overall player in the league. Everything he does just looks right. His dominance comes as no surprise, because his dad was in the actual, real-life major leagues.

That morning, Daniel had laid things out for me. "This team is like baseball royalty, an MLB All-Star coach, and his kid's a stud. Who are we? We are nobody. And nobody expects us to win. The Pinstripes are underdogs, and that's a good place to be."

Kai comes up next, fouling off pitch after pitch, feisty and slight.

"Another legendary Kai at bat," says my dad. "This kid knows how to battle."

Ultimately, after at least nine pitches—my dad and I lose count—Kai pops a ball straight up. Deacon springs up from his knees, jet-black hair poking out from his helmet. He turns his back to the field, locates the ball in the air, throws his mask into the dirt, and catches the baseball, using both hands, like it's nothing, his fine features expressionless.

"Damn. That kid is good, T."

"Good grab," says Leo's dad. Even opposing fans can appreciate that we are seeing something different, a catcher who controls the tempo, blocked errant pitches, and actually makes outs.

"What do you expect?" I say. "His dad won the Golden Gloves. I looked it up."

"No, that's boxing. He won the Gold Glove. Very prestigious. You know how good you have to be to even make it to the Show?"

Trying to be cool about it, I glance at Coach Orange. His arms are crossed loosely. He takes up room, feet planted wide, legs like tree trunks in shiny black compression leggings.

"No other dad could pull off wearing tights. No way," I say, staring. "I heard all the moms have a crush on him."

"Are you kidding, T? *I* have a crush on him."

"And you might think he'd be one of these supercompetitive asshole dad coaches, but look, he wants every kid to swing. Even the sucky ones," I point out. He's coaching his batters from right in front of our dugout, miming what he wants them to do.

"Hands up. Choke up. Step into it. Watch it in," he instructs.

My dad says, "He doesn't even put the 'take' sign on for those two tiny cousins at the bottom of his lineup. They make Andrew look like Randy Johnson."

"I don't understand. Does the 'take' sign mean take the pitch or leave the pitch? How am I supposed to follow this?"

"'Take' means leave."

Coach Orange reminds the smaller of the cousins, "If it's not your pitch, leave it."

As I watch this game, confused about taking and leaving,

marveling at how anyone can know when to do either, under pressure and under the lights, I think about leaving my mom the last time. I'd been so tortured by indecision, I couldn't actually move my body. My feet felt stuck to the sidewalk, like I was standing in hardening cement, just frozen there, right in front of a Starbucks on Geary Street in San Francisco. I clutched the handle of my red carry-on bag, trying to figure out my next move. It was not yet seven a.m. in Union Square, and I couldn't figure out if I should head to the airport and go home to Phoenix or go see my mom one last time.

The thing is, she'd been dead for an hour or so.

As you might expect in such a fresh-dead-mom scenario, I was sobbing, hunched forward at the waist.

"WHAT DO I DO?" I asked Daniel on the phone, open-throated, wobbly. I slouched forward with the phone to my ear. "I can't leave her. I just can't leave her." I kept repeating myself, inhaling sharply between each word. "I . . . JUST . . . CAN'T . . . LEAVE . . . HER . . . BODY." I was wailing, my body doing something between davening and capoeira. But it was Union Square, so nobody much noticed.

"You were there when it mattered," said Daniel. "She's gone now. You can come home. There's nothing else for you to do."

"Someone should be there."

But I knew she wouldn't want to be seen as nothing and nobody, just another stiff with a C. diff infection. "People ignore you when you're old, when you're not pretty anymore, or if they think you're broke," she'd told me when I was in middle school, somewhere around the time strangers stopped helping her push-start her VW Bug.

One of the times I'd stopped talking to her—and there were many—it was because she'd thrown a fit at a fancy vegan bakery in LA. The manager treated my mom like she had no clout. And my mom wasn't having it. The manager told her she couldn't get her money back for a giant, pricey cake she'd bought for a party celebrating my wedding. "Teresa, I went to that place because I know it's your favorite place, but that cake was dry and crumbly. It was just wrong. Nobody ate it. I think they left something out. I just called over there and that snooty manager told me I can't prove it, I can't prove they messed up the cake, and I said, 'WATCH ME. I'm on my way over there right now. One taste and they'll know.'"

In her passenger seat were the remains of the towering brown, chunky, desiccated apple dessert, which she'd shoved into a black plastic trash bag.

"Mom, I'm begging you, please don't. I go to that place all the time. I'll pay you whatever the cake cost NOT to do that."

"Okay," she said, hanging up on me.

But she ignored me. Which I learned the next day during the first hour of my morning radio show, when the call screener caught me during a commercial. "Some lady from a bakery is on the phone. She wants to talk about how your mom showed up yesterday with a trash bag full of cake, yelling that her daughter is a big deal because you're on the radio and they better pay her back for the cake or her daughter is going to blast them on the air."

"Just some wacko," I explained, looking down at my coffee and a stack of news stories. "Not my mom, but thanks for letting me know." I felt nauseous. The red numbers on the digital wall clock were counting down, forty seconds left until we were back on the air.

The call screener was confused. "The wacko lady with the cake in a trash bag specifically said, 'Do you know who my daughter is? She's Teresa Strasser from *The Adam Carolla Show* and she's a big deal.' They have a picture from their security camera, I guess."

I looked up at the call screener, begging. "Can I ask you for a huge favor and I'll never ask for anything ever again? Hang up. Tell them that it wasn't my mom and it was a misunderstanding. *Please*."

"Okay, but this would've been radio gold," said the call screener, clearly annoyed. She returned to the booth and got rid of the irate bakery lady, but I made my mom pay for the entire shameful episode. I called to berate her from my car on the way home from the radio show. "Do NOT go around asking if people know who I am. They don't," I told her, "and if they do know who I am, you're just embarrassing me AND you. I asked you to stand down and you didn't. You can't treat me this way!" I didn't talk to her again for months. It didn't seem fair for her to cash in on me as an adult, when I was finally interesting, when I wasn't just some needy crouton of a child.

There was no way to make it right now. If I could bring her back, if I could do it all again, I'd let her make scenes. I'd spin them into radio gold.

But back on Geary Street, one hour after the end of my mother's life, my sneakers were still stuck to the cement and there was no way to do anything all over again.

"I know it's just her body, Danny. But I can't leave her. I was the worst daughter." I let out a noise that sounded exaggerated and comical, bending so far over at the waist with my phone to my ear that I was folded like a motel cot. "I want a do-over, and next time I won't have any beefs with her."

If I left town to return to my family in Phoenix, there'd be nobody to see that my mom got the VIP treatment in the hospital's basement morgue. I thought about calling my brother for advice, but I was an only child, had been for four months, and it was just me, me and my dead mom going cold and stiff across town.

"Remember when the social worker called from the hospital?" Daniel said. "All your mom wanted was to see you before she died.

And you showed up, and you told her you loved her, and she was kind of Tammy about it, but she told you she loved you back. And now you can leave her there and come home. I just checked and there's a flight in two hours. I'm buying you a ticket."

"Okay," I said, only at that moment dropping the idea that I would be standing on Geary Street forever, until I died, and everyone in Union Square died.

I ordered an Uber and went home.

When I walked into my dead mom's condo in Las Vegas, I encountered a sea of tchotchkes, each one a decision I'd have to make. There was her cherry-red ceramic panther lamp. There were vintage Mexican silver bracelets, pastel Bauer nesting bowls, seven mint-green mid-century modern pitchers crowding the Mr. Coffee on her kitchen counter. There was a framed print of a Hawaiian hula girl hung next to a plaster of Paris orange, ruddy-cheeked and jaunty, winking like the world's creepiest citrus fruit. The place was tidy, but it was cramped, stuffed with a lifetime full of garage sale and flea market treasures. It smelled faintly of the inside of one of her worn leather Coach purses.

We had only one day to clean the place out before putting it on the market. The boys were bouncing around on the couch. Then they flung open the fridge, revealing four giant bottles of off-brand neon soda.

"Can we have some? PLEASE? CAN WE?" Nate begged. My mom had never kept soda in the house.

She must've predicted we'd all be at her place after she died. *And why shouldn't her grandsons have some soda if they want to? And who could even tell the difference between this stuff and the brand-name soda? And why not let the kids live a little on Grandma's dime?*

"Fine," I said.

As they poured bright orange soda into mugs they found on the counter, I wandered into her congested bedroom, looking at a silver tray on her nightstand covered with unopened mail, a few pencils, and a clay craft I had made one summer at some free neighborhood day camp. I remembered sitting with a bunch of kids I didn't know, doggedly rolling out pieces of clay into worm shapes, stacking them together in a circle, making a too-small lid, painting the entire thing pastel yellow and blue after they baked it, and handing it over to my mom.

"Well, maybe crafting is not your thing," she said, laughing so hard at the drooping clay atrocity in her hand that she had to wipe away tears with the other hand. I never, ever forgot that moment when she didn't notice that I wasn't in on the joke. I'd spent all week working on the bowl, sitting alone at the dodgy playground day camp. The whole time, I couldn't wait to impress her with my creation, and she'd shit on it. Now I held that bowl and thought about how long she'd kept it, how many decades, how many moves. She'd never displayed it before and I'd had no idea she'd kept it. I cried into that crappy craft, more hideous than I remembered it. I felt the paint, smooth and cool against my hands, brushed my fingers across the too-small lid resting at the bottom of the bowl. I showed it to my boys. Then I tossed it.

In the drawer of her nightstand, I found the manila envelope containing the custody appeal she'd saved for more than forty years. Underneath it was a brittle, yellowing copy of a now-defunct underground newspaper out of Berkeley.

"*See PG. 7,*" was written on the cover in blue ballpoint pen above the headline: "SINGING THE COWGIRL BLUES WITH TOM ROBBINS." Underneath the headline was a photo of Robbins, submerged in a hot tub, looking toward the heavens, a cigar, or maybe a blunt, between his fingers.

On page seven, a roundup of the best coffee shops in the Haight-Ashbury included her shop, which she'd bought with savings from working her dull government job. "Tamara Strasser, owner, thinks there are two types of people in the world: those who want to run a bookstore and those who want to run a coffeehouse. Being one of the latter, she bought the Sacred Grounds last year." The piece went on to say that "children often doze under burlap tables" while musicians and poets performed from the stage in the corner.

The ambience was "a pleasant change if you've just had some punk rock performer vomit in your direction at Winterland." And if that wasn't enough, the soups were top-notch.

My mom made those soups from her mother's recipes, in a giant stainless steel vat. I'd often eat a bowl of potato cream soup, then doze under one of those burlap tables, waiting for my mom to carry me to her car, still asleep, after she mopped the floors and put up the chairs at midnight.

I stuffed the newspaper into the manila envelope with the custody appeal. She was somebody. She was the kind of person who wanted to run a coffee shop. She had even "married" one of her longtime employees, a shaggy-haired gay man from Canada, so he could get his green card. He and everyone else stole cash from the till, and between that and the constant invasion of pests, she stopped being the kind of person who wanted to run anything. "Quick, get over here, Teresa. Get the spray. It's one of Mr. Wilkerson's friends," she'd whisper, when I was helping in the kitchen. That was code. Mr. Wilkerson was the exterminator.

After finding her jade pendant in the pocket of a winter coat, and putting it around my neck, I moved back into the living room, feverishly emptying the contents of her crowded wooden curio case into a plastic bin. The decisions didn't feel quick or intuitive. Sweat was making my denim shorts stick to the backs of my legs. I couldn't slow down time. I was just ready to stop reckoning with all her shit.

"Is my mom having a conniption in heaven because I'm deporting her Russian nesting dolls?" I asked Daniel, hoisting the dolls on top of a set of Scottie dog salt and pepper shakers. We'd hired our Realtor's nephew to take the stuff somewhere for donation, but I had a feeling most of it would end up in the Clark County dump.

I felt a pang every time I put one of her blue glass vases in the box, and a wave of sorrow when most of her stuff rode away in the truck of a stranger, things that had been precious to her, stuff and more stuff. The visceral remains of a life, start to finish, would probably be melting into a landfill in Henderson.

———————

As Team Orange tries to stitch things up in the sixth, my mom is at my house in a plastic bag from the Neptune Society, which has been placed in a decorative box next to a vintage Gucci address book she bought at a garage sale in 1987. It was one of the only other things I kept.

"Vintage," she bragged. "I paid five dollars for it at the flea market. *Real Gucci*,'" she crooned, displaying it like a game show hostess with a prize.

That faded brown canvas-and-leather address book is still filled with my mom's Post-it notes about appointments and insurance codes, lists of my brother's doctors and medication doses, things that will never matter to anybody ever again.

Across an entire page, in her familiar scrawl, in red ballpoint pen and blue ink and faded pencil and felt tip, are every phone number and address I've ever had in my entire life.

"Did you call me or did I call you?" she'd often ask, hearing my voice. "Hello? Is that you? I'm futzing with my cell phone and I don't understand how you're here. Did I call you?"

"No, Mom, I called you."

"But I was just picking up my phone to dial your number. Isn't that funny?"

It seemed funny how much she wanted me to call her, and come around to visit, once I was grown and didn't need anything from her. I never stopped wondering where all this care and concern had been when I was little, when I needed her to look out for me, or at the very least give me a ride.

I recalled traveling alone back and forth between my parents, first by plane, then, starting when I was around eight years old, by bus. Monthly and on holidays, she took me to the depot between Market and Mission Streets, an industrial neighborhood of warehouses and residential hotels, and stood next to me in the parking lot until it was time to board. She gave me a ten-dollar bill, then waited until she saw me wave to her from inside the coach, on the other side of the big window. In her gray-and-white wool poncho, Levi's, and tall leather boots, she'd wave back. She'd smile, big hair with a tight perm and glossy red lips. Pulling away from the station, I'd ache, just for a second, to think about the hours ahead without my mom, but then I'd stop, because I didn't know it was all right to long for that. It never occurred to me that she could have driven me in her car, or that I could have wanted that, or requested it. I'd stop feeling sad by the time the bus hit the freeway. Though I never once saw another little kid alone on the Greyhound, it would have shocked me to think that my mom was doing something that would later be illegal, that she could have chosen to drive me or ride along with me. Part of me still sees that as impossible, unimaginable. When you went away, you went alone. And when you returned home, it was the same.

During the course of those days on the open road, or at least Interstate 5, I was nowhere. I'd left one home for another, and in between there was only time to fill, the world outside the vast Greyhound windows changing from green to brown and back, rural to suburban and back again, industrial farm buildings far from the highway, strip malls up close, and then miles of brown emptiness.

Every time the bus lurched out of the parking lot, the time ahead felt hopelessly long, but it was broken up by stops in Salinas, San Luis Obispo, and Paso Robles.

The automatic doors of a Greyhound make a *whoosh* when the driver opens them from his big cushy seat.

"I'm leaving here in twenty minutes, whether you're here or not. So don't be late, because I am not waiting," the driver would say to me as I lined up to get off the bus. I'd nod. If this jowl-faced fool thought I didn't know how to get back to my seat on time, puh-lease. I'd been traveling solo since I was three, so I'd been doing it as long as I'd done anything, and I was never skittish about it. I jogged down the four stairs to the bottom without even looking down. I had it wired at the stops—buy food from either a vending machine or a lunch counter, count money down low by my hip and out of view, so nobody would know if I still had cash left to steal, avoid the metal benches where there was usually a couple fighting or someone nodding out, complete tasks quickly and with a confident facial expression—but there was attention to be paid en route.

For example, there was no telling what might happen in the dark underworld below the seats, so I always kept my backpack strap around my ankle, in case someone tried to jack my belongings from down below while I slept.

Not only did my parents not worry about the safety of bus stations; they didn't think much about exposing me to art meant for grown-ups. Neither of my parents ever took me to an animated movie, but my dad did take me to see *Yol*, a two-hour Turkish film about suffering.

When I was ten years old, my mom took me to see *Midnight Cowboy*.

"Wasn't Dustin Hoffman brilliant in that? He's a method actor.

He *becomes* the character," she said as we streamed out of the theater, she in a leotard and jeans, I in patent leather Mary Jane shoes. The devastation of Dustin's death in the final scene was so brutal, I couldn't speak. By the end of the movie, I was so attached to him, so uplifted by the humanity and salvation of his friendship with cowboy hustler Joe Buck, that I could barely breathe. I would have given anything to bring him back to life, to see him triumphantly soaking in the sunshine of the promised land in Miami, instead of dying right when he got there. (It dawns on me now that Ratso died on a Greyhound bus.)

Her book choices, like her movie choices, were never for kids. She took us to Yosemite every summer for a week and read a book to us in our cabin, one chapter a night, by flashlight. That same year, she read us *Slaughterhouse-Five*, which we loved.

But *Of Mice and Men* really did us in. One of two times I ever saw my brother cry as a kid was when I walked into our cabin one day and caught him reading ahead. He was on the last chapter, when George has to kill Lennie. We were so annihilated by the story that it was almost like that was the end of our childhood. I promised I wouldn't tell Mom that he'd snuck into the cabin to read ahead. And I promised I'd never tell anyone he cried. Last month, I read it to my boys (or to be exact, we listened to the book on tape together) and it was just as heartbreaking.

"I got you to look after me, and you got me to look after you," Lennie told George.

Of Mice and Men and *Midnight Cowboy* are both about the end of loneliness, about having that one person who cares for you and who has your back in a dangerous world. These are stories about brotherhood. Not literally, but I wonder now if both of us, Morgan and me, had the visceral experience of being part of a duo, then being alone, before we could understand the cleavage or place it in time.

Back on those Greyhound bus rides, I didn't read books, just

Mad magazine. For me, the heart of any issue was the feature "Snappy Answers to Stupid Questions," which I wouldn't allow myself to read until the monotony out the window broke me.

Unlike the lettuce in a bus-stop tuna sandwich, "Snappy Answers to Stupid Questions" was always crisp. Each cartoon panel showcased a person innocently asking a dumb question, and then a tightly written retort.

My very favorite Snappy Answer blew me away with its succinct brilliance: A woman barges into the bedroom of a man in striped pajamas who is facedown under the covers. "Are you asleep?" she asks, swinging the door open. The man replies, "NO, dead—leave the flowers and get out." When I discovered that one, I couldn't wait to show it to my brother. I folded the corner down to remind myself, and we would reenact it ad infinitum.

"Are you asleep?" he'd say as he opened the bedroom door.

"No, DEAD—leave the flowers and get out," I'd sneer as I popped up in bed. It wasn't as crushing when I said it, as my performance didn't capture the world-weary spirit of the cartoon. Still, I had a new private joke with my big brother and I wanted to freeze the scene in time. He liked baseball, I liked ballet, so there weren't many ways I could think of to engage him. And because I saw him only once a month, sometimes even less, he was a bit like a stranger every time. We were always starting over.

"Let's do the Snappy Answer again, Mugs!"

He leaves the room and closes the door. Then: "Are you asleep?"

And so it would go until I lost my unenthusiastic scene partner to a Dodgers game on the TV.

"Snappy Answers to Stupid Questions," as a work of graphic art, was in stark contrast to the work displayed at Greyhound depots. In particular, there was a poster of a teenage girl with long eyelashes and straight hair parted down the middle. She was there as long as I could remember, a black-and-white close-up of her face

on an ad for a hotline runaways could call if they needed bus fare
home, so they could avoid being prey for bus-stop pimps. The girl
was sun-kissed and pretty, while I was frizzy-haired, with calcium
spots on my teeth and heavy eyelids. My corduroy pants were too
short and the snap barely stayed closed at the waist. We were different, the poster girl and I. Plus she looked naive, not on her guard.
Her kind might need saving. I'd get where I was going.

"How could you put me on a Greyhound bus to see Dad or my
grandparents when I was so little, Mom? That isn't even legal now.
When I tell people, they don't believe it," I'd finally said to her as a
young adult, hysterical and unhinged, holding a box of tissues. "I
could have been groped on some bus, or left behind at the depot in
San Luis Obispo . . . or . . . stolen by some sex traffickers. I could've
been kidnapped and stabbed, Mom, and nobody would've known
it. *Stabbed alone in a bus station restroom.* I could've been chopped
up in little pieces and buried in a tarp near the slaughterhouse off
I-5 in Coalinga because I was a child. *I was a child*, Mom."

"What was I supposed to do? Take you there myself?"

"Jesus, Mom. Yes! YES! You were my mother; who else would
take me?"

She looked genuinely stunned. She wrinkled her brow at the
thought of it, of doing anything for hours on end that she didn't
want to do. Her daughter had turned out just fine. You could even
read her articles in newspapers or see her on TV, or hear her on the
radio. To her, little kids were insipid time sucks—everyone knew
it—and she'd figured out a way to do the very least of the yucky parts
of parenting and still end up with an adult child to brag about.

I was standing in my dining room in Los Angeles. She was sitting at the table, her arms folded. She looked up, dumbfounded,
annoyed, like *her kid had survived, so what was the big deal?*

That look on her face, like she was starting to feel sorry for herself because I was yelling at her—it made me throw the box of tissues at the wall. She flinched, narrowed her eyes, and slid down into her chair. Tears were falling from her jaw down onto her folded arms, dotting her linen sleeves. She did feel sorry for herself—*the fucking nerve!* She had always just done her own thing, while I had hardened into a sort of full-time unaccompanied minor. I'm still a loner, and still kind of hard. It became my natural state.

She wanted to pal around now that I was easy, now that I was an adult who didn't need anything, now that I could even do things for her, reflect a little glory her way, make it seem like she'd always been right there, on the sidelines. One summer, she had worked on a tree farm in Hawaii with some friends while I stayed with my grandparents, watching game shows and waiting for her to call on Sundays.

To her, I'd always been a little adult. What was the big deal about letting me fend for myself? She'd been there to wave goodbye at the terminal. And I'd made it home every time.

To understand where she was coming from, which I managed to do only after she died, I had to go back to her parents, who had fled Europe before the Nazis took over. My grandfather left his village in Ukraine after Cossacks—anti-Jewish rioters—shot his brother dead on the front porch. His toddler daughter died on the train to the boat to America, scalded by a tipped samovar. His older son later died in a gas station fire in Los Angeles. He met my grandmother doing Yiddish theater after emigrating. Most of the people they knew from back home were rounded up and killed by the Nazis.

Extreme free-range parenting maneuvers didn't seem so bad in that context. You want a snappy answer to a stupid question: Was this childhood safer than running from Cossacks, or from Nazis? I don't know; ask Anne Frank. I had food and ballet lessons. I had a scholarship to private school, and if it took two buses to get there, it still beat dodging bullets. My mom's whole parenting vibe was a shock wave still rolling outward from that porch in Ukraine.

And also, she wanted to have adventures, not parent-teacher conferences or all-day family bus trips down the I-5.

I used to press my father, too.

"I didn't know you took the bus. I didn't know. I don't remember."

"What do you mean you didn't know? When you lived in LA, you picked me up at a building where there was a huge sign with a dog on it above a parking lot full of buses."

"That was your mom's idea," he said. Then: "Aunt Julie is cheating at Scrabble," he'd add suddenly, tapping letters into his phone.

"But, Dad, you could have offered to pay for the plane. Or come to pick me up—"

"I wasn't mature enough to have kids," he'd mutter, wandering away.

"You were twenty-six when you had me."

"But I was like a kid."

Whatever reasons my dad had, he can't talk about them now. All he had to say about it landed in that roadside coffee shop somewhere outside Prescott, Arizona.

"I wasn't a good father. I was a terrible father," he confessed. "But she's a great daughter." He had never said either of those things to me until that day, a year after the season of the Purple Pinstripes, standing in a slice of dusty High Country sunlight.

My mom never reckoned with how she'd parented us as kids. But when my brother got sick, she poured all she had into caring for him.

My mom was Johnny-on-the-spot, as my dad used to say, from the day my brother was diagnosed to the day she tapped out, a few months before he died.

She stayed at his house for months at a time. She fed his kids breakfast and walked them to school, even when they were wild with confusion, their routines upset, adults always whispering.

My mom kept careful notes about procedures and insurance codes and medications. She regularly caught dosage errors at hospitals. She yelled at nurses sometimes, and there was always a bottle of Valium rattling around in her big leather purse, but I didn't blame her for vacillating between rage and sedation.

But then she went back to Vegas for a couple of weeks, like she always did, to check on her dog. And this time she sent an email to my brother. She wouldn't be returning, she wrote. And that email was her goodbye to her dying son.

"You can't do this," I screamed at her over the phone.

She was quiet.

"I'll be the only one left one day *when you're dying.* And I'll just send an email telling you I can't make it. You'll die alone." It's the worst thing I've ever said, and an empty threat. I was there, but only because her best friend, Kathy, asked me, "Teresa, has there ever been something you knew you just couldn't do, despite what anyone else thought? Until that happens, you won't understand. This was that thing for your mother. She just couldn't be there for the end."

"I know," I said. But I'd wanted better for my brother.

I was appalled she thought she could just tap out whenever she chose, and until Kathy phrased it like that, I always framed it as a choice she was making, avoiding when she should have approached, shirking her responsibilities like she'd done before, when it was inconvenient to drive us places or even find a job in Los Angeles so we could all at least live in the same town. I never thought about it as something she literally couldn't do, hiding out in the spare bedroom upstairs, Laura snapping at her if she used the wrong plastic cup to give the kids juice, everyone's patience worn thin, no hope for anything to get better, her child stuck in the basement, stuck in his body, the one she'd made and nursed and rocked, the child she'd already lost when he was just five years old. There was nothing she could do either time to keep ahold of him. The next time I saw my mom after telling her I'd never see her again was when I walked into the palliative care wing.

Kathy was sitting in a wooden chair next to her bed, all of my mother's gold jewelry in her lap, in a black velvet drawstring bag. She'd driven there from her home in Berkeley to wait with my mom until I arrived.

"She wanted you to have this," Kathy said, lifting up the bag of hoop earrings and gold rope chains and bangles. "She's fixated on getting you this gold. I promised I wouldn't leave until I personally handed it to you. So here you go. She wants you to split this with Morgan's kids." She hoisted the bag higher. "Take it. I feel like Berkeley's fiercest lesbian pirate with all this gold." I took it from her. It felt heavy in my hands. "All I need is a parrot on my shoulder." She stood abruptly and smoothed her knit vest. "I've been here since yesterday. I'm out of here. Keep me posted." She'd spent four decades eating Japanese noodles and seeing documentaries and hunting for treasures at flea markets with my mom. That was the last time she'd see her alive.

My mom was asleep in a patch of light coming in through the window. I peered into the bag of gold. Every precious thing she had left, she wanted me to have.

Major League Baseball Player's son is now on the mound for Team Orange. With a cushy lead, he's working out the feel for his new changeup. He's thrown Nate three balls in a row.

"If anyone would swing on a three-and-oh count, it's Natey," says my dad.

From the bleachers, Leo's dad calls, "Wait for your pitch, now." Deacon draws up his front leg, looking both grown-up and fragile, like a baby giraffe. He lunges forward.

"BALL FOUR," the ump bellows as Nate tosses his bat into the dirt.

"Disciplined at the plate tonight," I say, raising my eyebrows with surprise.

My dad adds, "Very."

Team Orange bests the Purple Pinstripes, 11–6. Daniel and the boys stay at the fields to catch the late games.

When we get home, Dad heads directly to the liquor cabinet, pours himself a couple inches of Kirkland tequila, downs it, and then grabs a box of pretzels and a nonalcoholic beer before he sits across from me at the table. "That's all the booze I need." He still has to ride his bike back to the Riviera. "Just one pop to round out the edges."

"How are you with that game? I'm actually okay. Nate hit a triple. We can't be sad."

Dad chews his pretzel. "I can be sad. I HATE LOSING." He grins, the tequila warming him up from the inside.

"We are so shallow, Dad."

"No, we're petty. There's a difference. HA!"

It's just us in the house, and it's so quiet, you can hear the sound of one of our cats walking toward the dining room table, claws clacking on the floor. Dad takes a swig of beer, wipes his mouth with his hand.

"They could've gotten the whole tumor the first operation. They could've just decided not to leave anything there, not a single cell. I wonder about that sometimes. He'd still be alive."

"He'd be in a wheelchair."

"I'd still have my son."

"I know, Dad."

"If they just took the whole thing, did the total resection, didn't have to show off what brilliant surgeons they were instead of trying to save all the nerves, those geniuses at Johns Hopkins."

He pulls another long gulp from the bottle, his fingers still wrapped around the bottle's neck. "And he wouldn't have suffered, all that cutting and cutting until there wasn't even enough tissue there to close up his back. Remember that plastic surgeon? What was his name? We used to make fun of it."

I thought for a second and it came back to me. "Dr. Holdhoff. *Hold off on doing more surgery.*"

"Holdhoff. That's right."

He looks away, as if to hide himself. "Morgan never missed a grounder at first. Not one time. He played every ball; it never played him."

"I remember that."

It's quiet again, just the humming of the refrigerator and Dad chewing and the Pottery Barn clock ticking on the wall over our heads. "It's out of order, him being dead, me being here." He picks up his bottle, then puts it back down and looks straight at me, like a little kid who can't understand some awful thing about the world he's just learned. "That's the problem. I should be dead and he should be here. It's out of order."

"I know, Dad." But I don't. I don't and I can't and I won't even try.

"I was scared about the yips, T. When Nate had that bad game, like it was happening all over again. One day Morgan was good; the next day he wasn't. It was all over."

"Nate didn't have the yips. It was just mechanics. Daniel fixed it."

The old man's shoulders narrow and slouch. "Yeah," he says, far away. Then he perks up.

"Daniel is the best. The other day, he said the nicest thing to me that anyone has ever said, in all my seventy-five years, in my whole life. I told him I hoped I wasn't a burden to you guys, now that I live here and I'm always around, eating your food, drinking your beer, tagging along to all the games. He said, 'You aren't a burden. You're a blessing.'" The old man's green eyes fill with water, the lower lids bulging and crimson. His gaze lands on one of our cats napping in a decorative bowl on the table, her paw over her eyes. "Look at that cat. What a beautiful creature, with all those markings. She's so pretty. Which one is that, Lolo or Biggie?"

"That's Lolo, Dad."

"A blessing."

"Dad, I know you don't like grief books—"

"Bunch of bullshit. Stages. Acceptance. Blah, blah, blah. There's one stage, the one where I'll never be the same. Not a day goes by that I don't think about him. And it isn't easier," he says, resigned. "It won't ever be."

I know what he means. I want to cheer him up with all my books, their soothing pastel covers. But there aren't stages for me, either, discrete slices of emotional states, movement from one paradigm to another. There's just before and after. One stage of grief.

The day my brother died, I felt myself propelled at great speed, shot out of my normal world into a sort of pitch-black galaxy where I now float around, waiting to land somewhere, weightless. My dad is a point of light in this big, cold, nowhere sky, a way to orient myself. And so is baseball, the steadiness of games, one after another, the way Nate lopes with my brother's walk, the way the anticipation of a game starts hours before the first pitch, the way Little League sweeps us up in a cosmos of small, intense dramas, urgent and serious, but free from the possibility of real malignancy.

"This one book by two hospice nurses, it doesn't mention any stages, so you might like it. Anyway, they say everyone wonders what they could have done different, you know, medically, but it doesn't matter, because that person was always going to die."

He doesn't care about some nurses and their book. I don't like the sound of myself trying to make things okay. *Leave it*, I think, hearing an echo from the bleachers.

Home safe, he texts later, after chaining his bike to the storage shed.

Scouting report on Team Navy, I text back, smoking my one cigarette in the Adirondack chair at the side of the house. **They have a losing record and their ace just threw 64 vs. Team Lime Green. He's burned. I smell a W.**

I wil ride w you if that's ok.

||||||||||||||||||||||||

CHAPTER TEN

Let the Old Man Ferry the Load

"I'm a very lucky guy. I had so many people help me
over the years that I never had many problems. If I
had a problem, I could sit down with someone and
they would explain the problem to me, and the
problem would become like a baseball game. You're
at home plate now, how do you get to first? How do
you get to second? How do you get to third? When
you get back to home, your problem is solved."

—WILLIE MAYS

"It was a Corolla." My dad always starts the story the same. "Remember that Corolla your mom had? Hatchback. Green. You were sitting in the front seat. You had that hairstyle. What do you call it?"

"Ponytails."

"Right. Ponytails. And you looked out the passenger-seat window. And I was standing in the driveway in LA. And you had your little flowered suitcase all packed up in the trunk. And I wish I hadn't looked. I'll never forget it. You had one little tear going down your cheek, just like this. Slow," he adds, tracing a line from his eye to his jaw with his index finger. "And we made eye contact through the window, and I saw the tear."

The one tear I cried when Pops gave me away, it was the star of the story, and this was the story he told me the most.

Like many of my dad's stories, a car is both tangential and pivotal. In this instance, it's the car my mom had before her push-start VW Bug. He grounds himself there, in the world where a mechanic could fix things, where you could tinker under the hood, rebuild the parts that are broken, resurrect an alternator, jump-start a battery, bring the whole thing back to life.

"That day you left in the Corolla. That was the worst thing. The worst thing I ever did. I won't ever forget that tear going down your cheek." He still tells it the same as when he started telling it, when I was four. "I just want you to know that I didn't give you away because I don't love you," he'd tell me. "I just couldn't handle two little kids. Morgan was all messed up because of the divorce. And I—your mom and I—we just thought it would be best for you, to live with her."

Daniel says that's why my dad always wants to pull the wagon to the car after baseball games, even when it's toppling with heavy gear.

"Let him do it," Daniel tells me. "It's penance." This must be a vestige of his Catholic upbringing, years of Sunday school and mass. But then he adds, "Penance. You know, like . . . Yum Kippur."

"Not *Yum*—it's not yummy. In fact it's the opposite, because you have to fast. *YOM*."

"YOM Kippur," he corrects himself.

"But it's too sad, Danny. He's old and bent over."

Daniel had observed us fighting over the wagon's handle, me grabbing it out of my dad's hands, Dad taking it back.

"He's fine. He's in better shape than any of us. Here's how I see it. He can't change the past. And he can't apologize. And he can't buy you anything. Lord knows, he hasn't set up a trust fund—"

"There's a trust fund. He trusts that I will fund him."

"Right. And that's not a good feeling for him, because he's your dad and because he likes to be a big shot and because on some level he knows he made mistakes. Let him pull the wagon. Stop arguing with him and let him ferry the load."

"Poetic," I say, impressed.

"I don't know why I just sounded like a classic rock deep cut. But I can see things better from the outside. I see he's trying to pay you back, and that's all the currency he has. He can't do dishes for shit."

So I do. I let him ferry the load. Even though he makes grunting sounds and does his *puff, puff* breathing. Even though Andrew sometimes sits right on top of the catcher's gear and black bucket of baseballs, adding more weight to the red wagon with the black handle, the one every family has.

Sometimes people comment. "Letting Grandpa do the heavy lifting, huh?"

"He earns his keep," I joke.

I realize that the penance began during the chaos of my brother's illness, at least in my personal ledger, anyway. All he did to help my brother, nights in hospitals and emergency rooms, it hit my heart like reparation in a slow drip, not just for giving me back to my mom and exposing me to Carol, but also for letting Carol do my brother dirty. "Nelson," she'd insisted, "if you don't set limits with Morgan, and I'm telling you because I know these things, he's going to be shooting people off a clock tower."

I didn't know what a clock tower was, but I knew shooting people was bad. Carol was so convincing, her tone unwavering and authoritative, it took me a couple of minutes every time she said that thing about the clock tower to decide it wasn't real. But she said it in front of my brother regularly, and my dad never corrected her or chided her.

On my brother's tenth birthday, Mom drove us out to surprise him, to my dad's house in Santa Rosa. It was the only time she ever visited the gloomy house across the Golden Gate Bridge. We walked into the kitchen, which was silent and empty, and saw a handwritten note from Carol on the counter:

Morgan,

You need to take out the trash
Do the dishes
Clean out the composting machine
Mop the kitchen
Clean your room
I am running errands.

Happy birthday

My mom looked at me, then at the note in her hand. Eyes wide, she put it back on the counter, almost gingerly placing it in the exact spot it had come from. It was only then we noticed him out in the yard, hoisting compost into a trash bag. My mom hurried out there in her wool shawl, shouting, "Happy birthday! Get your coat. We're going for ice cream! Ice cream for breakfast!" And we sang a loud, awful version of "Happy Birthday" in the VW Bug. The redder his cheeks got, the louder we sang. It's hard to explain how big that hurt felt to me, the way Carol didn't ignore his birthday but deliberately took a great big dump on it. We had to leave him in that house, to finish his chores alone. Driving back over the bridge, I stared out at the ocean, trying not to complain about being carsick. The curvy roads, and the sad sight of Morgan quietly wolfing down his birthday ice cream, the note, my mom's eyes when she saw it—it made me nauseous deep down.

Carol was a bogeyman in my dad's house. We had an unspoken agreement to scatter when we heard her footsteps. When we scrounged food, we carefully hid any remnants and covered our tracks. In her presence, we spoke only when necessary.

We never discussed how we felt about Carol, not as kids, not ever, the way we didn't discuss much other than the Golden State Warriors, the *Serial* podcast, and, later, any cute new things his kids were doing. And, of course, our dad, whose annoying habits only we really understood.

Maybe Dad hadn't seen that birthday note, because he was at work, but he'd certainly fertilized the garden that grew it.

Only during my brother's illness did I begin to feel an adjustment in the score I was keeping.

What the old man owed could only be repaid in ways I hadn't yet conjured before the cancer, reparations in sterile, buzzing medical facilities: leaning over my big brother, a vigil of agonizing tedium and breathtaking devotion; cutting his grown son's bagel while a nurse checked off a long list of medications on a dry-erase board. Dad left the room only if my brother was asleep; then he'd go for a jog around the hospital corridor. That's when he let himself cry, into the hem of his sleeve as he ran, *puff, puff,* pursing his dry lips to exhale. By the time he trotted back to his son's room, he was always ready, a clear vessel, upbeat. "Nurse, are you sure you can't get us a couple cold ones in here? The 49ers are losing again and we need a drink!" he'd joke.

He'd pat my brother's hair. "You doing okay, Mugsy?"

———

At this morning's game, the Pinstripes are coming off a two-game losing streak. Team Navy won't be facing Gavin, because he's at some church thing. Wyatt is out, having jammed his thumb playing basketball at recess. It's Caleb's time for the Little League pitching spotlight. And Caleb's mom doesn't seem ready to watch her kid on the mound. I don't know exactly what kind of engineer she

is, but probably the good kind because she has a strategy, has it at
the ready. She stands by the bleachers with a pair of running shoes
in her hands. When she sees Caleb throw his first warm-up pitch,
she says her goodbyes.

"I'm going for a run. I just can't watch."

She's my kind of people.

"It's okay," I tell her. "You just have PMS: Pitcher's Mom Syndrome." It's not that funny when your stomach is gnashing and
your eyeballs are starting to blur with nerves. She nods like *I get it,
ha ha* before speed-walking all the way out toward the basketball
court, not looking back. By the time she hits the parking lot, she's
at full speed.

I take my seat. "Dad, look. See that lady speed-walking way out
there? That's Caleb's mom. The engineer. She had to bail."

"Fight or flight."

"She flew."

"I don't blame her," says my dad as Caleb's last warm-up pitch
moves like a slow-motion dart. "Well, he doesn't bring heat, but he's
consistent."

"Consistently locating his throws in the dirt two feet in front of
the box. Shit, Dad."

"Shit."

It's a rough outing for Caleb. After two innings, we're already
in a hole. Coach doesn't have many options tonight, so he puts Nate
on the mound.

"Dad, do you have the pitch-counting thing I got you?"

He unzips his fanny pack and pulls out the bright blue plastic
counter I ordered for him. It's as basic as it can get: You click a
metal tab at every throw, and the number counter advances.

Nate doesn't exactly have command, but he's throwing Little
League fire this morning. He's making the most of his long legs, so
disproportionately long, his purple belt almost looks perched on his

nipples. His front stride is landing closer to the mound this outing. He looks sure-footed and stable, despite hitting just outside the zone.

"There's movement on the tail of the pitches," my dad notices. "He just needs to throw strikes. These walks. You know. They have a way of coming in."

"I know."

"But he looks smooth tonight. That one outing where he was terrible? There was no continuity to his delivery. My heart stopped at the top of his motion, every pitch. It was like you threw something into the gears of a machine. This is like watching an opera."

"I hate opera," I say. "Don't tell anybody."

After walking two batters, Nate strikes out the next three. Inning over. Now Team Navy's pitcher warms up.

"I'd rather watch this than Sandy Koufax himself," says Dad, gesturing toward the diamond, where his grandson, after gathering himself, throws strikes. "And I saw Koufax at Dodger Stadium. Saw him strike out eighteen Giants."

"You saw him strike out Willie Mays, right?"

"Koufax struck him out twice that night, the great Willie Mays. Mays led the league in home runs four times."

"You call Wyatt Caleb, and you call Caleb Wyatt, but your mind has retained all this?"

"Oh, and I remember the great Vin Scully, announcer for—"

"I've heard of him—"

"The great Vin Scully, announcer for the Dodgers, he said you get only one Sandy Koufax in a lifetime."

"He had arm troubles, right?"

"Oh yeah. That game he struck out eighteen, between innings he was rubbing hot pepper ointment on his arm, and they were draining fluids from his elbow. He played right through it. In the crowd, it was like we were in a trance. We couldn't believe it."

"Did he have a cool baseball nickname?"

"Oh yeah. They called him the Left Arm of God. Too bad the arm gave out and God couldn't fix it."

"Speaking of throwing too many pitches, how many pitches did Nate throw in that inning? I'm supposed to tell Daniel."

He looks at the counter.

"I don't know. I think I missed a couple."

"You had *one* job. Give me that." I grab the little clicker. "Well, somewhere around thirty. Isn't that too many for one inning?"

"It's not one-two-three, three up, three down," Dad admits.

When Nate comes up to bat, my dad says in a raspy voice, "Help yourself, Nate." Then to me, explaining, "That's what you say when pitchers are batting." And that's what Nate does, helps himself by hitting a single. He's on base. At least one hit today, and that's all I will need to be happy. I can breathe now.

The air is bone-dry and stinging for this early game. I cross my arms, hugging myself against the elements at Ingleside Middle School. "It was supposed to be warm this morning," I say. "Why am I freezing?"

"Take my fleece."

"No, thanks. You need it more than I do."

"I'm not cold. I'm actually hot." He wrestles himself free of his turquoise pullover and plops it on my lap. "Wear it. I told you to layer. You didn't layer."

"Thanks. I'm good." I drape it over his armrest.

"Put this on," he insists. It's nubby from use and dotted with a few random white threads and some lint, but I put it on.

"Fine. Freeze your ass off, old man. Everyone knows you're the toughest one in the family."

The phrase hangs in the air and I wish I could take it back.

My dad blinks hard. "Like Mugsy said."

It was in a flat, beige town in Kentucky, near the Ohio border, where he'd been transferred for a year. "I think he's lonely out there," my dad had said. "Let's visit. We can triple the total number of Jews in Kentucky." So we went, all three of us staying in my brother's small, bare apartment.

I was twenty-five. My brother was twenty-seven. My dad still had all his teeth and hair.

After we'd all gone to see a college basketball game and eaten dinner at Subway, Morgan addressed our father. "We could pretend something different is going to happen, but let's be honest. I'm sleeping in my bed and Teresa's sleeping on this couch, and you're sleeping on the floor. It doesn't seem right because you're the oldest, but let's face it. You're the only one tough enough to sleep on the floor."

My dad sat cross-legged near his backpack. He looked up at me, and then at Morgan, then cackled so loudly, I'm sure you could have heard it all the way down the hallway of the sterile apartment building on the drizzly, colorless street.

"I should feel guilty but I don't," my brother added, "because I have my bad back, and she's a girl, so that leaves you. You're the toughest one in the family." Morgan always had lower-back pain.

Dad threw his backpack under his head. "This is great," he said, like he'd just placed his head on a goose-down pillow. "The Three Musketeers."

"Oh, by the way," said my brother, "congratulations on being the first customer ever to order tofu at that Subway."

The sweet, mousy-haired teenager behind the sandwich counter had to look everywhere before she finally found a stack of tofu patties. "I'm sorry, mister. I didn't even know we had tofuuuuuuuuuu," she'd said with a twang.

Settling into the corner of the couch, I asked, "Quick quiz: How many syllables does the word 'tofu' have in Kentucky?"

"TOFUUUUUUUUUUUUUUUUU," howled my dad, in his Bob Dylan voice. "I'd say about six."

Anyone sitting in that Subway fluorescence, observing the skinny, tofu-eating man and his two kids, would have thought my brother and I were just normal siblings, a brother and sister who had grown up together. I got off on imagining people seeing us that way, and it was worth the trip to this beige town in winter just to form that tableau in the corner booth, just to be a little sister who shouldn't have to sleep on the floor.

On that trip, my brother's back pain was just some sort of muscle strain, something that could be controlled with the Advil he was always swallowing, just a consequence of the mild scoliosis he had inherited from our father. We didn't know it was the tumor that would kill him. But we did know we could make fun of our dad for ordering the tofu, and we knew we could make him sleep on the floor, because he could take it, and because we'd all be eating a thousand sandwiches together in a thousand places until Dad died first, in some very far-off future—because the man, as all of us knew, was tough enough to handle cold hardwood on a winter night with nothing but a backpack for a pillow.

It's a tie game after Nate's second and last inning on the mound. He throws a total of fifty-one pitches, but who really knows? It was enough for Daniel to pull him, saving his arm for the next game just in case.

My dad is feeling smug about his grandson, unabashed, letting the pride puff up his entire torso. "Struck out four, walked three," he summarizes, slapping the plastic armrests of his beach chair for emphasis. "Couple runs came in on passed balls, but only two kids hit the ball hard off him. Not a bad day at the office."

"I've seen worse."

Nate goes two for two with a walk. In the end, we can't overcome the early lead we gave up to Team Red and Black. They beat the Pinstripes, 11–10. But we've learned Caleb is better as a backup catcher, where his brave demeanor and quick hands help him block balls and stop those walks from turning into runs. And we know we can snap this losing streak when we face our next opponent, the winless Team Lime Green. We stand slowly, shaking out our legs, folding our chairs, placing them on top of all the gear in the wagon. The boys are getting Popsicles at the snack bar. So we take our time heading out to the parking lot. Dad ferries the load, and I don't say boo.

———————

The next night, with no game and no practice, we decide to pick up some takeout for dinner and head over to the Riviera. Dad is waiting for us in his plush green chair outside.

When we arrive, he shows the boys how Grandpa does chin-ups, then gives each kid a boost up to the bar, remarking, delighted, on their feats of strength.

"I put this bar up myself. Learned how to do it on YouTube. Isn't that something? And I never thought little kids like you two would have the upper-body strength that I do, because as everyone knows, I AM RIPPED. Feel my muscle!" The boys roll their eyes but giggle and poke Grandpa's tiny hill of a biceps springing up from his bony arm.

He hoists Andrew up.

"How does anyone so small do a chin-up? This kid is a specimen. Core strength, baby! He's got it all!"

He lets Nate go next. "You are a beast! Look out, world. Here comes my favorite lefty. Strikes out batters. Smokes the ball. What can't he do?" says my dad, sliding into a sports announcer voice.

After we eat Thai food on the card table outside, the boys collect rocks and bottle flip on the black asphalt road in front of the trailer.

The desert darkness lowers slowly over the patio's flimsy metal awning, until we pile into the car and Grandpa stands in the road to see us off. Nate rolls down the car window.

"Grandpa, I'm gonna be so sad when you die." I wait for the old man to crack wise about Green Acres Mortuary next door, to say, *When I die, just toss my body over the fence.*

But he just runs his hand over his blotchy bald head and says, "I know."

Nate's face is in my rearview as we drive away from Grandpa, who stands in the road of the Riviera Mobilehome Park, watching us until we disappear onto Hayden Road. Then he scuttles home in his moon boots, the fingerprints of his favorite sluggers on his front door.

CHAPTER ELEVEN

|||||||||||||||||||||||||||||

Obviously

"Never fuck with a winning streak."

—CRASH DAVIS, *BULL DURHAM*

On days without baseball, we march through routines, errands, and chores, long spring days. Sometimes, the predictable is pierced by the unexpected, grief coming at us until we can either regroup or fake it. For my dad and me, weekly baseball games are like lily pads. These are the places we safely land, bright and blooming spots rising just above the water. There are four games a week, if you include Andrew's stake-free coach-pitch Farm A scrums. In between, we direct our energy toward whatever diamond is next, where we will plant our feet in the dirt, in our own little grief bubble, focused only on the game happening right in front of us, very much alive.

And of course sometimes, we talk a little shit. Without saying so, we give ourselves a carve-out. Dad doesn't say, *I watched my son die of cancer. I bathed him like he was a baby. He died before I did. That broke the rules. Fuck the rules.*

He doesn't say any of that, but that's what I hear. And I answer, in this dialogue that both is and is not, *I got you, old man. It gives*

me a headache in the center of my forehead when I have to concentrate
on having social graces anyway.

In our grief bubble, anything goes.

"What's up with that kid's swing?" I asked after a kid took a bad
hack.

"Sheesh, T. It looks like he's trying to club a baby seal."

"Dad!"

"Am I wrong?" Dad asked. With a flourish, I pulled my phone
from the side pocket of my beach chair.

"Who are you calling?"

"Greenpeace."

He elbowed me in the ribs and cackled.

For Daniel, there was more than just sideline commentary and
hand-wringing. There was the primal, paternal duty to coach his kid,
and all the kids. It was his job to teach them to be mentally tough and
strategically shrewd. To me, Little League baseball was like a collective
bar mitzvah, and the coaches were the rabbis, even the (lapsed) Catholic ones. Daniel had drafted these Pinstripes, and now it was on him
to make players of them. I have many thoughts about when to touch
my lucky jade pendant for optimal juju enhancement, and how to
control the game by taking the correct driving route, but I don't have
many suggestions for Coach about the inner workings of his defense.

But I do have one.

Daniel is at the kitchen table eating toast, working on his lineup
for the next game.

"After Team MLB Coach handed us our asses," I say, repeating
the phrase he used to his assistant coach, "I was thinking about his
infield."

"What about it?"

"I thought catcher was just where you stuck kids to satisfy the
Little League rule about each player getting at least one inning in
the infield. Like, God bless any kid who wants to strap on the gear—

catchers are heroes—but you need your strongest gloves at short-stop and third base and first base."

"Yeah, that's right."

"But MLB Superstar Guy—did you notice he put his best players at catcher, including his own kid?"

Daniel picks up his toast. Then he puts it down without taking a bite. "Wait a second. You might be right."

"Who knows more about baseball than that guy? Why not steal a page from his playbook?"

Daniel stares off toward the window, seeing all the season's plays at the plate in his mind.

"You know what? So many runs are scored on passed balls, and wild pitches, and steals. I never thought about it. What if I move my best gloves to catcher? Could I do that?" he asks himself. "I could," he answers.

Daniel then clacks away on his laptop at the kitchen table, revising his lineup, moving around who will be where against Team Green. Then he stops and looks at me. "We need this win. Team Green has lost every game and we just can't lose to them. I mean, I know it doesn't matter, but I think it would just be too demoralizing for the kids. If we lose four in a row, including to those daisy-pickers Team Green, we may never come back, mentally."

Daniel thanks me and the next day finds a lefty catcher's mitt for Nate at a secondhand sporting goods store. "When I can, I'm putting one of my studs behind the dish. Let's see what happens."

———

Team Green will bat first. Their leadoff hitter is on deck, taking practice swings near the third-base line. Andrew and his band of younger siblings are screeching around the snack bar, playing tag, running across pine cones and crushed Big Gulp cups and the unseen fossilized remains of decades' worth of peanuts.

The battery facing Team Green will be Gavin at catcher and Finn as starting pitcher.

In the first inning, Finn looks unsteady. He's lobbing balls instead of throwing them. He gets a batter to a full count and then walks him. The unsteadiness continues into the second inning.

"Dad, how many outs? We need outs."

"None."

"None? I hate this game."

I hear myself and I remember the mindfulness book. I pause to sense my feet in my flip-flops, the warmth of my hands resting on my knees. I don't want to be a nervous wreck over a game, but I am. "Befriend what is happening," Victoria would tell us, fringed shawl over her legs as she sat in lotus position at a Monday night dharma talk. I can't be easygoing about Little League. I can't do it. I can't make myself do it. So I settle for noticing what a mess I am. Like Victoria said, "If you want to get from point A to point B, you have to be fully present at point A." So here I am.

We get into a deficit early, down a couple of runs. But Gavin is blocking errant pitches, reaching up to grab the high ones, not letting the low ones roll to the backstop. His technique is almost flawless and his demeanor unshakable.

"Just play catch," he calls out to Finn, reassuringly centering his mitt. "Right here." It's the most I've ever heard him say on or off the field.

"Gavin is stopping the bleeding out there," says Dad.

"You're absolutely right. This should be way worse," I reply, relaxing slightly because maybe I am an accidental baseball genius. It's the catching. It's keeping us in this game.

"I'm so happy I was brilliant enough to steal someone's brilliant baseball idea."

"I don't know why I didn't see it," Dad says. "Catcher is a critical position. The catcher is the point guard, the quarterback, the heart and soul of the infield. The catcher has to set the mood. If the pitcher doesn't have his stuff, it's the catcher who has to hit the reset. The catcher is a therapist."

Now he's speaking my language.

At this point in the season, baseball is about everything, and everything is about baseball. It's not just that pitchers need therapy. And it's not just Isaiah who has to stop flinching.

——————————

"Tell me more about your brother," said Ruth, the grief counselor I'd found thanks to Daniel's spreadsheet. I hadn't seen her in a few years, but I had returned earlier that week. Driving to her office through the manicured streets of Paradise Valley, I figured I was heading toward a place where I could work on what Buddhists might call "staying in the present moment," and what baseball coaches might call "staying in the batter's box." I had started to believe that I'd never feel better, but that I might feel different, and that would be almost as good as better. I thought about Ruth's prompt as I looked around her office, at the pink-and-white plastic dollhouse in the corner, the shelves full of grief books. "Tell me about a time when you were children."

"I can't," I said, stone-faced. "But can I say something? I think I'm grieving too hard. All I think about is death, and people's children dying, and how terrifying it must be to be cut open again and again, and legs that don't move, and wounds that don't close. I can't be this screwed up about losing my brother."

"Why not?"

"I don't know. I just keep being surprised that my big brother got cancer and died. It shouldn't feel surprising anymore."

"Uh-huh," she said, nodding. She patted down her poufy hair, didn't break eye contact. Ruth was pretty good at not flinching.

A memory finally came to mind, but I didn't know if it was

relevant. She crossed her slender legs and kept looking at me, so I started talking.

"Once, my mom dropped us off for a field trip with the Parks and Rec Department to go swimming for the day at a lake in Oakland, Lake Temescal. There was a big group of kids on a charter bus. We didn't know any of them, but we were so excited to swim. We had bathing suits under our clothes, and one towel to share, and bagged lunches."

"Sounds like a happy memory. Did you swim? In that lake?"

"I had a cast on my arm, because I had fractured my elbow. A camp counselor or chaperone or something was walking up the aisle of the bus, counting the kids, and she saw my cast. She said I wasn't allowed to go, but I told her it was okay. I showed her how my mom had wrapped the cast in a black plastic trash bag so it wouldn't get wet in the lake. The chaperone said it didn't matter. I told her I couldn't leave my brother. Next thing I knew, we were both escorted off the bus."

"So what did you do?"

"The bus left for the lake, and we were stranded at this city park, far from home. Our mom was already at work at Sacred Grounds."

"Sacred Grounds?"

"That was her coffee shop. She worked her federal government job half-time and then ran Sacred Grounds. They even had a softball team, the Sacred Grounders—and whenever my brother was staying with us for the weekend, he got to play with the team, which he loved. All grown-ups, except for Morgan."

"Oh, I get it," she said, poking her pen in the air. "The Sacred Grounders. Funny." She poked the pen at the air again. "So what happened?"

"We didn't have change to call our mom from a pay phone or for bus fare. I knew we'd have to ask for money from strangers walking by on the sidewalk. I found a busy corner with lots of foot traffic. And my brother, he was embarrassed. I didn't want him to have to ask for the money, but I didn't mind doing it, because I'd had to do it before a few times when I lost my bus pass or my bus transfer. So I told him I would handle it and Morgan stood back. These passersby on their way to work, I told them the story about the lake, and I had the cast to show them. I was cute, with freckles and a cast and a shy big brother standing six feet behind me, holding our towel and lunches. He was so innocent and guileless."

"How did you do?"

"We were a great panhandling team. We made enough change to call our mom on a pay phone, with enough extra for both of us to catch the bus to the coffee shop."

"Then what?"

"It took two buses to get there, but we made it. We had hot cream of potato soup. We helped work the cash register up front and serve black-bottom cupcakes on little white plates."

She looked down at my chart. "You were the older sibling?"

"No, he was eighteen months older than me, but I was more savvy somehow. I always looked out for him. Like, I always tried to do his hair, so I could make sure he looked nice. If he let me, I would wet it in front, then brush it with a black plastic comb. I didn't want anyone to make fun of him."

"You looked out for your brother."

"I did."

Ruth waited. I could hear a patient in the room next door, a young child's high voice saying something or other. Ruth looked through me, eyes soft.

Finally, I said, "That's why I should have protected him. You know, later." She looked down at her notes, pushed up her glasses.

There was a sudden sensation of falling, like down a well. My body felt both heavy and weightless, tumbling downward, flying through someplace dank and foreboding. My vision went blurry.

"You should have protected him from what?" She leaned forward. "From dying?"

"Yes." I could feel an avalanche of guilt, my chest collapsing in on itself. "I know it should have been me," I sobbed. "He was nicer. He was better." I cradled my head. I heard the kid next door again, and then a soothing grown-up voice from through the wall. I kept snatching tissues from the box. Balls of soggy Kleenex surrounded my knees on the chair. "I shouldn't feel this bad anymore. I'm not doing grief right."

"Not doing it right?"

"Can I ask you something? Why am I not getting better?"

"When you have two losses close together like you did, with Morgan and your mom, that leads to 'complicated' grief. That's what we call it. It can be more . . . challenging."

Don't "therapeutically reframe" this, Ruthie, I thought. *Challenging, my ass. I'm just a fucked-up fuckup, and I always have been, and I'll never get better.*

"And it could be complicated because of what happened when you were little, the separation from your sibling."

"But I don't even remember that happening."

"But your body does." Ruth squints. "I treat children all the time. Before you came in here, I was seeing a patient who is four years old. Her twin died two years ago. Do you think she has grief?"

"Yes. That's awful." I really want to know what happened to the twin, but I don't ask.

"I can tell you as a practitioner who treats many children that, yes, children grieve, even very young children."

I toss some balls of Kleenex in the trash next to me, then stare at the dollhouse.

"That's fucking sad—excuse my French."

"One twin choked in front of the other. They were sitting next to each other in high chairs." This is the worst thing I have ever heard. I picture the surviving twin, helpless, strapped into a high chair, and I feel so stupid. This is worse, way worse than losing my forty-seven-year-old brother and having been separated from him as a kid. I picture the parents of these twins, and it's all too much to think about, a whole world filled with ghost twins, choking and then disappearing. I imagine the surviving twin doing play therapy in the corner with the dollhouse. All her recollections of this time will be a patchwork of things her parents told her, and maybe some lingering, ineffable sense of sadness living right in her bones.

———

Leo comes in to catch for the third and fourth innings, and the game is tight, tighter than it should be against winless Team Green. We have only a one-run lead in the fifth inning. Because of the official Little League rule about games not going longer than ninety minutes, this will be the bottom of the final inning. We have a lead. All we have to do is maintain it.

Nate is coming in to play catcher now, warming up Gavin on the mound.

"Oh, a lefty catcher. You don't see that much," the ump says, giving Nate a playful tap on the shoulder. Nate looks up at him only briefly, eyes dark and serious.

The toes of Nate's cleats are pressed deep into the ground, his knees fanning out. His left hand is behind his back. Kai's dad comes over to let us know, "Looks like Gavin is dealing tonight." I make the gesture, sweeping one palm against the other, dealing my imaginary hand into the bleachers.

Please, dear baseball Gods. Give us this one.

"You got this, Gav!" yells his mom.

"We just need to hold 'em," yells Leo's dad. "Three outs. Let's go, boys."

"Balls in," yells Nate. "Coming down." The infield zips the ball around one last time.

Things are going fine for Gavin, who strikes out the first batter. But the next kid makes it to first base on a blooper hit. No big deal. We can still get out of this inning. Then Gavin throws one wide. Nate lurches to the side, trying to grab it, but the ball gets away from him. He scrambles to find it, unable to locate the ball in the dirt, not accustomed to seeing the world through a catcher's mask, black metal bars above and below his eyes.

"Shit, shit, shit," I say, spitting out the words.

"Get the ball, Nate. It's to your right. To your right," says my dad, but not loud enough for Nate to hear. He's just repeating it like a rosary prayer. "Get to it. Get to it. Get to it." The runner on first hesitates, unsure what to do as Nate fritters around, like a girl at the end of a party, drunk, looking for her lost earring in a shag carpet. The runner on first takes off toward second, capitalizing on the mayhem behind the plate.

"COVER!" yells Coach Daniel toward shortstop, at full baseball-coach volume. He's admonishing Leo to cover second base. Nate finds the ball and sees Leo covering second, foot on the bag, glove up. He knows he can trust Leo. From his knees behind the plate, Nate fires the ball, throwing it his hardest. Leo, right where he should be, catches the ball in a flash, lithe and graceful, twisting to tag the runner with his glove.

"OUT!" shouts the ump, raising his clenched right hand into a decisive fist.

"No way," says Dad. "NO WAY. Did that just happen? Did he throw a kid out at second?"

I raise my eyes and shrug, like *Of course that happened.*

The excitement of the play is charging through my dad's body. He shoves himself all the way to the back of his chair, stretches his arms over his head, then crosses them, then lays them over the armrests. He moves his sneakers back and forth in the dirt. The next batter pops one high into center field, easily caught by Leo at short. Inning over. We hold the lead. We win.

Nate goes three for three in the game, but it's hard to celebrate too much over that, as we barely escaped handing the Green Losing Machine their first win. (Team Green never again came this close to a victory, not for the entire season.)

But all my dad sees, all he sees until the next day, all he sees in his dingy bathroom with a yellow dish towel serving as a bath mat, all he sees when he rides his bike to the 99 Cents Only Store for some razors to shave his head, all he sees when he looks out the window of his trailer at Green Acres Mortuary over the fence, is redemption. All he sees is Nate, in his lefty catcher's mitt, losing the ball in the dirt, then finding it, with just enough time to make a play.

Dad texts me the next day, **RU kidding? Throws a kid out at second.**

And guess what, Dad? Some kid on Team Camo got strep. They asked Nate to play, as a sub. TWO games for Nate on Friday.

Double header, he writes.

Then: **Goody.**

Team Camo 5 PM. Purple Pinstripes 7 PM. Bike there or ride with me?

With u.

When a team in the Arcadia Little League is short a player due to illness or injury, that team can draw from a pool of available players from other teams. The borrowed player can't pitch or catch. The borrowed player bats at the bottom of the lineup. The substitute wears a plain white T-shirt. But they do get to play an extra game, so when Nate is invited to play with Team Camo, Daniel greenlights the temporary trade. "It will be nice to watch Nate play without coaching him," he says.

"THANK YOU. THANK YOU. THANK YOU for letting me. THANK YOU, DAD," Nate responds, the closest he gets to giddy.

After work on Friday, I'm still in my TV host heels and makeup when Dad and I roll up to Ingleside. I check the rearview mirror, and my blush looks mauve and sparkly and way too intense for this late-afternoon light. I smear it with my hands to try to blend it, but we don't want to be late. As we cross the grass, I take off my heels and we jog toward the narrow corridor between the North and South Fields, toward the bleachers.

I can't even watch Nate's first at bat. What if he screws things up for this team that borrowed him? And Team Camo is playing undefeated Team Orange. I know Nate wants to impress everyone: Coach MLB Star, his kid, all the cool fourth graders on the field, and their siblings in the stands. I put my hand over my eyes, fingers spread, like maybe I have an itch on my forehead, but really I can't look. I hear cheering, raucous and sudden. The sound of clapping fills the air. Dad yells, "GO, NATEY!!" I remove my hand just in time to see Nate rounding third in his white T-shirt, then touching home with his cleat, flinging off his helmet. Team Camo's dugout clears as all the boys jump on Nate.

"Can you EVEN??" Dad asks. "Can you even believe this? An inside-the-park home run."

Daniel does a good job playing it cool as other dads high-five him. "Obviously, the coaching is superior on this team," he jokes, humble. But I see his posture change. He straightens up, shoulders back, feet standing out wide. He adjusts his purple hat and lets the beginnings of a smile spill out onto his face.

Team Camo wins, handing Team Orange their first loss. But there's no time to rejoice or break it all down. Nate throws on his purple pin-striped jersey. Dad and I relocate our base camp to our usual spot at the South Field. You can see Papago Park to the south, where giant red sandstone formations jut into the now indigo sky. The clouds look like cotton balls hovering over the blue-gray evening.

Nate pitches three innings for the Purple Pinstripes. His performance isn't perfect, but it's clean enough. He hits a single and later a triple. "All the Purple Pinstripe bats are popping," says the old man, jubilant. Our entire bullpen is starting to get more consistent. The catching is tighter. And the Pinstripes put together their second win in a row, besting Team Bronze.

"Another day at the office," says Grandpa, folding up his chair. Three hours of watching his grandkid play baseball and he's bursting with all the good things he has seen. "Nate's batting average is gaudy. It's a gaudy number." I shush him. We can't be overheard baseball bragging, but it's hard to wait until we are out of earshot from others. And already, before my chair is stacked on the red wagon, I can feel the worry set in about the next game and how no night can ever be as good as this one.

"Don't forget, this is baseball, Dad. We can't get too high or too low. Statistically, he can't always have days like this. We have to gird ourselves."

"Nope," he says. "No girding."

"Dad, what's the thing you always say about Hall of Famers?"

"They fail six out of ten times."

But Grandpa is manic, stuffing his bandana back into his fanny pack, tossing his empty bottle of diet soda into a trash can with a nimble flick of his wrist. Forget statistics and facts. Today, baseball has convinced him that anything good is possible. Today, his grandson was smoking the ball and throwing strikes. That was all that mattered. A bubbling euphoria fizzes out of his body and into his voice; it motors him as he pulls the wagon across the grass, waving at parents like he's the mayor of Little League.

"What's that guy's name? The redhead's dad?" he asks me.

"Josh."

"Hey, Josh! Good luck in your game tonight!" he yells, magnanimous. "What a nice guy that Josh is," he says to me, an aside. Then he draws his arm across the sky, waving again. "Bye, Josh! Great to see you!"

I can't recall the last time I've seen my dad like this. His eyes are clear and sparkling, the spasms quiet. He pulls the wagon, which glides across the grass like it's filled with feathers. *Nate is the Chosen One*, he's thinking.

On a good night like tonight, it seems like baseball can resurrect the dead, and your heart, and hope.

Nate and Andrew are now walking ahead of us toward the parking lot.

Andrew asks his brother, "That was an inside-the-parker, right? Right, Nate? In the first game?" His tiny legs move fast to keep up.

"Yes, Andrew. Obviously."

"I know," Andrew counters quickly. "And you won, right?"

"What do you think? Yes."

"I know. I knew that," says Andrew. "You won both games, the one with the Camo team and the one with our team."

Andrew, still walking at his fastest clip, looks puny, with his floppy hair and his round baby face, keeping pace with Nate's leggy stride. Focused on not dropping back, Andrew still manages to slide an Airheads sour candy rainbow ribbon out of the package he got from the snack bar. He speeds up again, closing the space be-tween him and his brother. "Do you want one?"

Andrew holds out the candy. Nate stops. "I'll have one." He grabs the rainbow rope.

"Nate, why don't you give him one of your Jolly Ranchers?" I suggest, overhearing.

Nate looks back at us, thinks about blowing me off, but instead pulls a hard candy from the pack. Then he drops his baseball bag in the grass so he can focus on carefully unwrapping the candy, too tough a maneuver for Andrew. "I'm giving you lemon, because lemon is the best flavor." Nate hands over the Jolly Rancher, un-wrapped, and picks up his baseball bag again, the bat in the side pocket. They walk ahead into the darkness. Nate stuffs the sticky plastic wrapper into the back pocket of his pants as the lemon flavor explodes into Andrew's cheeks. It's impossibly sweet and face-puckering sour, but it's the best flavor. Obviously.

‖‖‖‖‖‖‖‖‖‖‖‖‖‖‖‖‖‖‖‖‖‖‖‖

CHAPTER TWELVE

HBP (Hit by Pitch)

"The best way out is always through."

—ROBERT FROST

In his next appearance on the mound, Nate hits a kid with a fast-ball. Hard. It's no way to start off the first inning, but his grandpa is unfazed.

"Kid should've stayed inside. Baseball is counterintuitive some-times, T. If you bail out, step in the bucket because you're scared of getting hit by a pitch, you actually get hurt worse. See, you open yourself out like that." Dad angles his shoulder back, demonstrating.

"He's okay, though, right, that kid Nate just drilled?"

The kid from Team Camo is rubbing his upper arm a little, but he's already taken first base.

"He's fine. This is baseball. Every kid is going to get hit by a pitch." Dad's eyes are darting from Nate to home plate. "Imagine how terrifying Nate must be to these batters," he says, delighted. "Big southpaw up there on the bump, throwing hard. And you don't know where it's going," he adds, his inflection lilting. "Did he lose command on that one pitch? Yup. So what? Keeps everyone off guard." Dad chuckles one loud "HEH," then continues. "Sometimes it takes Natey a coupla batters to get into his groove. Don't worry. He's going to strike out the next kid."

But he walks the next two kids.

And then, with bases loaded, he flings one toward Finn's mitt, but his delivery is off, his movements desperate and jerky. The pitch nails Team Camo's batter in the shinbone.

"Dad, what is happening?" I poke the old man's forearm.

"I don't know. I thought he worked out the hitch in his windup. He's all over the place out there. Can't find his release point. Can't find the zone." Dad's eyes twitch nervously.

The ump tells Daniel, "Your pitcher hits one more batter and I have to pull him. That's the rule. If you hit three kids in one inning, or four kids total, you're out of the game."

Daniel approaches the mound, along with Finn, who flips up his catcher's mask. They stand close to Nate, up on the small hill. Daniel says, "Do you want to come out? If you hit another batter, I have to pull you. Did you hear what the ump said?"

"Please leave me in, Dad."

Nate is shaken, his eyes glassy. It looks like he might cry at any moment. But he stays in the game, at least until the next batter, when he throws a ball so low that it makes the kid hop like he's trying to avoid a pack of scurrying rodents. The ump points at the batter's foot with his left hand and points to first base with his right hand, to signal a third hit batter. Daniel heads toward the mound to pull his pitcher.

Nate says, "Dad, that pitch went under his foot. I didn't hit him. It was a bad call."

Daniel says, "Stop."

Nate says, "I didn't hit him."

Daniel says, "Give me the ball," and puts out his hand. Nate drops the ball into his dad's palm, defeated, and trades places with Gavin at shortstop.

Team Camo scores five in the top of the first inning, thanks mostly to all the batters Nate either walked or hit with pitches. And the home team mercifully vacates the field by rule of the Arcadia Little League.

Daniel approaches Nate as he heads back to the dugout from the infield, trying to meet him in front of the first-base line for a private moment about the inning that went sideways. Daniel doesn't know what he's going to say, but it seems like he should say something. Before a single word comes out, Nate says, "Dad, I don't ever want to talk about this *ever again*," not even breaking his stride, continuing right into the dugout, a boy on a mission to pull on his batting gloves and helmet and forget that whole awful thing ever happened.

In the end, despite Nate's troubling, turbulent, and terrifying pitching performance in the first inning, we trounce Team Camo, 16–6. I wish I was a better person and I could be happy for the team's victory, for Gavin's mom in her visor and ponytail, smiling in the snack bar line, and for Leo's dad, high-fiving his kid, telling him, "Attaway, Six," beaming. But Nate avoids the snack bar, hustles out of the dugout toward the parking lot by himself, because he's so embarrassed. The world is now filled with kids he has hit with pitches, or who saw him get yanked for being so dangerously inept that the Little League of America itself had to put a stop to him. And I don't like myself for being so selfish, unable to celebrate such a lopsided victory, especially when we had to come from behind. *I'm a bad sport,* I think, folding up my chair. I should just be happy for the Purple Pinstripes.

"Sympathetic joy" is a phrase I remember hearing during one of Victoria's Monday night dharma talks at the church. "The Buddhists call it *mudita*, the ability to find happiness in the success of others."

Victoria leaned forward on her meditation cushion and explained,

"There isn't even a word for this concept in English. I guess we have a word for the opposite, right? 'Schadenfreude.'" All of us sitting in the church pews nodded in recognition. "I guess that's technically a German word. Anyway, we all get it. Someone we don't like gets fired from their job, we light up a little. Someone wipes out or faceplants, and assuming they're not seriously hurt, who hasn't been tempted to laugh? It's not Buddhist, but it is human." She sipped slowly from her tea. "*Mudita* is the ability to find joy in other people's joy. We all feel jealousy, because that's being human. This practice just asks us to notice it: Oh, I'm feeling really envious. That awareness becomes the path toward cultivating a sort of delight when good things happen to others. It's one of the ways to dissolve the illusion of separateness."

When I heard that dharma talk, I thought about baseball, about games like this, when your team wins but your own kid tanks, so you can't find joy in other people's joy because you're all wrapped up in your own kid's momentary baseball grief.

And I also thought about actual grief, how at the moment of impact it feels like you can never be happy for anyone else ever again. People going on with their lives—celebrating, even—is a confusing affront. It's like you're stuck marching in some garish parade and all you want to do is yell at everyone to shut up and go home.

At least, that's how it felt to me when Morgan died.

I was sitting in a conference room at a hotel in South Beach, trying to convince television stations to buy the syndicated show I was cohosting out of Phoenix. That morning, I'd put on a bright turquoise dress, clipped in my hair extensions, and covered all my blemishes with concealer.

We were meeting with a full slate of television station executives from around the country, one after another, to pitch our show: "It's a fast-paced roundup of all you need to know to stay in touch with pop culture!"

I'd been flying back and forth to see my brother, but it was hard to time my trips with his death, and I wasn't sure he would want me there anyway; it was too intimate for us, a deathbed scene. He was too private—I knew he'd just want to be with Laura—but I was on high alert that day in Miami. He'd outlived his six-month prognosis by ten days.

"He's gone," Laura texted, in the late afternoon.

She'd been texting me updates throughout the day, including the video of my brother's death rattle that she'd sent the hospice nurse.

I was with three television executives and two of my bosses, who had flown in from corporate headquarters. My cohost was there, too, a former British pop star whose boyfriend had flown out to meet her for a night on the town.

Time of death, 4:18 PM

I didn't shift my position on the couch in the hotel conference room. I put the phone down on top of a throw pillow. There was a platter of sliced fruit on the coffee table in front of me. I can still see it, the most mundane of details, the black seeds in the kiwi, the stacks of pineapple triangles, me in that room floating above myself, stunned, logging the physical details in the soulless hotel meeting room almost against my will. *When my brother died, this is how the world looked.*

After the meeting ended, I walked outside to head back to my hotel a few blocks away. Night was falling in South Beach. The ocean was to my right. Cars were barely moving, stuck close together in Miami traffic. My cohost had already gotten a taxi to meet up with her boyfriend.

People wearing bright party clothes filled the streets, the happiest people I had ever seen. I hugged the curb so I wouldn't brush up against anyone.

Do you people not care that my brother just died? How can you drink mojitos when a videographer went to my brother's house eight months ago to record him reading a bedtime story to his kids for when he was no longer there to do it himself? The hospice people said this was a good idea, along with telling the kids things he would want them to know about himself, maybe deliver some fatherly advice they might want later. Heading toward my hotel, I pictured Morgan holding the book. I heard suede boots and stilettos clattering along the sidewalk, and music bumping out onto the street from open car windows. "Goodnight moon," said my brother to the camera, cheeks swollen from steroids. "Goodnight comb and goodnight brush."

I stopped to make sure I could still breathe. I looked down at the texts again on my phone. **He's gone.** Then I looked up at the sky, craning my neck.

"Goodnight, moon. You asshole piece of shit."

I decided never to think about that video ever again, the bedtime story read by the dying father. I swore never to think about the advice he was asked to deliver to the camera, something for his kids to watch on the occasion of their high school graduation and other milestones. I don't know what he said; I still haven't watched the video. Laura told me his eyes got teary only once, when he said, "Soon, I won't be here anymore." At this point he was still well enough to sit in a regular chair. "You will have to grow up without me," he said to the lens, and to the future versions of his children. And afterward, he slept the rest of the day. He hadn't wanted to make the video because he didn't want to concede to dying, just in case it wasn't really going to happen. The hospice volunteers said that was a common reaction but to do it anyway, because best-case scenario, you have this beautiful video to commemorate the miracle of recovering from cancer. I still wonder if it did the kids any good to see their dad wearing flannel pajama bottoms, reading them a bedtime story from so far away that he could never come home again. They watched parts of it, once or twice, just after Morgan died. They didn't ask to see it after that.

That night in Miami, I hid out on the cold tile of the bathroom floor, as far as I could get from the street noise oozing in through my windows. Buddha himself wouldn't have expected a newly bereaved sister to delight in the gleeful doings of a Friday night in Miami.

I remember being hungry. The hotel didn't have room service, and there was no way I could go out into the jubilant world as this new person, the girl whose brother had died—died just that day during a snowstorm in Arlington, Virginia. I couldn't even go as far as the lobby to get a prepackaged salad in a world where I couldn't save my brother, and he didn't exist anymore, and all that remained was his ghost, sick and swollen, reading aloud.

> Goodnight stars
> Goodnight air
> Goodnight noises everywhere

––––––––––

I don't ever want to talk about this ever again.

When we get home from the game, Nate sits at the kitchen table, bereft. I don't know if I should ask him what exactly happened on the mound or just say nothing. I don't want him to know how attached we are to this baseball thing, and especially to him playing well. How we live for it. It isn't fair. It's too much pressure for a kid, and he puts enough on himself.

Nate's mood now, slouching at the kitchen table, is the same as when his candy hearts toppled back in kindergarten. Trying to paper over how I'm feeling, I act casual, getting a can of sparkling water from the fridge, popping the top in the quiet of the kitchen, then sitting across from Nate. *Nothing to see here* is how I'm acting, because my teeth have sunk into his grief from losing, his disappointment. And I don't like to feel the monster's breath on my neck, the yips monster, who appears inexplicably and suddenly, and I don't want Nate to know I'm scared, and that there's some kind of emotional umbilical cord connecting us, transporting all the frustration of losing from his heart, and from his pitching arm, directly into my bloodstream.

Suddenly Nate bursts out, "Ryder said I suck. He said I suck as a pitcher and that I wasn't going to strike out his brother. He said that to me when I was warming up. He was walking by the bullpen. And he kept saying it, saying I'm a terrible pitcher. So I bet him twenty dollars that I could strike out Miles. After the game, he told me I had to pay up." Ryder Insdorf is two years older than Nate. He always wears an oversize flat-brimmed Under Armour cap and a gold chain. His mom has already gotten him professional headshots and he's booked a couple of modeling jobs. That preteen heartthrob little twerp got into my kid's head.

There is nothing I can think of to say other than "I told you betting is for suckers." Nate slowly rises from the chair, goes to his room, and flops facedown on his bed.

"Daniel, did you know about this?" I ask.

"No, but now it all makes sense. He was trying too hard because of the bet."

"Why did you let Ryder even talk to him? I hate that kid. He's a dipshit. Keep kids away from Nate if he's in the bullpen."

"I didn't see it," he answered. "Anyway, we can't keep dipshits away from our kids. There will always be dipshits."

"I know, but I don't want there to be dipshits making my kid lose it on the mound."

"Who is this Ryder?" Grandpa asks, drinking two fingers of Kirkland tequila from a plastic juice cup.

"You know, Dad, *that* dipshit: good-looking kid, dark eyebrows, always wearing a chain and hat."

I turn to Daniel. "Doesn't he have to pay that dipshit? He did lose the bet."

"Technically, no. Nate was pulled before Ryder's brother even came up to bat. So he never faced Miles. The bet is moot."

"Nate!" I holler back from the kitchen toward his room. "Come out here." He ambles out, wearing just his baseball pants, his face pink and puffy.

"Daddy says you don't owe Ryder anything. You never faced Miles. Because, you know, you hit all those kids."

"But Ryder is going to say I lost the bet and he's never going to stop saying it."

Daniel says, "Tell him if he wants his money, come to me. I'll explain it to him. And listen to your mother. Betting is for suckers. He's two years older. He should pick on someone his own size. Okay?"

"Okay," says Nate quietly. "Can I go back to my room?"

He sleeps in his baseball pants, on top of the covers, feet dangling over the side of the bed in dirty purple socks.

———

Team Dark Teal drafted a stud named Otis, who would've been the best pitcher in the league, except his parents wouldn't let him pitch in the league.

He played club baseball, traveling to tournaments all over Arizona, California, and Nevada with an elite band of boy baseball wonders. His parents let all the coaches know ahead of time that they could draft Otis, but he wouldn't be pitching in Little League because he was already throwing a maximum number of pitches in tournament games every other weekend. So, even though Team Dark Teal has the stud of all studs, they aren't very good.

The Purple Pinstripes take an early lead against Team Dark Teal but fritter it away with a few errors and some sloppy play.

It's now our team's last chance to hit, the bottom of the sixth. We need one run for a tie, two to win.

A new pitcher is warming up.

Otis.

Whispers go through the crowd.

I thought he wasn't playing. Nobody can hit that kid. I heard his club is the best in the state. Well, that club team isn't playing this weekend for some reason, tournament got canceled or something, so his parents are letting him pitch one inning this game. One inning. And that inning is now.

When Otis's first warm-up pitch hits the catcher's glove, it's the crispest *thwack* we have heard at Ingleside, sending shivers through our lineup. Otis's next practice throw is too hot for the catcher. It hits him in the chest plate, knocking him back several feet. Warm-ups stop while Team Dark Teal's coach checks on the scrawny catcher, and all the players take a knee until he bravely crouches back down into position, dusting off the back of his pants. The crowd applauds. There is no batter in the box yet, but Otis is pumping strikes, an assassin in Dark Teal with fluffy hair and braces.

First up to the plate, Isaiah. He watches three pitches go by him, steps out and away every time. Strikes out looking. One out. No way he wants to risk getting hit by one of these withering Little League heaters.

"This pitching is next-level," says Dad, awestruck.

We are back to the top of our lineup now. Leo actually gets his bat on the ball. It's a weak tapper, but he makes it to first base due to an infield error. "The only good news is that with Otis pitching, Otis can't also be at shortstop. We have only one out," says Dad. "The tying run is on first."

Nate comes up. He swings at and misses two fastballs. He simply doesn't have the bat speed to catch up to Otis's velocity. "You're late on it," says Coach Daniel. "Load early." Third pitch, Nate makes contact. The ball sails out low, hugging the third-base line, and lands barely inside the chalk. The ump signals *Fair ball*, waving his arm toward the field of play. It's a double. Nate is on second. Leo is on third. (I didn't know it at the time, but Otis was working on his changeup. I didn't even know what a changeup was back then, how it looks like a fastball but comes in slower, and I wouldn't have known one if I saw one. Otis's club team had him working on it, treating this Little League game as a live bullpen session. The slow speed is the only reason Nate was able to get his bat on the ball. Daniel explained all of this later, but at the time I filed it under "BASEBALL MIRACLE.")

Gavin comes up next. He gets a hit on another changeup, for the walk-off.

"I love that kid," says my dad magnanimously as all the players clear the dugout and run out to pounce on Gavin, who smiles shyly.

"Let's go, KID! You walked it off!" screams Isaiah, slapping him on the back.

It's our good luck that Otis chose this night to practice his changeup in the bottom of the sixth. And there is more good luck in the next game, because with Leo pitching we get a huge early lead against Team Black and Navy. I can relax with a lead. And I can moderate my anxiety when Nate is playing first base, deftly catching even off-target throws, and only occasionally neglecting to play the bounce on a grounder.

Coach Daniel knows this is a good opportunity to try out some other arms. "I'm looking ahead," he explained to me earlier. "Mathematically, we need more arms if we happen to make it through the first round of playoffs. If I can keep my aces under fifty pitches, they need only two days of rest. Otherwise, they're burned for four days. I'm going to have to put some rookie pitchers out there, see how they do under the lights."

This is that chance.

Zander Davis takes the hill for the Pinstripes. He's been out in left field lately, but his arm is decent and it's time to see how he looks now. I notice his mom, the public school art teacher, stand up, fluff her skirt nervously, sit back down, and then rise again, pacing. She dresses better than anyone at the ballpark, in chic, vintage flowered fabrics, with cool red lipstick. She steps behind the bleachers, but not too far, just far enough to place more distance between herself and this Little League crucible. Zander walks a few kids but is saved by a divine double play, God's gift to a struggling pitcher. And the Pinstripes win 13–0. It happens so fast that there is still at least half an hour left with lights on and umps on duty. Coach Black and Navy offers Daniel a deal.

"I'd like to get my kids more reps in the field. And I want to give my pitcher a chance to throw to a few more batters. If your guys want some extra batting practice, this is good for both sides. If you're in, the ump says it's okay."

Daniel swings open the metal door to the dugout and explains the situation to his players.

"We won, but we're going to keep playing." The boys are confused at first but then psyched. *More baseball.*

"I have only one rule," he adds. "*Nobody walks.* Swing your bats. If you walk, I will send you back to the dugout. Swing at anything. If it's a three-and-oh count, I don't care if you have to throw your bat to touch the ball."

Easton and Zander strike out. Their bats never leave their shoulders and I can see Daniel is starting to get agitated.

"NOT ONE SWING, GUYS??" he asks, incredulous.

Now Isaiah is up.

"He's not swinging his bat. Not even now, when it doesn't count. Not ever," says Dad.

Coach calls time-out as Isaiah comes to the plate. "Remember what I said, Isaiah. I don't care where the first pitch is. If it's ten feet over your head, if it bounces in the dirt five feet in front of the plate, you are swinging at this first pitch."

"Got it, Coach."

Daniel takes his post near first base. First pitch, right down the middle. No swing. Second pitch, Isaiah steps into the bucket, doesn't move his bat. Daniel takes his purple hat off decisively. "ISAIAH! WHAT DID I JUST SAY?"

"You never hear Dan raise his voice," Dad says wonderingly.

"That's his Philly voice," I explain.

Isaiah looks at Daniel, looks him right in the face. "Sorry, Coach. Sorry."

"Isaiah, you are swinging at this pitch."

For Daniel, the dharma of Isaiah is now in crisis. His self-protective refusal to swing is now baked into him. He can't step toward the pitcher because fear has become one with his body. In the past are his failures, freezing his muscles in time and space. And in the future is the frustration of striking out looking, without taking so much as a single hack. And then there's the fact that every kid is going to get hit by a pitch, no telling when, and it's probably going to hurt. My husband is no Buddha, but he knows his job is to make this kid live in the present. Approach, don't avoid. *No risk it, no biscuit.*

As the third pitch heads toward Isaiah, Daniel takes off running down the first-base line toward home plate, waving his hat, bellowing out the word "SWING!" The pitch flies high above the strike zone. Isaiah doesn't swing, and now one of his hands is off the bat. The baseball is already in the catcher's mitt, but Coach is still running hard toward Isaiah, screaming with his Philly voice, startling him so much that he has no choice but to meekly swing the bat with one arm while the other dangles limply. The ump is confused by the one-armed swing, because the ball is already tucked safely into the catcher's mitt. After a beat, the ump calls, "Swing and a miss. Strikeout." It doesn't matter to Coach. Daniel squeezes Isaiah with all he's got, embraces him so hard, the kid's cleats come off the ground.

Daniel puts him down, bending his tall frame forward to look right into Isaiah's gold-flecked eyes. "You went down swinging. Sort of. But good. Good job, kid." Daniel taps the top of Isaiah's helmet. The child looks dazed, still taken aback by his mild-mannered coach running toward him and yelling maniacally. And he's surprised by his own body, going down at least half swinging. And then there was the unforeseen and sudden hug, momentarily levitating him, a victory hug over a strikeout.

"Thanks, Coach. You're crazy, though, Coach," he says, shaking his head.

Warmth is saturating my chest, like a heating pad has just been switched on inside my body.

For a few seconds under the lights, it's like the boy and his coach have won something. It won't be on any score sheet, but their joy is my joy, and I can feel that half swing with my whole heart.

||||||||||||||||||||||||

CHAPTER THIRTEEN

Rehabilitation

"When we are no longer able to change a situation,
we are challenged to change ourselves."

—VIKTOR E. FRANKL, *MAN'S SEARCH FOR MEANING*

I don't remember which of the four acute-care rehabilitation centers
Morgan was in when Dad and I had our worst fight.

He walked briskly, the keys to Morgan's house on a lanyard
around his neck, his backpack slung over his shoulder.

My brother had been shuffled around to these sour-smelling
facilities, places you didn't notice until you needed to. They looked
like mid-price airport hotels, with names like Future Care and
Genesis. After eight surgeries, multiple skin grafts, ongoing infections, a few spinal fluid leaks, radiation, and then the ministroke,
it was now a matter of negotiating with hospital social workers and
insurance companies to find beds where my brother could get
twenty-four-hour care. There was some talk of getting him well
enough for chemotherapy or to qualify for a clinical trial in New
York City, but until then, Laura and my parents weren't equipped
for the level of care he needed.

Angrily stamping the soles of his Nikes on the sidewalk, my dad
was venting. "He has cancer and all they do at these places is feed
him shit food that causes cancer.

"Do these people think Salisbury steak is rehabilitation? Do they even read anything about nutrition? *U.S. News & World Report* just put out an article. They said sugar, and red meat, and especially processed meat, are no good if you don't want to die from cancer. What do they give him this morning? Bacon and sugared cereal."

"Well, Dad, I'm sure the asbestos milkshake they're serving for lunch will be delicious," I said. His gaze remained low, the corners of his mouth tense. "At least they're letting him stay here. Maybe just stop complaining. Aren't the Fruity Pebbles the least of his worries right now?"

"I wrote a letter to the head nutritionist at Johns Hopkins."

"Great. I'm sure they're going to drop everything and start pricing lentil patties."

We had found a bagel shop within walking distance of whatever acute rehab facility Morgan was in at the time, and we were headed to get my brother his usual: an everything bagel toasted, with cream cheese and tomato. "Is a bagel healthy?" I asked provocatively.

"At least a bagel is real food," my dad said, charging ahead through the muggy streets of Baltimore.

My mom had toured all the facilities in the area, and the only one she vetoed was the one my dad called "Ventilatorville," for obvious reasons. But she was back home in Vegas that week, taking a rest.

"We did all his exercises today, lifting little dumbbells in his wheelchair," he continued, striding harder and faster down the sidewalk. "The idiocy. We have to do this alleged physical therapy so the insurance company will let him stay here, as if he's going to get better! Making my son do biceps curls when he has a tumor on his spine. Fucking stupid," he added sharply.

When the tumor starting growing again, seven years after it was first removed, there had been lots to track and coordinate, treatment plans and options and specialists, because this was going to be hard, sure, and maybe my brother wouldn't have the quality of life he'd had before, but survival was very much on the table. *Come back for a follow-up in two weeks*, that kind of thing. Now, although he hadn't yet been officially diagnosed "terminal," he was in bad shape and nobody knew what to do. Our strategy was basically to stall, to keep him in these acute-care places as long as we could, because he felt safer there than at home. There were emergency procedures at these joints. If you spiked a fever from an infection, or the pain pills stopped working, you didn't have to take an ambulance through a crowded city with an open wound, your nerves exposed, jostled about, terrified.

My dad, charging ahead on the sidewalk, wasn't done. "They still got Mugsy on too many medications. They should take him off everything—the steroids, the antibiotics, the cholesterol medications, the blood pressure drugs. He needs chemo, but they won't do it until the wound closes, but it won't close and the VAC is still suctioning out so much fluid. And he doesn't look good. He's not himself. It's not just the stroke. He's down. His color is off. He's always tired. They can't manage the pain. These fucking genius doctors can't fix a fucking thing."

"Wrong way, Dad," I said, looking at the map on my phone. "We've been walking in the wrong direction. Were you just going to truck ahead with complete confidence until you hit the waterfront or what? You said you knew where this place was. If you don't know something, just admit you don't know."

"I *do* know. I walked here yesterday and I had no problem."

"You don't know, and now we're twenty minutes away from the bagel place instead of being there, which we would be if you had bothered to pay attention to your surroundings."

"I don't need your shit right now." My dad had never spoken to me like that.

He started doing his *puff, puff* breathing, speeding down the sidewalk in his battered old running shoes.

He'd had his moment of desperation and surrender after Morgan's stroke, but it had passed, and he'd returned to being optimistic. Over the course of my brother's illness, from the first surgery to remove the tumor through the second round of surgeries and treatments, my dad had rarely become testy or discouraged. He'd sat patiently in whatever padded vinyl chair in whatever hospital or facility, reading or playing Scrabble on his phone, waiting for reports from doctors, or lab test results, or for the nurse to find the television remote so he could change the channel to whatever game was on that day.

He always knew everyone's name.

"This is Lila," he'd told me that morning in Morgan's room. "She's the night nurse. Her shift is about to end. She has the most beautiful singing voice. Sometimes, when she's just humming, it's like our own concert."

Lila blushed, bursting out of her lavender scrubs. "I sing in church sometimes."

"I bet you're the best singer there," he said sincerely.

Now, somewhere between the rehab facility for his child who was probably never going to be rehabilitated and the nearest bagel shop, my dad was no longer hearing grace notes in the background music. He was lost—lost on a dreary morning on a dreary block a mile from a dreary corporate warehouse of the sick and dying. And I would have known he was breaking, except I was breaking, too.

"You don't need my shit, Dad? Nobody seems to care that I'm going through this, too, that my brother is dying. I'm also your child, and you should care how I'm doing instead of snapping at me. I didn't do anything to you but show up and try to help, even though I have my own kids at home, and a job. And I'm all screwed up about this, too. And you know why? Because I didn't really get to know my own brother growing up because of you. Because of you and that witch Carol."

I heard the nastiness I hadn't meant to unleash, but I couldn't stop myself.

My brother was too well for home hospice care and too sick to go home. So we were stuck in this no-man's-land. And we were turning on each other.

"I can't listen to that stuff about Carol anymore," he said. "It's over."

"It's over for you, Dad. It's not over for me. Why did you let all that happen?"

"I can't go over this again. It's in the past. Stop, just stop," he barked, taking a sharp right at an intersection, just to get away from me, so he wouldn't have to stand next to me waiting for the light to change.

"That's the wrong way. DAD!" I jogged toward him, and he jogged away, securing both straps of his backpack over his shoulders.

"You let Carol hurt us! How could you do that?" I shouted, jogging slowly, out of breath. "It's like you just didn't feel like inconveniencing yourself, having to find someone new to cook your food and tell you what to do, so you let this abusive dragon lady run your life."

"She wasn't abusive."

"No? She threw a lamp at my head."

"I don't remember that."

"Do you remember that she sent me away? And she convinced you that it was for my own good. She said we were too close. And she insinuated—you know."

He ran faster.

"Dad, stop making me run. You can't act like a baby anymore," I said, panting. "STOP RIGHT NOW."

"No."

My lower back was covered with sweat, collecting in a pool at the waistband of my jeans. He slowed down to a walk, pumping his arms.

"Carol made you give me away because she proclaimed herself to be the Grand Poobah of Mental Health, and she said we were too close and that it wasn't 'appropriate.' But she never got a degree. She didn't know anything about anything. *She just wanted to get rid of me.*"

"Well, I don't remember that and I don't know what you're talking about."

"You don't? You don't remember who made you give away your own child?"

"It was because Morgan was too crazy, because he was all messed up from the divorce, and your mom couldn't handle him—"

"No, Dad. That's just you parroting back more of Carol's bullshit psychoanalysis. She died a long time ago, and you're still her puppet. When you repeat her Big Important Insights like you thought of them yourself, I *hate* that." My throat felt raw from shouting. Then I began to mimic my dad, my voice high and loud, my face mashed into itself. I wagged my chin from side to side. "*I'm a gullible idiot and I believe anything Carol tells me because I can't take responsibility for myself and if she says to give away my daughter, I guess I should just trust someone who's never held a job of any kind, not as a child development specialist, not as a two-dollar-an-hour babysitter,*" I screamed. "The court awarded you custody. You were the *parent*, Dad. You should've protected us." There were red flashes of light in my eyeballs. All of me was clammy and damp. "And you never should have separated me from my brother, because now it's too late, and he's going to be gone!" I yelled. Life, death, decorum, hope, civility—it was all for nothing.

Dad set his voice to its top volume, which I'd never heard him do. "I can't apologize anymore! GET AWAY FROM ME."

We slowed down but kept walking another block in the wrong direction.

"Dad, take a left here."

He followed me all the way to the bagel shop in silence.

"Make sure it's toasted, with extra tomato slices if you wouldn't mind," he told the clerk. "It's for my son."

On the way back to the rehabilitation place, I said only this: "Except about Morgan, I don't want to be in touch with you ever again."

A few weeks later, I got an email from Dad saying my brother had been moved back to the inpatient rehabilitation center at Johns Hopkins; it was the best of the acute-care places, a five-star palace compared to the others. They'd previously expelled him because he wasn't getting better, and their whole deal was to prepare patients to return to their lives, healed enough to live independently.

Laura had figured out how to sway the bureaucrats toward letting him slide through a loophole and return to Johns Hopkins. She convinced Morgan's oncologist and neurosurgeon to write letters on his behalf stressing that his situation was "medically complicated," which is one of the specific categories of care listed on the facility's website. Laura was unfailingly organized and competent. She was persuasive but never hysterical. It also helped that some of the doctors had gotten to know him over the years, especially his world-renowned brain surgeon, the mustached, Turkish-born vice chairman of neurosurgery at Johns Hopkins. I think the famous brain surgeon, and other physicians treating my brother, came to like and admire him, his gentle manner, the way he never complained, the way he'd gone from being a single guy with no kids to being a father of two, all since first being diagnosed. They liked the way he let his kids climb all over his hospital bed. During visits, the little ones were always eating these special lollipops from Argentina.

Laura stockpiled them, these treats from her home country, saving them for when she really needed the kids to be good.

And it was hard to resist our delightful brother-sister singing act. At least once per hospital stay, we would regale medical personnel with a rendition of *"You can kiss my acka-backa, my soda cracker, my B-U-T, my booty whacker . . ."* I'd pull a chair as close as I could to his bed, and we'd look at each other for a second before launching into our routine, like musicians in an orchestra waiting for the conductor to wave his baton. We'd always start at the exact same time. Morgan couldn't do the "booty-shake" move, so he'd shimmy his shoulders in the bed. *"My belly aches. My back's too tight. My booty shakes from left to right, ALLLLLL RIGHT,"* we'd finish in unison, just like we'd done since we were kids.

Everyone probably thinks their sick relative is the hospital staff's favorite. But for whatever reason (probably Laura's devastatingly thorough, fine-print-reading tenacity), he was back in the Four Seasons of rehab.

> They don't seem to be pushing hard to throw Morgan out, at least not yet. And another day passes. I saw a great blue heron at the waterfront. It is the only one that I have seen at the harbor. Tomorrow, Morgan is going to take me down to see the legendary statue of Jesus. Ten feet tall and made of one single block of marble. It was already made when they realized it was too tall to bring in, so they had to dig a hole and get it through that way. PT took him there today, and his assignment is to take me. Later, Dad

I'd said so many awful things to my dad. I felt nauseated thinking about him walking around alone, clutching his sagging backpack, wearing out his sneakers.

And another day passes.

There was a statue of Jesus to see, marble arms outstretched in the lobby, and a great blue heron.

Dad must be talking your ear off about the blue heron he saw, I texted my brother.

He might have mentioned it once or twice, my brother texted back.

That's a topnotch hospital, so after he talks your ear off, we can get you an ear transplant. We should at least get you on a waiting list.

Ha.

I wanted to think of something clever but I couldn't. And then I worried he was tired and would feel pressured to text me back, so I put down my phone. I picked it back up and searched "blue heron," even though I had never cared much about birds, tuned the old man out whenever he blathered on about red-winged blackbirds or white-throated sparrows. In some of the photos I found, the herons did look almost blue, with their deep gray plumage, standing tall on stick legs.

Can't believe you saw a blue heron, Dad. Majestic. Way better than a seagull, I texted the old man.

Beautiful creatures.

Nate strikes out during his first at bat against Team Sedona Red. The darkness inside us is coming in fast, like a rolling fog. "He has to stop swinging at those high ones, T."

But the next at bat washes everything away, a rag across a dry-erase board. Nate hits another inside-the-park home run, with two RBIs. Dad and I are on our feet, giving each other double high fives, like somehow this was something we did. The memory of

Nate striking out, swinging awkwardly at all the high ones, the debacle three games ago against Team Camo, the ill-advised bet with the chain-wearing dipshit, the wincing faces of a trio of hit batters—that's all gone now. And we have the lead. Team Sedona Red has been five-run-ruled. Inning over.

Now Nate takes the hill to pitch the third inning. I look sidelong at my dad and grimace. He grimaces back.

But Nate's only a little wild this outing, walking two kids. And then he nails one.

"Here we go," I say, clutching the armrest of my chair. The batter looks down at the side of his ribs, touches them to see how bruised they feel, before ambling to first base. Dad and I grit our teeth, but Nate doesn't hit anyone else that inning. The frightful, winking apparition of my brother's long-ago and unexplained yips appeared but blew by like a storm that never touches down. And in his next and last at bat, he hits an RBI triple. "Can you believe this, Dad?" I ask, exuberant. "Who has it better than we do?"

"Nobody, T."

"I can't exhale yet, though. Nate still has another inning to pitch." And in that inning, though he sprinkles in a few strange, slow lobs and allows two runs, he doesn't bruise any flesh with his wandering fastball. Instead, he manages to hold the lead for the Pinstripes.

The Purple Pinstripes are clicking now, beating Team Sedona Red 8–5. The players line up on the first-base and third-base lines to shake hands, as they always do.

"Two hits for Natey, T. Not bad at all."

"Three, Dad. If you count hitting that kid in the ribs."

"HA. One hit batter? That's nothing. He usually takes out half the lineup," Dad says, cracking himself up. It's all okay now, all of it: the beaned batters and the worries about the yips, my brother's yips and Nate's yips. A win washes some things away. Errors and

strikeouts, mistakes and mishaps, now cleansed and forgotten, pu-
rified by the thrill of getting away with one.

Dad rises from his chair, groaning with the effort. He shakes
out his stiff legs and asks, "Is it just me, or was that our sixth straight
win?"

"Yup," I said. "We're heading into our last few games of the
regular season on a winning streak."

"Feels good, T."

"We versed Team Sedona Red and we won," says Andrew, hopping on top of a stack of gloves and balls and chairs and catcher's
gear piled high on the red wagon. Andrew has borrowed his phras-
ing from Nate, who always says things like "Dad, who are we vers-
ing tomorrow?"

After hauling the wagon to the car, Dad heads back from the
parking lot to Ingleside's bike rack. He flings the green sheet off his
ride, stuffs it into one of his panniers, and heads home through
Scottsdale toward the bike trail.

He turns onto the Indian Bend Wash Path, flying down the first
hill. He's lifting off his seat, and all he can hear is the wind rushing
into his ears, whistling and ringing. Beneath him, the yellow letters
painted on the bike path spell out **SLOW**, but he ignores the in-
struction, as usual. The old man is flying, exhilarated. He's immor-
tal. Redemption and resurrection are possible. They happen on the
baseball field. He's seen it for himself. He sees the boy now, on the
dark path lit only by city streetlights and a wash of light from his
headlamp. He sees Nate, first striking out and then hitting a home
run, just like that.

The old man takes a sharp left at full speed and then cruises when
the path straightens out. One day, and he knows this, knows this as
well as he knows the curves of this bike path, his grandson will be
hitting real home runs, over the fence, going yard, moon shots into
nights like this. *A winning streak*, he hears his daughter say.

The warm wind is hitting his shoulders. He eases back down on the seat, pedaling in rhythm with his heartbeat. He thinks about his grandson pitching, only hitting one batter this time, getting command, how one day he might be like Randy Johnson himself. He might be a tall lefty, like the Big Unit. *All Nate needs is a mullet.* He smiles big at the thought: a mullet. He doesn't usually smile without putting his hand over his mouth, on account of his missing teeth, the cavernous gaps, the gums pink and vulnerable. But nobody can see his face on the empty bike path. He pedals his hardest, and then coasts. But then there's a lurching sensation, his body feels weightless, moving slow now, like he's skidding and listing and teetering through an ocean of molasses. He's sideways now, disoriented on the path, his helmet on the concrete, the sound of the wheels spinning in the silent, salty air. He's wiped out somehow, skidded from vertical to horizontal. He's pinned beneath his bike. Reflexively, he unclicks his cycling shoes from the pedals, picks up his bike by the handles, snaps his feet back into the pedals, and cranks his legs, shaky and slow. The next stretch of the path is uphill, and his muscles burn with the effort. The wheels feel heavy, and home feels far away.

What happened? He didn't even fall going his top speed, on the downslope, on that first precipitous decline. He sees a can of Mountain Dew, tipped and spilling on the right side of the path. He couldn't have seen something like that. *Did litter do me in?* Looking down at the dimly lit path, he regards a fistful of pebbles as he rides by it. Would it have been pebbles taking him down? Or maybe it was a thicket of weeds cropping up right through a crack in the concrete, an unseen hazard in the night.

This was the explanation, he decided. Weeds.

But what if this was the beginning of the end? A sign of his deterioration, the loss of his balance and his marbles?

He passes the sports bar on his left, with the outdoor volleyball courts covered with sand. Was it sand? That got under his tire? At a table under a green Heineken umbrella, a group is gathered, half-empty beers in their hands. He rides by them, reviewing his fall again and again, this possible turning point, this to-be and probably not-to-be, this flash of a future when he won't be able to stay in the saddle anymore.

Speeding up now, past the fishing pond, he thinks again that it was probably weeds. Or a can or a crack in the cement.

But what if he just lost his balance for no good reason?

Endorphins. That's what he needs to get rid of this feeling. That's what he always told his daughter; he always told her you can't be sad when you're cranking down a path on your bike, or jogging. He pedals as hard as he can, passing the El Dorado Hermosa apartments, the empty basketball courts in El Dorado Park, with their sagging nets.

He passes a yellow sign with block letters, **CHILDREN AT PLAY**, and then a playground, beige slides, green beams, sand. *Was it the sand?* There are monkey bars and swings. He remembers being at playgrounds like this with Nate, when he was just a toddler. He had tried to help his daughter with the child, but Nate was restless and miserable. You placed him in the baby swing and after a few back-and-forths he just wailed. He wasn't happy until T-ball, the precursor to baseball, *a thing you could win.* The old man chuckles to himself again about Nate.

Competitive little fucker.

What would happen with the boy? Could Nate make it to the bigs? Someone had to. No, no. That was too much to ask. Too unlikely. But maybe he could play in high school? That would be enough. The old man wonders now if his fall, a fall out of nowhere, a fall on a level path, if it meant he would miss all that.

His calf throbs a little as he passes a picnic area. He's scanning the road carefully. There's a clump of dirt mixed with rocks and glass. Had it been a clump like that, earlier? His eyes weren't so good. Especially at night. Maybe he hadn't lost his balance for no reason. Maybe it was dirt. An obvious culprit. Could've happened to anyone, really. Even someone young. *I dare anyone my age, any of the* alte kakers *I see at the 99 Cents Only Store, to ride as many miles as I do. They're old farts. I'm a goddamn vegan. Except I do eat a doughnut sometimes, and sometimes I have cream cheese on a bagel. But LOOK AT ME*, he thinks, and then rises out of his seat, legs fully extended. *I'm not on statins. Who else my age can even say that? I'm not strong or fast. I wasn't good at sports like my son, like my grandson, but nobody can stop me out here.*

He feels the wind on his torso as he pedals. It feels cold on his skin, because there is sweat evaporating across his arms and chest. He usually didn't break much of a sweat at night on the way home. Not like this. *Is it from falling? Some kind of stress reaction?*

He stops to regard a small smashed pine cone on the path. That was it. That was probably it. That was the culprit. But he'd ridden over dozens of pine cones and never gone down, skidding out in the dark. He grips the handlebars tight, coasting, and feels something warm on the back of his leg. A trickle of blood, he realizes. *So what? So. What.*

He leaves the path at this usual exit, rides through the city streets to Hayden Road, passing a huge self-storage facility. KEY STORAGE, says a sign in boxy purple letters across pale bricks. CLIMATE CONTROLLED.

He's almost home now. He sees the three cacti, each as tall as the American flag at the entrance to the Riviera Mobilehome Park. He crosses the threshold, slowly rolling over the speed bump just inside the entrance, which has been covered with a glossy new coat of white paint. "SPEED LIMIT 10," says a sign he usually ignores. But not tonight. He glances over at Green Acres. "When I die, just toss me over the fence," he always says to his daughter. But it isn't funny now.

He chains up his bike outside and then pours himself a double shot of E&J brandy. His skin still chilly and moist, he allows himself the luxury of plugging in his little space heater, letting it warm up his body in the old tin can.

"Got home OK," he texts his daughter, like she asked him to.

———

The next morning, before Andrew's game, Dad comes over so he can ride to the field in my car. He's half an hour early, so he makes himself at home. He grabs an avocado from the fruit bowl, looks in every drawer for a knife, even though he should know very well where the knives are by now, and slices it open. He places a couple of hard cubes of unripe avocado on a heel of bread.

"This isn't ripe," he says grumpily. He chews with his mouth open and then settles on a chair with a loud groan, placing his feet up on an ottoman. "Tastes terrible. No flavor," he gripes, clicking away on his phone, playing Scrabble.

"Hey, Pops," Daniel says, looping Andrew's belt into baggy white baseball pants, getting him ready for his game. "Don't forget you can mute your phone."

"I know. Sorry. You told me that already."

"Dad, why not just take another avocado that's ripe? Why eat this one and then complain about it?"

I open the refrigerator, and there's the old man's half-eaten, unripe avocado.

"Seriously, Dad? First of all, how about putting it in a baggie? Secondly, why'd you save it at all? If it isn't good."

Click-clack goes his phone. "Dad, mute."

"Okay, I'll throw away the avocado," he says petulantly, getting up. That's when I notice an abrasion along the back of his calf, with a line of dried blood flowing toward his ankle.

"What's that on your leg?" I ask.

He throws the avocado in the trash, then sits back down. "I fell off my bike last night. I don't know why. I've taken that trip a million times. There wasn't a rock or litter or anything on the path, not that I remember. I can't figure it out."

"Is that why you're in a mood?"

"I'm not in a mood."

"Why don't you put a Band-Aid on that thing?" I head toward the first-aid kit in the junk drawer. "Let me get you one."

"I don't need one."

I try to feel the cold air hitting my nostrils. "Breathe in, and know that you're breathing in," like my guided body scan says to do. "Breathe out, and know that you're breathing out." I know I'm breathing, and I'm also keenly aware now that my stomach is twisting and seething with resentments, Dad's cluelessness, his relentless ineptitude, the way he eats the heel of the bread instead of a regular slice. *Who does that? Normal dads don't do that. They don't eat what isn't ripe. They understand about baggies or Tupperware.* I inhale again slowly, even though my lungs feel heavy, sagging under the pressure of containing the urge to detail the old man's failings, to turn around to his face and give him what for. He should throw away his own trash, not leave it for me. *He's the parent. He's not supposed to be some heel-eating buffoon who doesn't know how to handle a bad avocado and leaves me to manage his mess.* I close my eyes and stand still for one more breath.

"Nobody has ever died from not scratching an itch," Victoria reassured us once during a dharma talk.

But that was the hardest thing about meditating sometimes, overriding the compulsion to scratch, to be absolutely still, when I'd always been a nail-biting, pencil-chewing, neck-stretching, knee-bouncing, ponytail-twirling, itch-scratching bag of nerves.

"Guess what happens to the itch." She paused, and looked at us in the pews, and sipped tea from her thermos.

"It goes away. If you keep scratching itches, you won't have a visceral experience of how everything changes."

When it came to my dad, I had always scratched itches into welts. I didn't know how to leave things alone, how to reconcile the dad who listened to my every problem and glowed over all my achievements with the guy who'd been a passive oaf as a father. There was the guy everyone wanted to be around, who quoted Shakespeare and Leonard Cohen, and there was the guy who didn't recall if he should pick up his three-year-old at Burbank or LAX.

The year I moved to Hollywood, I had four hundred dollars and a Honda Prelude my dad gave me that someone had left at Delta Battery. "It's so slow, I call it the Honda Quaalude," he announced, but that car ran just fine, and it took me to all my first auditions. I lived in a tiny studio apartment in the flat, dirty part of Hollywood. My dad and Morgan came to visit for my birthday that year and we all watched the Lakers on a little television balanced on a milk crate. Dad gave me a card with a cat on the cover. It said, "You are the coolest cat I know." I knew he chose that dime-store card because that's how he genuinely felt, that I would land on my feet like a goddamn cheap birthday card cat. When I was down, he was the person I called. I looked forward to seeing him, and we mostly got along when we were together a few times a year, but then something would remind me of Carol, and all the errors in his past, and I'd get irritable and short-tempered. This season, though, I'd gotten practice being with my dad, sitting through a dense concentration of innings and uncontrollable outcomes together. The Pinstripes and a little bit of imperfect, irregular meditation had delivered me, not all the way somewhere, but a few inches closer to something.

Every morning on my bathroom mirror I saw the list of mindfulness concepts from the class, a piece of paper curling up at the sides, taped down. *Let it be.* This was the dad I got. I could love him, the snaggletooth smile, the way he rooted with his whole heart for my sons, or I could miss everything that was happening, at Ingleside Middle School and everywhere else. I could miss out on the dad who had cared for his sick child with all the delicacy and compassion of a thousand monks, and who could mourn with me, not with prayers or services, or even words, but with the shared experience we had of my brother. If I could let the past be a tickle on the skin, something that caught my attention but didn't require me to react, I could stop waiting for him to issue me a full and detailed accounting of his fatherly wrongs. He couldn't repair what had broken; nobody had the parts anymore. This junker wasn't running like new, and it never would. There was gunk in the gears, and the bearings were damaged, but maybe it could still get you home.

And I tell myself, *Wait this out. Let it be.* I'm still riled up, like my whole body is rolling its eyes and stomping its feet, a fist that won't unclench. I sit down at the table, my heart rate slowing, feeling my palms on my legs. *Maybe he's picked a fight because he's shaken up, unnerved because he fell off his bike.* The fist loosens.

I don't force him to put a Band-Aid over the road burn. He doesn't want it, and I know he doesn't need it.

He looks up at me, eyelids heavy over his green eyes. "I just don't want this to be my last season." He speaks it solemnly, like a confession, and then he folds his hands in his lap, daintily. "I want to see Nate play in high school. I want to see Andrew play in the Little League Minors. At the very least, I want another season."

"Jeez, Dad. One fall and you're worried about ending up at Green Acres? *Puh-lease.* You're way too tough to die anytime soon," I say.

But I know he doesn't have forever. I'm always doing dead-dad baseball math in my head. He's seventy-five; if he lives five more years, Nate will be a freshman in high school and Andrew will be playing Little League Majors, so that's pretty good. But if he lives eight more years—and why not?—the old man eats nothing but tofu and avocado (never mind about the booze; lots of old people drink a little), then the boys will both be in high school, and wouldn't that be something to see, brothers playing on the same baseball team, maybe? And now I realize Dad has probably been doing the same calculations. The fall from his bike changed a variable in his actuarial model, and the updated forecast is bleak. To him, when you die, you don't watch your grandkids from a heavenly cloud or send lucky pennies or communicate through ravens or butterflies or blue herons or dreams or angels or fairy dust. To my dad, death is the sound the field lights make when they shut off after the last inning of the last game of the last season. There's nothing left but darkness and eternal quiet. Game over.

"Dad, it would also be really selfish of you to take a dirt nap anytime soon. Think about *me*. I've been through enough," I kid. He laughs a little, glances down at his leg. I think I know why he sold his truck, and why he only rides his bike, and it isn't just because "nobody leaves a smaller carbon footprint than I do," like he'd tell you. He pedals his bike through the Arizona desert—even in summertime—to prove how alive he really is.

But one season, he'll be gone. That's the surest thing there is.

I picture myself sitting in my beach chair alone along the first-base line, turning to the ghost of my pops to ask, *What's the count?* I'll turn to jab his bony forearm and demand to know if it's 2 and 2 or a full count. And there will be nobody there, nothing but a scrim of red dust. And I'll hear him sing, *Two and two, whatcha gonna do?*

Daniel is too sane to care like we do. To us, every hit is a rebirth; a do-over; my brother risen, rejoice all ye faithful; spring after winter; a new bud swelling on a bare branch; a saguaro flowering in the desert outside the car window; a blackbird with a beak full of twigs and green blades of grass building its first nest of a new year. Only my dad and I let ourselves get this swept up in it, inning after inning, when we know it's just kids swinging at balls. And Daniel is too sane to shoulder the losses with me like my dad does. The depth of our caring is stupid, I realize, but it lives in our bones and tissue along with the sorrow from the before times. My dad understands. He understands how one little bad thing can be connected by thousands of miles of invisible thread to another, way back in time, and that you might not want to feel so bad over something that's already happened, but that's what your body does sometimes, and at least we can be fools together, unhinged over goddamn baseball like goddamn lunatics. Gritting our teeth together is also a do-over. Every at bat, every pitch, every pickle, we get another go, a to-be-or-not-to-be that always ends in being.

I put this vision away, of me reaching out to touch my dad's bony forearm, him vaporizing, leaving only red dust. I cram it in my back pocket like a handful of sunflower seeds. But I know it's there, a visitation from the Ghost of Baseball Future.

"Dad, we just have to *Tuesdays with Morrie* this. You know, appreciate every day, blah, blah, blah."

"Better yet, we Victor Frankl it," he chimes in, perking up. Frankl was a psychiatrist and Holocaust survivor who wrote one of our favorite books, *Man's Search for Meaning*, which chronicles his experiences in concentration camps. He argues that eventually suffering becomes nothing more than a remembered nightmare. You survive it by having authentic interactions with others, by communing with nature, by controlling your own perspective, and, of course, the main thing, by identifying a purpose, something or someone outside yourself, and immersing yourself in that purpose.

"Man must find meaning. And my meaning," he says dramatically, "is baseball."

CHAPTER FOURTEEN

Sudden Death

"Winning is wonderful in every aspect,
but the darker music of loss resonates
on deeper, richer planes."

—PAT CONROY

Streaks of neon pink slash the deepening blue sky over the Riviera Mobilehome Park. "Is it just me, Dad, or are the sunsets in this low-rent trailer park, like, million-dollar sunsets?"

"Every single night is a masterpiece up there," he says, craning his head up toward the flowering green tops of the palm trees, blinking his twitchy eyes at the fuchsia brushstrokes in the sky. "You know me. I love the desert. It's always felt like home, since the day I got here."

Andrew, Dad, and I are on the winding narrow road outside his trailer, throwing a football around.

That afternoon, Andrew said, "Can we go visit Grandpa? It's been a long time since we've seen Grandpa." But it had been only three days. I called the old man. "Hey, Dad, how are things?"

"Good, good. You know me. I'm just as happy as if I had good sense."

"Can we come visit? We can bring you a blueberry muffin. Andrew is requesting an audience with you."

And he said, "Of course, come over. But I don't need a muffin."

I told him we'd be there in half an hour. "It's funny you called," he added after a pause. I could hear him turn off the fan on his end table. "I never really get lonely, but I was feeling lonely today." I thought about the possibility of Andrew intuiting this from across town, the way little kids can pick up on things sometimes, like incipient psychics.

Nate was busy throwing pitches with his dad against the side of our house, so just Andrew and I headed over to see Grandpa with a football, stopping on the way for the expensive muffins Dad told us not to buy.

"Hey, Dad, where's Alan? I don't mean the dead one," I ask, tossing him the football. "I mean the other one. You know, lives right up there?" I gesture toward the single-wide up the road, with a front yard full of rocks and a metal sculpture of a baby owl and a wind chime hanging by the door. "Alan? You helped him fix his bike or something?"

"Oh, you mean Alive Alan?"

I nod.

"He died last week," Dad says matter-of-factly, then soft tosses the football to Andrew.

"I told him not to eat all that crappy food and put down the cigarillos, but he didn't listen," he adds, shrugging. "Management already cleaned out his trailer . . . and now . . . his ghost . . . haunts the Riviera," he says theatrically, like the narration in a horror movie trailer. He lets out a few staccato guffaws, delighted by his dark bit about Dead Alan, but Andrew's eyes get big, so Grandpa reassures him. "I'm kidding! I mean, Dead Alan is dead, but he's not a ghost."

If death wasn't already in the air, wafting over from Green Acres next door, the proximity of the second Dead Alan and his empty tin can brings it home.

We sit down to eat our muffins at Dad's folding card table, just a few feet from the storage shed where he keeps the box of photos of my brother. As the sun dips, the old-fashioned streetlights along the road turn on, illuminating the deep black of the smooth gravel road. You can hear the wind rippling through Alan's wind chimes.

"Sudden death," says Dad. He's eyes are fixed on the shed, but he isn't talking about my brother. Or Alan.

He's talking about the Arcadia Little League Minors playoffs.

I know what he means as soon as he says it. This season, because we've sat together through so many games, it's given us a shorthand. I can follow him without transitions or context. The postseason tournament is single elimination. Lose one game, hang up your jersey, and wait until next spring. *Sudden death.*

He bends over to break off the top of his muffin with his fingers and daintily stuffs it in his mouth, chewing fast, like a mouse gnawing through drywall. His eyes land again on the shed, the disintegrating metal door.

"I still can't look at pictures," he admits.

Now he is talking about actual death, not sports death, and I set my muffin down on the table. He looks so old with his missing teeth and bald head, his scrawny, stooped shoulders. But he also looks young to me in this moment, like a scared little kid, afraid of the shed, and embarrassed by his own fear of it.

"It's okay, Dad. You have the pictures in your mind." *God, that sounded syrupy,* I think to myself. *I wish I wasn't an idiot.*

"It's too much," he says, looking away from the shed. He sighs, stretches out his legs, and stares at his slippers.

I want to talk more, so much more, to know what he thought about keeping five-year-old Morgan, then giving him back to Mom nine years later, and what it was like going through all he went through when my brother was sick all those years, and how he manages to be okay, despite living so close to a bin full of photos of his dead son, how he cheers his way through innings and games, how he's able to be with his grief, not push it away totally, but keep it in the shed. I want every heavy detail, how much he misses going to visit my brother in Arlington, when Morgan would take time off work so they could ride bikes together around DC and visit museums. Dad would look for blue jays and red-tailed hawks. He would call me from Morgan's guest room at night, breathlessly telling me about all the things they'd seen: the chess set of John Quincy Adams, the Apollo lunar landing module, Chuck Berry's 1973 red Cadillac Eldorado, a black-throated sparrow landing on an urban shrub.

"I can't believe our next game is our first playoff," I say, instead of asking anything about Morgan. Sometimes talking about my brother just seems to make it hurt worse for my dad. *It's too much*, as he'd said about the pictures in the shed. He seems to know that about himself, seems to accept that, for him, opening the shed all the time doesn't help or heal. It's too much to look at things directly. The wound won't close no matter how long you stare at it. So, instead of pressing him to engage, to do grief my way, blubbering and bleeding out, I let him be. We meet halfway, between his way and mine. We meet in the middle, where baseball is our grief group. There, we can experience big upheavals of emotion, ride them out until they fade, know it's all only a game, and do it all again. *Reps.* Baseball is an excuse to be together, my dad and me and the open wound we share. On the sidelines, we are in total communion, not grieving alone, each of us at separate altars. We share every win and every loss in real time, in physical proximity. We care together when it comes to baseball, a fire hose of care that is pure and powerful, pointed in the same direction. Fear and helplessness dig their fingers into us, but we are always released. Over the course of this season, I've come to admire how my dad does grief. I'm in awe of how he's tender with himself.

He keeps grief close, but not too close.

Sometimes, he screams it out onto the bike path, howling sadness into the night, and other times he manages to be just as happy as if he had good sense.

"I don't think we should worry about losing the last three games," he announces with vigor, perking up in his folding chair. "Danny knows what he's doing. He's a big-picture guy."

The last three games of the season were a blur of losses, something my dad and I were used to off the diamond, which made Little League losses easier and harder at the same time. In this case, though, in the case of the Purple Pinstripes, there were productive losses. There were losses you chose and planned for, losses that got you closer to wins, losses that showed you what you had, at least in terms of your bullpen. Coach had used the last few games to determine which of his second-string pitchers might be effective in a playoff game, should the team make a deep run in the postseason. The guy who had made me a detailed "Grief Counselor Options Spreadsheet" and who approached the drafting of his Little League team with mathematical precision was not going to march into the playoffs without gaming out all the possibilities. Pitch-count thresholds—implemented by the Little League of America in 2006 to protect young arms from overuse—had to be considered. You couldn't just ride your studs until their elbows burned and their arms fell off. There were strict guidelines.

With this in mind, Daniel had to see what he had, just in case his aces hit their pitch counts, just in case we somehow won our first playoff game, and then our second and third. He wasn't going to thrust some kid on the mound under the bright playoff lights without giving himself a chance to see how they looked as the regular season came to an end. That's why he'd started Caleb on the bump against Team Chartreuse, an outing as tough to watch as kids playing baseball in jerseys the color of soiled diapers. The sweet-faced kid gamely pitched us into a 9–2 hole after two innings, before Leo came in to right the ship, allowing us to mount a comeback that came up short. But Coach was okay with it, because the loss had taught him that Caleb probably should stick to catching.

Next, we lost a rematch against Team Teal. Isaiah and Kai got looks, but not much had improved since they pitched earlier in the season. Nate struck out the side to end that game, which ran up against the ninety-minute time limit after only three innings of long and tedious walks, but it was too late. We took the L. Adding to the sting of that particular loss: Ollie Reed struck out Nate, cheered on by his boisterous and overbearing assistant coach and father, the one my dad pegged as too intense. For our last regular-season game, we faced Team Red. They were a tough opponent, even with Leo pitching. He didn't have his best stuff that game. Finn came in to close, but he was shaky. He was better than the rest of the relief pitchers Daniel had tested on the mound in those last few games, but still inconsistent. Nate hit a home run in the last inning, when the outcome was no longer in doubt. Grandpa said, "Not a bad day at the office," as we packed up our chairs and went home, a bittersweet ending to the regular season.

Dad swats a mosquito with his hairy arm and then rips off another piece of muffin. "We could've beaten Team Teal."

"Damn straight."

I know one thing. If Dad starts in again lecturing about the poor parenting of Coach Reed, and how he's making his kid crazy with all his baseball corrections, I'm just going to agree and team up against him in our own private, unilateral trailer-park shit-talk war against the beefy-chested, loud-voiced assistant coach. It did make me cringe how boisterously he'd cheered when his kid struck out my kid, not that I wouldn't have done the same thing. "Coach Glory Days needs to take it down a notch," I'd whispered during that game, signaling that I was on my dad's side now. Reed was working my nerves, too. "Use your legs, Ollie! Get it down in the zone! Let your defense work for you! It's nine against one! Don't aim it, now! Good miss, kid! That pitch was gas, Ollie! Get him on the next one. Get him right here!" He was relentless. My dad had been at least a little bit right about Reed, even if I thought Nelson Strasser was in no position to judge. When Ollie finally struck Nate out, my dad looked sour and despondent, and for a flash I hated him for needing so much from Nate, and a second later I hated myself for feeling the exact same way, for believing everything in the world would have been sparkling and beautiful if Nate had only hit that baseball.

We move back into the trailer when the Riviera mosquitoes start to bite our ankles. Dad says nothing more about the heavy-handed Coach Reed, although I'm ready to back him up, guns blazing, us against everybody. Despite all the times he let Carol off the hook, he was still the one person who had my back more than anyone, and there was nothing like it.

When I was living in Los Angeles, I had a screen test for a reality competition show, a weekly network series in which young filmmakers would compete for a million-dollar development deal. I'd made it through the first cuts, and it was down to just two candidates for the job.

"Dad, the executive producer makes the final decision, and, Dad, *Dad*, guess who it is!" The minute I found out about the screen test, I called Delta Battery.

"Wait, hold on." He put the receiver against his chest and yelled, "Abbas, can you help this gentleman? Bring around the Ford. It's ready, sir. NO! The blue Ford, the pickup. Sir, my guys will have that truck to you in two minutes. Sorry, T. Tell me. Who is this famous producer? You know I don't know who anyone is in Hollywood."

"Have you heard of a guy named . . . STEVEN SPIELBERG?"

"ARE YOU KIDDING ME?! You're going to get this job. I can feel it. You are the coolest cat I know. Just a second, T. ABBAS! The blue Ford! It's behind the Fiat. Hold on, some idiot is calling here on the other phone because they don't know I'm busy with my daughter, who is about to be discovered by the *E.T.* guy. *Spielberg.* Wow. Hold on a sec. Delta Battery, can I help you?"

"Still me, Dad."

"Shoot. Hold on." He picked up the other line as a new customer wandered into the garage.

"Delta Battery, please hold. Uh-huh. Uh-huh. It was making a noise? Uh-huh. Just pull in right here and we'll take a look at it. I'll stay here after we close if my guys can't get to it. Just give me two minutes." He got back on the phone with me until I was ready to stop hyperventilating over my big break. This was how it was phoning Delta Battery. Even when the business wasn't making money, it was chaotic. But Dad always put customers on hold when Morgan or I phoned. We would imitate these calls together our entire adult lives, Dad shouting at his guys, yelling out car parts, makes, and models, saying "Uh-huh, uh-huh, uh-huh" while listening to a description of a customer's car troubles, an impression nobody else on Earth would ever appreciate: Dad answering the phone at Delta Battery.

The next time I phoned it was to tell him the other girl had gotten the job.

"Thank God. I didn't want to say this to you before, but Steven Spielberg is a putz and you're lucky he didn't hire you. I hated *E.T.* That movie was an overrated, schlocky, schmaltzy piece of shit. He sucks." I told him, "No, that guy is a national treasure, and he didn't choose me, so it's obvious *I suck*," but it felt like being resuscitated by a defibrillator through the telephone. His voice coming through the din at Delta Battery was like a paddle hitting me with a shock of blind faith that normalized the rhythm in my heart.

From now on, I want to take his side, just to feel the way I felt when he sided with me against Spielberg, just to feel that allegiance to each other. He was in my corner like that a lot, when it didn't involve Carol, or after she was just ashes in a candy tin. And even during her reign, he was conflicted at times. Carol was some kind of genius at being an evil stepmother. She had a way of keeping most of her cruelty just slightly beneath an invisible line, within the confines of what my dad could ignore. She knew how to hurt you without leaving much of a mark.

When I was in fourth grade, I tried to make my dad a special meal for Father's Day. I remembered how much he had liked kasha *varnishkes* when my aunt made it for him once. It's a Jewish dish of buckwheat and bow-tie pasta. I could barely remember how it looked, but I tried my best to find the matching grain and pasta among Carol's mason jars. I had never been taught how to cook, not by my mom, who was too busy, and certainly not by Carol. Confounded by the rows of dry goods, I threw some kind of grain on the stove, in a pan without oil or onions or seasoning. Then I added a handful of uncooked bow-tie pasta until the whole thing started to steam. Looking at the brown crunchy grains and scorched pasta, I knew it wasn't right, so I found some hot sauce to pour over the top of it. I knew my dad liked hot sauce. I had to work fast and do all the cleanup while Carol was out on her errands, because she wouldn't have liked me in her domain. And my heart raced as I cleaned, because I knew if I left a single crumb she would be furious. Dad got home from work and sat at the table. I set the plate in front of him and waited apprehensively. He took a bite; I could hear it crunch in his mouth. "Oh, it's good," he said.

Carol was back now, watching closely from the doorway.

"You can't eat that, Nelson. It's raw. But Teresa got you a present."

Earlier that day, she'd called me into the kitchen, saying she had something important to tell me. She had done me a huge favor, just this once, she whispered. From a brown paper bag she pulled a clear glass beer mug filled with popcorn kernels and covered with cellophane. The mug said WORLD'S GREATEST DAD. "You didn't even remember that today is Father's Day, did you?" I hadn't. "You don't even have a gift for your father. So I got you this from the store. You can pay me back next time you visit." She held it up briefly so I could see it, then stuffed it angrily back into the drugstore bag and hid it in the cupboard. It wasn't the kind of thing I'd have chosen, or that he'd like. He would never use that beer mug— he always drank out of the bottle—so it was going to be obvious I hadn't picked it out for him, and he'd know immediately that I'd forgotten, that I was a bad daughter and stupid and selfish for not having bought a Father's Day gift. I tried to cover it up by making my own gift, the kasha *varnishkes*, because that was the kind of thing he would like, something creative, but I'd failed. Carol smugly grabbed the popcorn mug from the pantry and stuck it in front of my dad in the paper bag. I don't remember where my brother was during any of this, but I can clearly recall Carol announcing grandly, "This is from the kids. I had to get it myself from the store, even though I was busy today. They didn't get you a thing, not one thing. I had to do it."

I'm still glad she's dead.

She wasn't the worst stepparent, not even close. She didn't, say, set the house on fire with us in it. She perfected a long, slow burn, a simmering disdain for us that rarely came to a full boil, so it could remain off my dad's radar. Her first order of business was to get rid of me, and after she'd successfully wished one of us away, it was just a matter of asserting her awesome dominance over the other. Anyone paying attention would have noticed, but my dad wasn't. It didn't register with him that we didn't have warm bedding, or toys, or books, or games; that Carol was never in touch with any of the other moms from Morgan's school, never set up parties or playdates so he was isolated from other kids. It was easy to miss the fact that though she never had a job, she was "too busy" to take us anywhere.

It was easy to overlook how delighted she was when one of us failed, the way I'd failed to remember Father's Day.

Dad dipped a piece of raw pasta into the hot sauce and crunched down on it. "I like the way you made this, T. It's not the usual way. It's different," he said, looking at me, then at Carol, who was bracing her thick arms against the kitchen doorway, a red scarf in her hair. She rolled her eyes and stormed out, thick ankles stomping away in espadrilles, and then she angrily ran the vacuum over the hallway rug. "I like these bow ties," Dad shouted over the noise of the vacuum, holding one up to his neck. "I'm going to wear this tomorrow. What do you think?"

World's Greatest Dad.

———————

"Grief is cumulative, you know," Ruth explains. In the break between the regular season and playoffs, I have some free nights, so I figure it can't hurt to see her again. I like it in her office: the pail of markers, the turtle pillow, the feelings chart.

"What, like a GPA?"

"Maybe," she says, a slight confused smile widening her lips. "What that means is that if you have multiple losses, either all at once or in succession, they pile up. And maybe there's a forgotten grief from the past, and a new loss can bring that back up. So there can be a kind of grief overload."

"Worst band name ever."

She gives me a courtesy laugh. I try too hard to be funny so I can be Ruth's favorite grief counselee.

"Grief doesn't go away. It just changes. At first, it's like being up close to a bright light, one of those giant floodlights; it's all you can see. Over time, the light softens, moves farther away from you, so you can see other things. And just as every relationship is different, every loss is different—all grief is different."

I knew that to be true, because grief over my brother and my mom was still sharp and fresh, lights so bright they were a full-frontal assault on my retinas.

Then there was my stepfather, Ron. My grief at losing him had softened almost immediately into a sort of halo around his memory, a warm, candlelit grief that never blinded me or made me turn away.

"Upper-left-hand corner," he once told me, putting down a heavy moving box filled with my books. He rubbed his beard, ebony with flecks of gray.

"What's that mean?" I asked.

"That's where a piece of music starts. You have to start over sometimes. You take it again from the top."

He was helping me move after a breakup. I was twenty-five and devastated. I had to move home with him and my mom for a few months, until I found a place of my own. I was waitressing then, and he would help me count out my tips at the kitchen table. And he would make his chicken and dumplings and put a whole huge stainless steel pot of it in the fridge. He didn't mind when I came home late from a dinner shift, got out a big wooden spoon, and picked out all the dumplings from the pot, wolfing them down in the darkness of the kitchen.

The next morning he'd peer under the lid of the pot and say in his distinct vernacular, "You let those dumplings get good to you," and he'd smile with his big-cheeked trumpet-player smile and shake his head.

"Well," I said to my mom, "Ron's making too much food and then he's secretly proud when I eat it all. He's officially Jewish."

His was the first and only funeral I'd ever attended before my brother's.

In fact, I planned it. My mom wasn't really up for logistics. She just wandered around her living room, pulling toilet paper from a roll and wiping her tears. She was maxing out her Valium, so I let her stay home and drove across Vegas to select a casket for my stepfather.

The casket salesman had red hair, not much of it, dyed and slicked back.

"The cream model with the silk interior is a nice choice for your . . . I'm sorry—what was the deceased's relation to you?"

"My stepdad. Ron was my stepdad. But he was like a dad. He even taught me how to drive, and that wasn't pretty, believe me."

"Uh-huh. Just sign here," he said, handing over a pen with his long, pale fingers.

From the office of the Vegas casket salesman, I went to Woodlawn Cemetery to choose a plot in the area for Black burials, a small section Black leaders had fought to establish back in 1939, when the cemetery promised the grave sites would be well cared for and not strewn on the outskirts of the place like they had been, covered over by weeds. This was where Mom thought he'd want to be, and even though she wouldn't be buried there next to him (she planned to be cremated and didn't give a hoot about the afterlife), she liked that Woodlawn wasn't far from downtown, where they'd spent so much time together, near the lights of Fremont Street, and the funky casinos on Glitter Gulch, which lacked the patina of the strip. The nickel slots at the Golden Nugget, the free photo you could take in front of a pyramid of cash at Binion's Gambling Hall—that was their kind of Vegas. And now Ron, who had always loved watching old Westerns, wouldn't be far from Vegas Vic, the forty-foot-tall neon cowboy saying howdy to anyone outside the Pioneer Club. Ron's final resting place at Woodlawn was also near eight Civil War veterans and a gunslinger named Diamondfield Jack Davis. I found a shady spot for him that I thought he'd have liked. Ron's grown sons came from Baltimore for the service, but they couldn't get there in time to plan it, or choose a spot for their pops. We never did see much of them, grown by the time he moved in with us and still living in Cherry Hill, the struggling Baltimore neighborhood where they grew up. I think as much as Ron was a do-over for me, a chance to have a stepparent who loved me, I was a do-over for him, a chance to be a different kind of father from the one he had been when he was young and always on the road. He didn't talk about it—he didn't talk about much—but I knew he wished things had been different with his own kids, that he'd been around more.

I had no unfinished business with Ron. He'd been nothing but kind to me. He'd taken the edge off my mother, and her loneliness and her moods. He'd diffused the tension in our house without ever being overbearing.

I told my favorite Ron story at his funeral. It was a big crowd, packed with musicians, and my mom's friends from her bridge club and the dog park, and old hippies from San Francisco and distant Jewish relatives.

It was when I was a teenager, and my mother and I were screaming at each other because I hadn't replaced a broken taillight on my car like she'd asked me to. The fight was getting louder and more hostile when he wordlessly walked past us and out the front door. My mom was still screaming at me about how irresponsible I was and I was still screaming at her about what a shitty parent she'd always been, and why was she all of sudden so interested in my personal safety, when he returned, carrying a brown paper bag from the auto parts store. "The car is fixed," he said softly as he casually walked by.

That's how he was. He solved what problems he could without making pronouncements about how anyone should be acting. I can still see him carrying the brown paper bag with the old, broken bulb and tossing it in the trash, while my mom and I started laughing at ourselves, how we were too busy fighting to notice what Ron had been doing outside in the driveway. You had to start over when you could, buy a new bulb, and throw away the old one. Upper-left-hand corner. It wasn't so complicated to mourn Ron. I could begin again, just as he'd told me to.

I have a printout of what I wrote for the funeral pamphlet, as well as the photo I chose for the front cover. In it he's wearing his favorite hat and a burgundy shirt my mom had bought for him, the collar perfectly pressed. I looked down at Ron's smiling face and knew that he was smiling at my mom. She wasn't in the frame, but I could tell, because that was how he always looked at her. The look said, *You're crazy, but I wouldn't have it any other way. You said you didn't want a mudslide tonight, but I knew you did, so I got you one anyway. Don't let it get good to you.* He always brought one of her sweaters when they went out for the night, even when she didn't think she would need one. In return, my mom knew he had bad habits but she let them be. She knew he used to walk down to the liquor store on the corner and buy one single cigarette from an old plastic licorice container that the owner kept just for him. And she knew that he knew that she would be poking her head out of the bay window to make sure he wasn't standing outside the liquor store smoking, so he worked out a deal with the owner to smoke that cigarette in the back of the store. If he could let her be crazy, she could let him have his vices and pretend not to see them, even if he had a bad heart and bad kidneys. He hid things from her that would upset her. She agreed not to see those things. He didn't get into her business, her ongoing feuds with me, her occasional freak-outs at customer service people who disrespected her, the way she sometimes got depressed for weeks at a time and watched television in bed all day until she fell asleep, and left the volume turned up high all night.

They fit here on earth, in the old Victorian in San Francisco, in the rent-by-the-month hotels in Vegas, in the condo where they eventually settled for good, a quick drive to Fremont Street. They were good together, but not alike. He was easy with people, social, chatting with every musician he knew from every band in every casino lobby, hopping onstage with his trumpet when invited, casually referring to old bandmates as "cats," and fist-bumping my elderly Jewish great-aunts as they giggled and jostled to stand next to him.

But their roads diverged when it came to dying, because Ron had a big party, and my mom wanted nothing to do with any of that.

When it came to funeral arrangements, my mother's wishes were crystal clear.

"No funeral," she whispered hoarsely from her hospital bed, four days before she died.

"Okay, Mom."

"I'm serious. No. Funeral," she repeated, and it took her a minute to catch her breath.

She didn't want to have a funeral because of a birthday party sixty years earlier. That's what her best friend, Kathy, told me, just after Mom died, and I remembered hearing the story of the birthday party that went so sideways it followed her, followed her all the way to her eternal home. My dad wasn't too broken up about my mom dying (probably griefed out from Morgan's death), but even he understood why she never wanted anyone to throw her a party ever again. And he didn't blame her.

Her immigrant parents didn't understand American birthday party customs. They barely spoke English and didn't know about RSVPs, so they didn't realize no one was coming. My mom waited at the dining room table for hours, elbows folded on a lace tablecloth, the weird European food my grandma had made getting cold, a skin forming on the potato soup. My mom stared at the door in a paper birthday hat, but not one kid showed up, because she was the weird girl with foreign parents, parents the age of other people's grandparents. She wore hand-sewn dresses and didn't even get to watch *The Ed Sullivan Show* on Sunday nights, and couldn't joke about it with everyone at school the next day.

All these years later my mom could still see that door, feel the isolation and shame, her parents speaking Yiddish to each other, wondering why nobody showed up to eat the soup, or what to say to their daughter. They finally put away the food and said nothing. Cumulative grief, a forgotten loss coming back, sparked by a new one. That's how Ruth described it: the way grief piles up, how it changes, goes from bright to dim but never goes away.

"Grief from childhood lives in the body," Ruth said, rearranging the strands of orange and brown beads around her neck. "It's like a picture, but it doesn't have a time or date stamp."

I imagine pictures floating in your cells, in the broth of your body, photographs from the past that develop in the chemical baths of the present.

I wonder if that's how my mother's grief for my brother felt. When he died, was there already one of those snapshots floating around from the first time she had lost him, when that bullshit motherfucking judge gave my dad full custody?

The day I cried the single tear in the passenger seat of her Toyota Corolla, the day my dad was always talking about, she probably also had a clear memory of that day. And I realize not only was she picking me up to take me home with her; she had to leave her other kid behind. Morgan had to have been there, in that tableau. I try to place him there, black bangs in his eyes, standing behind my dad, his mother backing out of the driveway, taking me and leaving him, a picture with no time stamp.

There's a photo of our family, when my parents were still married, taken at a park somewhere in Los Angeles. My dad is holding my brother and my mom is holding me. She looks worn-out, a yellow headband in her hair, and she holds me away from her body, more like you might hold a sack of flour than a pudgy baby. You can sense grief in the photo, the grief she'd already absorbed from her parents, the half sister who died on the train coming to America, the half brother who died in the gas station fire decades later, the second-generation refugee grief, all the relatives left behind in Europe, a picnic of mysterious ancestral sadness and survivor guilt right there in the park. And when I look at the photo now, I can see in her face, far away and pale, the little-girl version of her, the one that waited in her paper party hat.

Grief is cumulative.

I wanted to throw my mom a funeral, a blowout for the lonely girl without a birthday party, for the reluctant young mother suffering through a picnic in the park. I wanted to make it all better for her.

There'd be chocolate mudslides and a live band at this fantasy funeral, a top-notch band with a big horn section. And I'd say to the heavens, *Look, Mom. Everyone came.* But I was also scared nobody would show, and I couldn't do that to her.

If there's a eulogy, it's not the big formal kind I'd speak in front of a crowded room, wearing a black dress. It happens in daily bursts, moments only she would hear as elegiac verses, when I repeat things that she used to say, with her exact intonation. It's a eulogy when I look in the fridge and announce, "If we had eggs, we could have ham and eggs, if we had ham." When I wrinkle my nose and say "*FEH,*" looking at some disgusting food, I pay my respects. And when I walk behind my kids and sing out, just as she used to do, "What a cute little tushy!" I miss her as hard as the hour she died, when I was bent over wailing on Geary Street.

It was around the time my mom died that Ruth recommended a grief book for my brother's kids. I bought a copy and sent it to them.

In the book, a mother reassures her anxious children during a thunderstorm, telling them that even if they aren't sleeping with her, even if she is in the next room, that she is still connected to them by an invisible string. You can't see it, but you can feel it with your heart.

The way Victoria might frame it, in one of her Monday night dharma talks, is that Buddha also believed in invisible strings, "the interconnectedness of all beings," as she would explain it to us.

I resented the book because I didn't want my brother's kids to need it, but I still think about it, how grief now connects me to other people who are grieving, strangers who tug at me, the couple at Green Acres driving away in the newly washed white pickup truck. Strings connect me to dead relatives I never knew, or can't remember knowing, crisscrossing a map of space and time, like yarn wrapped around thumbtacks tracking a never-ending crime spree.

Baseball is also a kind of invisible string.

It connects us to Morgan. It connects Morgan to Nate. It connects the Purple Pinstripes to millions of other kids playing this season. It connects every hand-wringing parent or grandparent or sibling to every at bat. We feel the strings go taut, yanking at the hook in our hearts, the string that can't be seen, but also can't be broken.

||||||||||||||||||||||||||||

CHAPTER FIFTEEN

Quantum Entanglement

"You can have the nine greatest individual ball
players in the world, but if they don't play together,
the club won't be worth a dime."

—BABE RUTH

Dad and I march briskly across Ingleside's outdoor basketball court and toward the baseball fields. We know we are leaving the normal world, because even the air is different. The closer we get to the bleachers, the more we inhale the thick smell of Little League, like melted crayons and ocean water and the inside of an old leather handbag. EVERY SEASON STARTS AT DICK'S SPORTING GOODS, says one of the vinyl signs tied to the chain-link fence. A pennant banner of red, white, and blue triangles hangs above it, across the length of the fence.

The powerlessness I feel about the Purple Pinstripes and their first playoff game is collecting between my lower ribs, where it gnaws and twists. My chest is heavy. I walk faster to try to shake loose this feeling, outpace it, and Dad keeps up with me in his Nikes, doing his *puff, puff* breathing.

I'm grappling for composure. But I've got to hide it from all the parents and grandparents and players streaming by, some arriving for our game, others leaving after the previous game. You can always tell which team lost by their faces as they lug their wagons and baseball bags toward the parking lot, and in this case it's more dramatic, because for the losers the season has ended. We see faces smeared with dirt and tears, a dad walking with his arm around his son's shoulders, a player limply holding an ice cream sandwich, unable to even bother eating it.

"Sudden death," I mumble theatrically out of the side of my mouth, turning toward Dad. He just raises his eyebrows and keeps walking.

"Danny says he's going to start Leo on the mound," I continue, keeping my voice down, breathless from walking fast. "And if things go well, he can pull him after two innings, keep him under his pitch count for the next game. If there is a next game. Knock wood." I knock on my head, since I'm not near any wood. "And there's a good chance he's going to pitch Nate."

Dad looks just the way he does on an airplane when he's clutching a plastic cup of tequila and trying to pretend he isn't afraid to fly. His upper lip is moist, and his face is almost the color of jaundice. Dad picks up his pace and announces, "Endorphins, T! Let's get those endorphins going! Hey, since we have twenty minutes before the game, you want to walk around?" So we do, putting down our bags and chairs and then speed-walking around Ingleside's fields, pumping our arms and reviewing Coach's lineup. Andrew scuttles off to hang out in the dugout with his brother's team.

When it's close to game time, Dad and I settle into our beach chairs along the first-base line and watch the end of warm-ups through the fence, where spiderwebs trap clusters of pine needles in the galvanized steel wires.

Our opponents, the Black Pinstripes, look sharp and ready. We beat them earlier in the season, but they've been on a winning streak. And their skipper has acquired a new nickname.

"Coach Bunt" has been telling the kids at the bottom of his lineup not to swing but instead to gently tap the ball so it will land just feet away from the plate and make it hard for the pitcher to field. According to Daniel, this is nothing short of a mortal Little League sin. "Forcing your worst kids to bunt, that's like telling a kid you don't trust him to swing the bat," he told me last night, when several other coaches called to warn him about Coach Bunt and his sinister bunt dealings. "These kids all want to hit, even at the bottom of the lineup. And if you don't know that, you shouldn't be a coach in the Arcadia Little League." But I know he isn't really all that annoyed, because part of what makes Arcadia Little League the centerpiece of our entire neighborhood every spring is that it's a soap opera. And all good stories need bad guys. "Oh, all the coaches hate this guy. He even tells kids not to swing. We are going to have to throw strikes, because they aren't giving anything away."

Coach Bunt makes a good villain. He's a cigar-chomping real estate mogul who played college soccer and always runs a hand through the coiffed white streak at the front of his wavy hair.

Daniel isn't much of a pregame-speech guy, but this is it, single elimination, and he knows the boys are on edge, wound tight. "Listen up, guys," he says. "The biggest thing here is that no matter what happens at any point in any of these playoff games, you have to stay positive. If we get five-run-ruled in an inning, it doesn't matter. We can always come back, just like we've done all season. Play the whole game."

"Balls in, coming down!" shouts Gavin, who's squatting on the toes of his cleats, knees out. He flips up his catcher's mask, and I rub my palms together.

"Let's go, Six!" Leo's dad hollers out, sitting right up against the fence just behind the plate.

Leo throws his first pitch of the playoffs, and it's a strike, right down the middle.

Team Black Pinstripes' leadoff hitter tattoos the pitch, hits it squarely with the sweet spot of his bat, blasting a shot that soars out toward dead center. There haven't been many towering, high fly balls hit out there all season. Coach had hidden Wyatt Reyes in the outfield because his glove was weak, and just prayed nothing would come to him.

The ball hovers, soars, and then Wyatt, a speedy basketball kid with the longest legs on the field, wheels toward it. It's still so high, I can't locate the fly ball in space. He's settling where he needs to be, just under it. But if he can't catch it—and he hasn't caught a fly ball all season—he will have to hunt it down as it skitters around unpredictably in the outfield, from the grass to the warning track just in front of the fence. He will need the arm strength and where-withal to get it to his cutoff man, just like the team practiced during the preseason, so many weeks and months and games ago. Odds are, by the time the ball gets home, the runner will have beaten it.

It's falling in slow motion. Wyatt puts up his glove.

And he catches the ball. He catches it like it's nothing, which is something. The Little League of America banned bats with too much springiness (aka "juice") back in 2018. Not many kids could jack the ball to deep, deep center with a dull, safe, regulation Little League legal bat. But this kid had done that. And Wyatt Reyes had caught it.

"I fucking love baseball, Dad."

"Miracle catch."

I get up to high-five Wyatt's mom, Natalie. Earlier that morning, she'd written in a parents' text chain with Finn's mom, Should we wear purple? For good luck tonight?

No, responded Finn's mom. We shouldn't start doing anything new.

Agree, I texted. So everyone wore their regular lucky pants or shorts or whatever, same as they had all season. And I wore my jade charm, which I squeeze between my fingers as I take my seat again.

Leo keeps dealing, confident, pumping strikes. He also sprinkles in a couple of walks, so there are base runners when Coach Bunt lives up to his name.

After the miracle catch, we forgot all about the previously looming prospect of Coach Bunt's players bunting. Sure enough, Ari O'Brien, a redheaded kid with a high, congested voice, built like a thick rectangle, tries to lay down the game's first bunt. He swings and misses.

"I don't know what this coach is thinking. It ain't easy to lay down a bunt," my dad tells me. The old man prophesied it, and it comes to be: The squat redhead kid can't time it right, can't get his bat around sideways and lateral. Three attempts, and it's curtains for the inning.

Now, it's the bottom of the first inning, and we start hitting.

I don't know if it's Daniel's pregame speech, or the miracle catch, or the slow, deliberate, predictable pitching of Coach Bunt's hapless starter, but our dugout oozes with confidence. "Everyone hits!" a few parents yell out, encouraging. And everyone does. Gavin and Nate reach base on hot grounders. Ethan sends one right up the middle. Little Kai fouls off seven pitches before hitting a dribbler toward the pitcher, who can't field it cleanly. I look at his dad and shrug, like *Just another day at the office*, and he shrugs back, beaming. Easton awkwardly chops one down like he's a bespectacled lumberjack taking down an oak tree. The swing isn't pretty, but it's powerful, and even with his gushy, lollygagging waddle, he makes it to second base. Isaiah swings on almost every pitch. He stays in the box, and he finally makes hard contact *for the first time all season*. Coach Daniel grabs him by the shoulders and yells, "YES. GREAT. KEEP DOING THAT," even though the Black Pinstripes' shortstop caught the ball. Coach doesn't care if he ever gets on base. He just wants to see him swinging. We cheer so hard, our throats are raw in the dry air.

After two innings, we are ahead, 6–0. To save Leo for a possible next game, Daniel takes him out, keeping him under his pitch count.

That's when I see Nate throwing a final warm-up pitch in the bullpen, heading toward the mound. "Fuck," I unintentionally blurt.

"Don't worry, T. Look at him. He's got his stuff." I can't tell, because my eyes go blurry. I can't predict what's going to happen once the game resumes, and I grip the plastic arms of my chair with all my strength.

I think most of us are too ashamed to admit it, but when I see some dad pacing out behind right field, I know he's got his reasons. And I know how he feels, and that it's probably not how he wants to feel, but he manages it the best he can.

Then I remember how the meditation tape says, "Allow things to be exactly as you find them." I know I have no choice, but I don't like how I find things—namely, feeling overwrought and desperate. I watch Nate warm up, and I catalogue how many things could go wrong. He could give up six runs, easily. Nate could blow this entire lead for the Purple Pinstripes, and there is nothing I can do to stop it. Sudden death, *all his fault*. If he hits too many batters, then he'll have to be pulled, and we'll have to use Gavin. So even if we win, Gavin and Nate will both be burned for the next game, which we will lose, let's face it, because of my kid.

"What's the count?" I ask Dad, trying to stay in the present, as much as I don't like it. I want this game to just be over so I can stop worrying.

"Three and two," he answers.

"Whatcha gonna do?" we chant in unison, nervously.

Nate is wild, but not his wildest. He's hit only one kid with a pitch so far. Somehow, he gets out of the inning, leaving runners stranded on first and second. I love the way it looks when he throws that last strike and those two Black Pinstripes trot back to their dugout, no runs scored. It's so beautiful.

I exhale.

"Everyone hits," shouts one of the dads again. And they do. Our lead is growing.

After only three and a half innings, we are up 11–0. If a team is up by ten runs after four innings, the mercy rule is enacted, and they win. Everyone in the stands is buzzing about it. This could be it, right here. Nate slings the heat and it's game over. All he has to do is hold them to one run. But he's been so unpredictable all season.

"Anything could happen, Dad."

"That's baseball. But I know Nate. He's not getting the yips. Not when it's do-or-die."

"Whatever happens, Dad, it's good for kids to learn how to tolerate failure and frustration, so it's a win either way."

He looks at me, incredulous. The old man knows when I'm fronting.

"What's the count, Dad?"

"Nate hasn't thrown a strike. Missing high. It's three and oh." The kid walks.

"Great," I chirp.

The batter tries to bunt on two strikes. He gets the bat in front of his body, with both elbows bent, but he misses the ball. Strike three.

"Coach Bunt," Dad says conspiratorially. "Hoisted by his own petard."

We just need two more outs to advance to the next playoff game, with my baby on the mound, sudden death hanging in the balance. *Please, Jesus, Moses, Elvis, the Buddha, and the Babe, get us out of this inning.* I squeeze the jade pendant. *Mugsy, do me this one more thing*, I ask, knowing he probably can't hear me. But it can't hurt to try.

Nate is far from solid. He walks the bases loaded. Then, with two outs, he fields a ball hit toward the mound, throws it to Leo, who is manning first.

We win, in an improbable combined no-hitter. I'm so jubilant, I have to contain my inner Coach Reed.

Dad and I are wrung out, exhausted. We've been through something small and big together. "I'm going to have a little nip of brandy when I get to your house, if that's okay," he says. "Big win. BIG."

"So big, Dad. Can we never play ever again?" He throws his mouth open, not even shy about all the missing teeth, lets out an open-throated "HA."

"Survive and advance," Dad intones, snapping his beach chair shut like he always knew we'd win.

Andrew is in the dugout before the game, just like he was for our first playoff against Team Black Pinstripes. Since that was a win, the players have determined that he's good luck. He sits in the dark cavern of baseball bags and water bottles and sunflower seeds and batting helmets and gum wrappers. Dad and I are early again, for our second playoff game, and we watch as Andrew ingratiates himself with his older brother's friends, his floppy blond hair around his chubby cheeks, mostly shutting up so he doesn't say anything stupid.

The night before, I had put a stack of Nate's old clothes on Andrew's bed.

The little one looked at the pile of worn hand-me-downs on his red comforter and asked, "Are these for me?" I thought he'd be upset, that he'd rather get new clothes of his own, bought especially for him.

Instead, his mouth opened slightly; he was awestruck. He squeezed his eyes and pumped his fists, like he'd just hit a walk-off in the World Series. It was near bedtime, and he requested permission to sleep in his brother's old clothes. Maybe, he seemed to be thinking, he would sleep in the worn cotton costume of his hero and wake up having absorbed some of his superpowers.

Though Andrew is right-handed, he stepped up to his first baseball tee batting lefty like his brother and has been hitting it southpaw ever since. Whether it would have been natural to him or not, I'll never know. But to me, looking at Andrew in the dugout, there are the two boys, but also there is a third entity. There is a brotherhood that doesn't include me but to which I am a witness.

Andrew's stubby legs dangle and kick on the dugout bench as the Pinstripes head back in there to grab their batting helmets and gloves, check the lineup sheet hung up on a clipboard attached to the fence by a carabiner. I'm so happy for Andrew that he gets to be in this Pinstripes nucleus, right up close to the action. There are so many things I didn't get to do with my brother, big things and everyday things: We didn't trick-or-treat, or make pillow forts, or do homework together. We did watch TV on Saturday morning when I visited once a month, mostly sitcom reruns. Sometimes we fought over what show to watch. Once, Morgan wanted to watch *Gomer Pyle* while I wanted to watch *Alice*, and I tried to change the channel and we wrestled on the floor. Bigger and faster, naturally he pinned me down, but I bit his wrist, which was holding down mine. I jolted up fast, trying to get loose, and bonked my nose on his chin. I didn't cry, but my nose bled. He didn't apologize or help me clean the blood from the floor with paper towels.

I sat next to my brother, solemnly watching *Gomer Pyle*, blood streaked between my nose and lip, going dark and crusty.

When my dad got home, he noticed it.

"What happened?" he asked, popping the top off his Dos Equis.

My brother looked at me nervously. Dad never got angry and he never yelled, but this was the sort of thing that would disappoint him, a bigger kid hurting a smaller one. I held all the cards, and Morgan knew it, too.

"Nothing, Dad. My nose just started bleeding."

My brother looked over at me again, just for a second, to make sure this was really happening, that I wasn't going to tattle. He didn't thank me later, or ever mention it again, but I knew I had impressed him. I could've snitched, but I didn't.

"Remember that time we were fighting over *Gomer Pyle* and I got a bloody nose, but when Dad came home, I covered for you?" That was the fantasy of the story we'd tell when we were older, how we had covered for each other when we were kids, and of course how that was a precursor of how we'd act as teenagers, helping each other sneak out of the house, him buying me beer. But it was never like that. I remember the first of the few times my mother forced him to drive me to school, when he was sixteen and I was fourteen. It was the opposite direction from his school, but it was raining hard, and for some reason she noticed and intervened. He was so irritated by this chore that he found an AM radio station that was almost nothing but static and blasted it on full volume the whole ride, just to ruin it for me. At a stoplight, he looked at my face and yelled over the static, "Is that a mustache?" I flipped down the mirror. In the morning light, you could see fine blond hairs above my lip. I was mortified, but, on the other hand, my big brother was making fun of me! That seemed almost sweet, the sort of thing big brothers do, hazing little sisters. I would obsess about the mustache and eventually remove it with Nair, but it was worth it, because I considered it a private joke between the two of us. "I didn't even know I had a mustache until my brother pointed it out, giving me a ride one day," I'd tell people all the time, making out like that was the sort of thing that happened regularly, my big brother giving me rides, me by his side, him teasing me, like big brothers do.

"Okay, get out," he said when we got to the parking lot of my school. I grabbed my backpack and didn't thank him for the ride.

I didn't know if he even remembered any of that. All the times I visited him when he was sick, the hours I sat on the red couch pushed up against the wall of his makeshift basement hospice, we didn't talk about Carol or being separated. We didn't talk about the transformation he'd undergone after moving in with us, the sessions with the child psychologist, the way he went from failing out of school to graduating second in his class, the way he made friends with Phil. Then they made two more friends and formed their own circle, playing Dungeons & Dragons for hours. I had felt so happy that he was finally home with us, that things were going to be okay for him. I knew we weren't like most siblings, who had a lifetime of day-to-day shared memories, tricking the babysitter about our bedtime, plotting ways to steal cookies from the cookie jar, conspiring to lose the matching pajamas Mom bought us for a family photo shoot. These were my private notions about regular siblings. My brother and I were more like cousins. Sure, we knew each other, but we didn't have all that much to say. I couldn't have explained it to anyone at the time, or made sense of it myself, but I was both relieved I didn't have to worry about him anymore, didn't have to feel like I'd left a man in the field, and also grieving, because it was too late now for us to grow up together.

In the basement just a couple of months before he died, he said, "You seem pretty happy."

"Yeah," I said, "I guess I am." But then I didn't know if I should highlight all the flaws in my life, so he'd feel better about dying, or emphasize all the good things, so he wouldn't worry about me. I didn't know which way to go, so I did the thing that came more naturally: I started complaining. "Sometimes, I worry too much about the kids and I get too anxious about things. And the show where I work, it's not hard news. You know, not exactly winning a Peabody over there." He looked worried. I backtracked.

"But I'm grateful for the work, you know, because I'm a million years old in television host years." The tension in his face released; at least maybe I thought it did, a little. "And the shocker, to me more than anyone, is I think I'm turning out to be an okay mom. So, that's good. And Daniel. Everyone loves Daniel. I think Dad loves him more than he loves me," I joked. Morgan shifted in his bed and looked uncomfortable. That was it, end of deep life-overview talk.

Dear Morgan,

What the fuck with not answering my letter? The one I wrote when you were dying. Dude, did you not want to say anything to me, your only sibling, on the way out?

That was part of a letter I wrote, what Ruth called a "therapeutic letter." She suggested I put all my thoughts down on paper, even the angry thoughts. I put the letter in an envelope addressed to Morgan Strasser, c/o Heaven. I don't believe in a puffy-cloud heaven. Nonetheless, I stuck it in a mailbox with a stamp and everything.

The letter was just a way to be mad at a dead person, to express it and release it so the anger didn't clog up all the grief valves. I never wrote a therapeutic letter to my mom—didn't need to. I'd had no trouble telling her right to her face all the ways she'd disappointed me when she was alive. I wish sending the letter to Morgan was a mystical experience, knowing I'd communicated with the universe that, yes, I was mad at my brother even though all he had done was heroically bear pain, and the terror of knowing he was dying, and that he couldn't predict if he'd just be death rattling into oblivion all by himself or ascending into some glorious eternal resting place. Sending him the letter didn't make anything worse, but I don't know if it helped. Not like baseball. When it was game time, you had to get yourself together, not blubber about who hadn't loved you right in the past, or how you weren't going to have your brother and your mommy in the future. Baseball wasn't a clinical exercise. It was survive and advance, unfold your chair and know that sudden death is possible, but so is anything. An infinite number of glorious possibilities await us out there, me and my dad, our team, scribbling a salutation to the baseball gods, a letter with a million possible happy endings.

Coach Patel wasn't to be taken lightly. Although we'd beaten Team Black in our third game of the season, Daniel had deep respect for the coach, an anesthesiologist who was also a numbers guy shrewdly managing his roster.

However, to get through his first playoff game against Team Camo, he'd had to burn two of his best pitchers. There wasn't much left in his bullpen, but this was baseball, and you never knew what could happen.

Team Black gets off to an early lead. We just aren't hitting, and Leo, with his second playoff start, gives up four runs in the first two innings.

"Let's go, Six!" I always love it when Leo's dad calls his son by the number on the kid's jersey, their family shorthand, but he's nervous now, clutching his commuter mug, sitting low in his chair, pulling the brim of his hat down over his eyes. It's early and Leo is already looking tired, his arm soft and flimsy.

I'm rooting for him because he's one of ours, and his success is our success, but also, the longer he can stay in the game, the less chance there is that Nate will have to come in to relieve him.

"Only four runs scored, Dad. That could have been worse," I say as the Pinstripes get ready to bat.

"Way worse."

Then our bats come alive, just as they did in our first playoff game.

Ethan hits a hard ground ball up the middle. Our sweet-faced backup catcher has gotten so consistent at hitting, Coach has moved him up to leadoff. Almost every at bat, he knocks the ball to the exact same place, past the pitcher's mound, past second base, and then into center field, the same trajectory every time, including now. The next few batters all put the ball in play, Gavin, Finn, Nate, Caleb. Because everyone hits, because the Purple Pinstripes are connected in this way, like there's some kind of quantum team physics I can't explain. My dad says simply, "Hitting is contagious." And that seems right.

But defensively, Leo continues to struggle.

After he walks two batters, Coach Daniel takes Leo off the mound. To save him for a possible next playoff game, and because sometimes you just don't have it.

I see Nate head toward the mound. We are down 4–2.

There's a constriction in my heart. The feeling is of a sacred scrim separating me from the field. On the other side is a place where I can't help my baby, can't protect him or make him the hero, can't help him resuscitate this game, our second sudden death game. And next to me is my dad, who knows this feeling more profoundly than I do. We are together on this side with all the other parents who can't protect our kids from life.

It's dark now as Nate ambles toward the mound. Camelback Mountain, the palm trees on the horizon are all just dark shapes. A thin sliver of a moon hangs over the field. In the next two innings, he walks a few kids, and Dad and I mumble "Shit, shit, shit" each time, but the Pinstripes don't allow any runs. With our hitters mashing the ball, we take the lead going into the final inning, 11–4.

"Who's winning?" asks a group of sixth graders wandering over from the game on the North Field.

"The good guys," says my dad. He laughs loudly into the wind.

In the final inning, Team Black seems to adjust to Nate's pitching, and the top of their lineup gets a few hits. Still, I can feel a lightness come over me. One run has come in, but there are two outs.

"No way this team can score six more runs here, right, Dad?"

Andrew is in the dugout, cheering every play, eating sunflower seeds, his legs dangling off the bench in his brother's old Phillies socks. He wears only Nate's hand-me-downs now.

"No way, T. I think we got this one."

And we're right.

We win 12–5 and jubilation explodes on the field, the players running toward the mound, high-fiving their gloves in the air, Andrew somewhere in the middle of it all.

Afterward, Nate and some of his teammates stay to watch another game at the South Field. Andrew stays, too, tagging along, cheering only when Nate cheers, repeating what he says.

Nate: "That was a tank!"

Andrew: "A tank!"

Nate: "That should've been a ball! It was a mile outside!"

Andrew: "It was so far outside. It was a mile outside." He shakes his head at the injustice of the ump's call. He doesn't really understand the intricacies of baseball yet, can't interpret what the ump saw, what's inside or outside. He just sees Nate. And he believes with all his heart that the ball was a mile outside.

My dad came up with a theory, shortly before my brother was officially pronounced terminal.

For more than two months he'd been basically living in Morgan's room at some rehab center or other and he emailed to ask how I was doing. I responded:

> Between Googling ependymoma survival rates and feeling in my bones that it's me who's actually dying and hearing the words "palliative care" over and over in my mind and mentally rehearsing the end, and being without my only sibling on earth, I'm having a ball!!!!
>
> Jk.
>
> It's weird. We maybe were never the closest, but there's a bond that makes me feel the shock and sadness in a very physical way. I can't complain to you, because it's worse for you and Mom.

He wrote back:

> There is an unbreakable connection between you and Morgan that is apart from how close in proximity you are or how much you are in contact. You know, there is this phenomenon in quantum mechanics called "entanglement." Two particles can be around the world from each other, and if you measure one, the other one kind of "comes to attention." These particles are said to be "entangled." Physicists are aware of it, but they do not really understand it. You and Morgan are "entangled."
>
> Love,
> Dad

He thought we were linked, like subatomic particles.
And I liked to think we were, too.
The way it works is that once particles are "entangled," they

remain as one, even across great distances. If you measure one, you know something about the other. They are no longer wholly separate entities.

I think my dad wanted to believe his children were fundamentally entangled in a way that couldn't be undone, not even by him. He wanted to believe there were forces so powerful, they couldn't be interrupted by the bumbling custody decisions of one freshly divorced car mechanic and his unlicensed therapist/girlfriend. The universe was made up of relationships that were stronger, and more mystifyingly beautiful, than anything Nelson Strasser could break.

If Dad had told Morgan about this theory, my brother would have looked it up, like I did, and he might have concluded that it was all "spooky action at a distance," which is how Einstein described it. But maybe he would have shrugged his shoulders and conceded, like most current-day theoretical physicists, that these connections may be cryptic and complex, but they are undeniable. Change one entangled particle, and you change the other. They are attached by subatomic *invisible strings*. Maybe that's why it felt like I was dying some days, actually disintegrating right along with my big brother— why I could hear sirens in my head on the nights he was riding in the back of an ambulance, way across the country, *spooky action at a distance.*

CHAPTER SIXTEEN

IIIIIIIIIIIIIIIIIIIIIIIIIIIII

Nice Cut

"My motto was always to keep swinging. Whether I was in a slump or feeling bad or having trouble off the field, the only thing to do was keep swinging."

—HANK AARON

Every pitch goes low, until it's walk after walk, stolen base after stolen base. And everyone whispers, as they always do when a Little League team starts to crumble defensively, "It's the *Bad News Bears* out there."

The winner of this game goes to the championship. And the loser goes home.

Nate isn't available to pitch; he threw too many pitches against Team Black. And Coach needs to make sure Gavin is available for the finals, just in case we get there. His plan is to keep Gavin under thirty-five pitches. That leaves Leo, but there's no way Leo can get through six innings in under seventy-five pitches, so Finn got the start in this game, our third playoff game, and it's agonizing. His throws are blazing hot, but he can't throw a strike; he can send missiles only into the dirt in front of the plate. He's like a baby dragon that hasn't learned how to control his fire breathing. When he tries to breathe just enough fire to heat up dinner, he incinerates the entire kitchen.

Jen is pacing behind the bleachers in her lucky white jeans.

Finn was already five-run-ruled in the first inning, and now he's walked two more batters. There are no outs.

Daniel calls a time-out and there's a mound visit.

"How you doing, buddy? How do you feel? You want to stay in?" Quiet Finn with the low voice and shy smile, he wants to keep pitching. His eyes are welling up. But he isn't giving in to the despair. With no hesitation, he looks up at Coach, choking back tears.

"YES."

"Okay," says Coach. The players return to the field and Daniel says, "Deep breath. Look at the catcher's mitt. Nice and easy. Take a little bit off of it. Throw ninety instead of a hundred percent." Finn nods, stern-faced.

The ump calls the next pitch a ball, but it's close, too close for Gavin's mom, who has something to say about it.

"Hey, Blue. Why you squeezing him? Where is your strike zone? Just tell us where your zone is, so we know," she calls out, testy but not belligerent. I envy her, because she has a right-size attitude toward sports. She cares, but she doesn't over-care. And she knows baseball. Her brother pitched in college, and that's why she speaks it fluently.

A few months ago, I wouldn't have understood that sentence, but now I know an ump is called "Blue" because of the color of his shirt, and if he's calling the game tight, he's "squeezing" the pitcher. It puffs me up knowing this, speaking enough of the language of baseball to belong in this world, close to real baseball, beyond coach-pitch and T-ball, kids pitching the entire game. I'm remembering the season opener, the sound of all the baseball parent yells, a symphony of confusing directives that swells across baseball fields everywhere. I have come to translate these coded messages more fully over the course of many gusting, dry nights by the first-base line. "Nice cut," I hear some parents yell from the bleachers when a player swings and misses. And I understand that it also means,

Kid, you missed the ball but that isn't what matters. Your hands were pulled back, middle knuckles lined up on the bat, shoulders level, bat slicing through space on an even plane. It means, *You did all you could, and nobody hits the ball every time, but your swing can still be beautiful—necessary, even—to get you closer to a hit, to raking, mashing, or hitting nukes, tanks, dingers, and moon shots.* I know "good eye" celebrates the art of restraint, not swinging at pitches that you can't drive. I know a "circus catch" is what Wyatt made in center field in the first playoff game. And "gotta protect" is what you holler at a kid with an 0-2 count who needs to *swing at anything close, don't strike out looking, protect the plate, because now you can't be picky. You have two strikes on you and it's time to expand your swing zone, swing at anything close, protect yourself from the whims of an ump calling it tight.* And when your pitcher is lost up there, "Let him hit it" means just throw a strike; your defense will back you up. And that's what we call out now, the Greek chorus of Purple Pinstripe fans, willing Finn to focus and fire, to get anywhere near the zone.

Finn walks the next two batters. Daniel calls another time-out. He puts his hands on Finn's shoulders. "Leo is coming in," he tells his pitcher. But Finn begs to stay on the hill. He just wants to redeem himself. He's desperate to make right what has gone so wrong, but it's too late now. He knows it, and his coach knows it. It's not his night and there's no way around it. Looking at his cleats, he hands the ball to Daniel under the stadium lights and the moon, everyone watching, hushed. Then Finn takes his place at third base, replacing Caleb.

As a starting pitcher in the semifinals of the Arcadia Little League Minors playoffs, Finn recorded zero outs. The Pinstripes are down 0–7.

"I think it's over, Dad. Finn just couldn't right the ship."

"No. Steered it into an iceberg. Poor kid. You never want to see that happen."

Finn is slouching, despondent, but he has no choice now but to find some kind of game face. He's got to be ready. He's now in the "hot corner," as it's called, where balls fly toward you from right-handed batters so fast, you don't have time to mope about the hole you just dug your team into.

My heart breaks for him, this low-voiced kid who turned out to be so fierce, even though he couldn't find the zone. He never stopped trying. And my chest explodes with awe for Daniel, who doesn't flinch or panic. Coach still seems to trust his own game plan, starting Finn, letting him throw as long as he can.

I can't even look at Jen, because the level of baseball mom sadness will be too much.

Finn opens his stance a few steps behind the bag and gets in position, knees bent, weight on the balls of his feet. His glove is open and close to the ground. He has to forget everything that happened so far this game. He's here now, at third base, and there's no use slouching anymore. You can see him adjust to this in real time. He exhales. I see his shoulders rise and fall. His knees bend lower.

The next batter hits a low pop-up that goes foul, heading just outside the third-base line. But instead of letting it land in foul territory, Finn races toward it at his top speed, almost crashing his lithe body all the way into the fence. Somehow, he fully extends his arm while sprinting. The ball came off the bat so low that Finn has to keep his glove down around his ankles as he approaches it. He yanks the ball from the air and squeezes it hard, trapping it in his glove. He does all of this while simultaneously putting on the brakes with his legs, screeching to a halt inches from the fence, like a train grinding to a stop just in time to save a damsel tied to the rails.

This is our first out of the entire game so far, and the play electrifies the team, the fans—all of Arcadia Little League seems swept up by it—for a second, anyway. No matter that we're down seven runs. It was the space-time proximity of Finn's disastrous pitching to his heroic playmaking that made us all stop and pay respects to the baseball gods. The bases were loaded when Finn stepped off the mound. It was Finn who had placed the team in peril, and it is Finn who might rescue us.

"If you're keeping score, that's the second circus catch of the postseason!" exclaims my dad triumphantly. Relief pours out of us as we stretch out our arms and legs, settle back into our chairs.

"Circus catch," I repeat, just because I like the way I sound saying it.

One of the joys of watching baseball with my dad all season is knowing that something great could happen at any moment, just like this. A little piece of our hearts knows that baseball saves room for redemption. It isn't over until the last out, no matter how awful things look.

Leo strikes out the next two kids.

Team Red's pitcher mows us down, just as he did the inning before. Three up, three down. "This pitcher's a stud," says my dad as the kid coolly drops the ball on the mound.

"Total stud," I repeat, watching him tuck his red jersey back into his white pants and nonchalantly step off the hill, marching confidently toward the dugout. "We might be looking at a shutout, Dad."

Team Red's coach is an intimidating presence, with his thick arms and big shoulders stretching out his coach jersey. He's the other Little League coach who used to be a major-league player. In Arcadia, it isn't strange that more than one Little League coach used to be an actual major leaguer. The neighborhood is full of former professional baseball players, because it's in the backyard of spring training, where the Arizona Cactus League Baseball Association oversees ten nearby stadiums in what's considered the most highly concentrated baseball region in America. I guess players get to know the area during spring training and then settle here when they have the chance. The sport permeates Arcadia, not only because of those stadiums all around it, the tall lights shining down on diamonds across the Valley of the Sun, but also because of the soft-toss nets you drive by in front of so many houses. After a while, you barely notice kids swinging at tees in front yards on every block.

Coach Other Major Leaguer brings in Chris, a big kid, very round in the middle. He's keeping his ace, the total stud, below the max pitch count so he's fresh for the finals. That's how sure he is that he's winning this game.

Dad watches this kid warm up and I'm worried he's going to start pontificating about how his parents are abusing him by letting him get fat. I'm prepared to zip it, keep my thoughts to myself. But he doesn't lay into round Chris. Instead he says, "We can hit off this kid."

"But mass throws gas," I say, because I read that somewhere, that bigger kids throw harder.

"Not this mass," he counters.

He's right. We get a few hits off Chris in the third inning.

"Finn's sisters want Gatorade," Andrew says, suddenly appearing next to our chairs. It's the first time he's been out of the dugout in two games. The backs of my knees are warm and wet with sweat. Even in the shade, it's sweltering. Finn's little sisters are part of the younger-sibling tribe that has sprouted up around the Pinstripes. They have also become a sort of team.

The little girls look red and puffy from the heat. "Okay, fine. Ask the girls which color Gatorade they want. Order their drinks first, before you order anything for yourself. Say 'please' and 'thank you' to the guy working the snack bar and look him right in the eye. Don't be fidgeting and looking around when you speak. Okay?"

"Okay, okay, okay," he says, fast and breathless.

I obsessively remind my kids about manners, because I had to learn manners from movies and by studying other people, the way a Martian might upload the rules of human etiquette. Carol never taught us manners; she just criticized us for having none, and she was right. Once, I brought a pink comb to the table because I was worried she'd say my hair was too ratty. I pulled it out of my pocket right at dinner and combed the knots out of the frayed ends. "Nelson! Tell her to stop. She has no manners. It's disgusting," Carol shrieked. She stood and backed away like she'd seen a rat.

With Carol, children were to be neither seen nor heard, but they *should* know about table manners. Her "gauche" stepchildren (that was the word she used) were an extension of all that was wrong with her life, along with her shithole house, and my dad, wandering the earth in a mechanic's suit with grease under his nails for everyone to see, announcing to the world that he did manual labor, which to her was the province of imbeciles who didn't know any other way to make money.

My mom couldn't be bothered with niceties. She thought rules about salad forks and folded napkins were empty and meaningless. It was pointless for me to ask for her help, and I was too ashamed to bring it up to her anyway. I just knew I was beastly and clueless, and I still feel like an imposter every time I unfold a cloth napkin in my lap. I don't want this for my kids.

"Andrew, come back here for one second," I yell. He returns, agitated. I push his bangs away from his forehead. Then I check the rest of his face for smudges of dirt.

"Okay, Mom. *Bye.*"

"You're good," I say, giving him a final once-over.

"THANK YOU!" He grabs the crumpled ten-spot and I have no idea what happens after that, because when I see him next he is back in the dugout with a neon-yellow Gatorade. Isaiah is sitting next to him, Easton on the other side. The little brother is giggling.

The heat is getting to Chris, too. Sweat is streaking down his cheeks. His arm is a noodle now, lobbing pitches through the air like beach balls through molasses.

"All of a sudden, we got ourselves a ball game," says Dad, eyes darting around the field. After three outs, it's 7–5.

Leo is locked in now. I look toward Kai's dad on the other side of the bleachers. He doesn't even have to do the card-dealing motion anymore. He just tilts his head and smiles and shrugs his shoulders, and I know what he means. Leo is dealing. He gives up only one run, pitching all the way through to the fifth inning.

It's hard to watch Chris, who's sweating so much it, almost disguises the fact that he's crying now behind his black plastic glasses that look almost like goggles. He's like a giant round snowman melting onto the mound as he gives up his team's seven-run lead. And his coach is just leaving him out there, poor Chris, weeping and pitching and perspiring and wiping tears from his cheek and jaw with his forearm. Everyone knows that, besides the stud, Coach Other Major Leaguer has another solid arm in his bullpen, a kid with good command. But apparently he's saving both of his two best pitchers for the championship.

By the time he pulls Chris, the score is 12–8, and the Pinstripes have the lead.

"Why did this MLB guy try to get so cute with his pitching, T?"

"He's been saving his pitchers for the championship because he's that sure he's beating us."

"He's not."

"*Dad!* That's bad juju!" We both knock on our heads, to appease the baseball gods.

They have one more chance to catch up.

It's the bottom of the sixth, and Leo has thrown seventy-five pitches. He's burned.

Gavin takes the mound to warm up. Coach OML figures we're

down to the dregs of our bullpen. He doesn't remember that Gavin was the kid who caught a pop-up with his forehead and had to go to urgent care after the regular tryouts. He doesn't remember anything about Gavin and his parking-lot tryout months ago. Coach OML figures this is it: his time to clinch a spot in the finals. But then he watches Gavin throw his first warm-up pitch.

Staring at Gavin, brawny and square-jawed OML mutters a single word: "Fuck."

Then, in one single crisp motion, he pulls his hat down by the brim and lowers his head before marching to his station at first base.

He has every reason to curse out loud in front of God, the umps, and the entire playoff crowd gathered at Ingleside Middle School. He knows baseball. And he knows when you're fucked.

Gavin strikes out the side.

That's the ball game.

The next morning, after Andrew's last T-ball game, Dad sits drinking coffee with me at the kitchen table.

"We have Nate and Gavin still available to pitch," I say in a low voice, making sure Nate is outside. "You never know which Nate you're going to get, but Gavin has been solid."

We chat more about who should play catcher and whether Daniel should tinker with his batting order.

We've been through fifteen of Nate's games, and a season of Andrew playing T-ball, and I think I've figured out how to talk to him about Carol, to present a question without putting him on his heels. He's in a good mood, so it seems like a good time to ask. I'm careful about my tone. I don't want to try his case again. I'm just curious.

"Dad, can I ask you something? No judgment. I just want to

know. Other than the one time after she threw the lamp, did you ever think seriously about splitting up with Carol?"

He looks at his hands, folded on the table.

"She caused me so much trouble because she didn't get along well with you kids. But I was a mess. I'm glad I had you two, but I wasn't ready to be a parent, or even an adult. She was like my therapist. She helped me. If it wasn't for her, I'd still be fat like when I was a kid, and I never would have started jogging or eating health food."

She was older, he says, a guru to him with all her psychology paperbacks and her vegetarian cookbooks. Her way was going to save the planet, even if he'd find candy wrappers in the car sometimes. A neighbor once called Carol a "fat bitch" during some protracted war over something or other to do with her garden in Santa Rosa. Her weight did fluctuate wildly, from chubby and stout to portly and square. I remember that war, and how many times Dad told the story of Carol's last stand. When the neighbor called her "fat bitch," she clapped back, "I could lose this weight. But you'll always be stupid." "ZING," Dad always said when he recounted the scene. Wasn't she brilliant? She was so worldly, riffing on that famous Winston Churchill riposte when some fool accused him of being drunk, and he told her he'd be sober the next day, but she'd still be ugly. ZING.

"She made your life so . . . complicated," I respond carefully, "because she didn't like us. She didn't like your sisters or your parents. Nobody came to visit because Carol would confront them about their issues, and they'd never come back."

He says nothing.

Then, meekly: "I tried to kick her out another time. I told her to go stay with her sister. But I felt bad for her. Her dad molested her when she was five or six; it's just terrible to even think about. Then he left the family and never came back. Then she grows up and marries a guy who was abusive to their kids, and then he ended up living on the streets. So *he* wasn't going to help Carol."

"How did it go with her sister?"

"Oh, even though I told her to leave and go to her sister's house, she never did."

"What happened to her abusive ex, who lived on the street?"

"He died young, not sure how." Dad wraps his hands around his coffee mug, warming them, eyes downcast.

"She just wouldn't leave. I thought about calling the sheriff's office to put her out, but I just couldn't do that to her. She'd be on the streets." He is still looking into his coffee, shoulders curling forward. I remember how he was when Carol died, lighter and looser, relieved she was no longer suffering. But maybe he was also relieved that she had finally moved out.

"That's a pickle for sure, Dad." I try to see it like that, envision the pickle my dad was in, but the image creeps in of a sheriff standing guard while his deputies put Carol's suitcases in the driveway and take her far away, ZING.

"Where are the coffee pods?" he asks, scuttling toward the kitchen counter to make himself a second cup. He stares blankly at the coffee maker, which sits beside the basket of pods.

"Literally right in front of you. Where they always are."

I'm still mad at him for not getting Carol out of our lives, but a guy who can't find a coffee pod that's right in front of him had a million reasons not to see the damage Carol was doing to his children. *Why be irritated that he doesn't know what's right in front of him?* I think. *That isn't going to change.* He had seen every single Little League game of the season. That had to mean something.

I try to picture my dad before he was my dad, when he was just a guy in the San Fernando Valley without much going for him. He was schlubby, an average student, while his older sister, Diane, was an academic superstar. He played Little League but was so bad, they had to send him down to play with the younger kids. Once Carol moved in with him, he'd get home from work and jog, then eat vegetables and tofu. He became the skinniest guy, the most fit. That was his *thing*. He was the person who had given up meat to help the planet, who could tell you all the reasons why tofu would end world hunger. He had a claim to fame now, and Carol had made it happen. He was done with his past, his mom comparing him to his more accomplished cousins: this one who went to Harvard, that one who was an orthopedic surgeon. He jogged and ate ratatouille and fixed cars. He just couldn't call the sheriff. But he did think about it, and I like knowing that. I don't know if it was a nice cut, but maybe it was.

"Big news," Daniel interrupts, tramping into the kitchen, looking at his phone. "Jackson is burned. Team Gray had to ride him to beat Team Orange. So, in the finals of the Arcadia Little League Minors, we're facing a Jackson-less Team Gray." He pauses dramatically. Dad and I stare at him. "It's winnable."

Nate will get the start. Gavin will close. This is it.

All the time my dad and I had spent together during the season of the Purple Pinstripes would end, one way or another, after the next game. I thought about all the hours in our parallel beach chairs, all the big emotions. The games were like a warm compress, bringing everything to the surface. We'd felt grief: first the kind that's so in your face, it blinds you, and now the kind with a slightly softer light. We'd felt panic, euphoria, jubilation, wild openheartedness, petty jealousy, empathy and awe, irritation and rage. We'd known unquenchable wants and attachments, fears, nerves, yips by proxy, and relentless, breath-stealing helplessness. We'd unfolded our beach chairs feeling anticipation, concern, care, and wellsprings of *nachas*. There'd been a sense of separateness, the two of us in our grief bubble on the sidelines. And there'd been a sense of oneness, the two of us dissolving into the team. The team gave us belonging and purpose, a communal schedule, someplace we needed to be no matter how we were feeling. And the games gave us a different way to think about errors. We learned that mistakes were okay—in fact, at least in baseball, mistakes were essential. "I threw a lot of balls and walked a lot of batters. Not something I'm proud of, but something I learned from." That's the Randy Johnson quote on a white vinyl banner tied to a fence at the Arcadia Little League field. We strode past it all season.

We'd known loss and frustration in ways that felt both cosmic and tangible. And maybe, more than anything, my dad and I had come to feel like those particles he had described in his email. But we weren't just connected to each other. Entangled atoms exist in pairs, but they also sometimes consist of hundreds or even millions of particles that become one entity, a subatomic family, a team, a spooky unit of interwoven states. They affect each other, whether they're separated by a diamond of grass and dirt or by billions of light-years. They're entangled.

As we head into our final game, the mysterious relationships of quantum worlds seem to explain our team, the way hitting is contagious, the way the outfielders have come to trust their cutoff man. It encompasses our connection with the Purple Pinstripes, with Daniel and the Roychester Royals, with my brother and the Santa Monica Angels, and if you believe in this sort of thing, with every kid who has ever stepped up to bat, dug his spikes into the dirt around home plate, and swung for the fences.

||||||||||||||||||||||||||

CHAPTER SEVENTEEN

Eighty-Three Problems

"It's the mathematical potential for a single game to last forever, in a suspended world where no clock rules the day, that aligns baseball as much with the dead as the living."

—BILL VAUGHN

Hundreds of neighborhood kids are now swarming Ingleside. Teachers, parents, cousins, grandparents, aunts and uncles, and coaches have parked their cars and passed by the outdoor basketball court, through the blue gates, to stand in clumps behind the bleachers or congregate in the cramped clusters of chairs by the dugouts. Since it's the championship, there are four umps tonight, and two are by the snack bar in their heather-gray pants, Little League patches on their sleeves. They are taking sips from huge jugs of water as the commissioner announces over the PA system, "Welcome to the Arcadia Little League Minors Championship game. Kids, a reminder: Anyone who brings a foul ball to the snack bar gets a free small Icee. And don't forget that tonight we are offering the surf-and-turf special. Get your surf and turf at the snack bar. A hot dog and a bag of Goldfish crackers." There are some groans in the crowd.

"He needs new material," says my dad.

"I have to say, Dad, I like it. That's actually a pretty good bit for the occasion."

He shrugs. "It breaks the ice."

"No. It breaks the Icee," I say. My dad opens his mouth wide and lets out a loud "HA."

"I was thinking about it, T. I really like Leo batting cleanup. He's been swinging a good bat. Ethan bats leadoff—that kid is automatic right now. Keep Nate in the two spot. Gavin after that. This batting order will be tough to stop."

"We just need these bats popping," I say, like he always does.

Earlier, I had called to tell him my car wouldn't start.

I was at a used-car lot, filming a television story about how to buy a used car, and in my nervous baseball mom state I didn't shut my car door all the way. When I went to drive home and get ready for the game, I turned the key and nothing happened. They jumped it for me and I called my dad on the way home. "Remember that time I left the car door open and it drained my battery? In the driveway in front of Mom's house in San Francisco? I was a teenager and you drove all the way in from Santa Rosa just to fix it? I did the same thing just now. Can you believe it? I think I'm too nervous. I know I am. I'm too nervous, Dad. I hate it. I can't even function."

"I felt that way, too, when I woke up, T. But then it just faded. I'm at peace now. I'm not nervous at all. Because I just realized, whatever happens, it's been a great season." I can hear in his voice he's not faking it. The Tao of Dad has been activated.

"Don't forget, the surf-and-turf special is still going," booms the PA.

"It gets funnier, Dad."

"You know, you're right."

Someone has brought a small speaker for the Purple Pinstripes dugout and it emits a tinny version of "Old Town Road" as the infield whips the ball around. The outfielders play catch, and the catcher warms up Nate. "Well, this is it," says my dad, eyebrows arched. "This one is for all the marbles."

My mind understands this isn't a true emergency—wouldn't be even if Nate were the starting pitcher in the World Series—but I'm light-headed. Though it's near dusk, I feel around in my bag for sunglasses, grateful for a task. I unzip the side pocket and gingerly open the case so I can stretch the time it takes. I wipe down the lenses of my scratched aviators like I'm about to hand them to an action star for a tight close-up, and I slide them onto my face. I can feel my heartbeat in my eyeballs. *Stay inside*, I say to myself. *Way to battle.*

Fifth graders are crowded behind home plate. A mist hits my cheek from some little sister's plastic portable water-spray fan. The Purple Pinstripes are lined up for one last chance at batting practice. Daniel throws up a soft toss from the side, and each kid hits it into a portable net. Isaiah steps up; his setup is looking solid. He delivers a series of self-assured cuts. Next, Nate taps his bat on the dirt, lifts it, bends his knees low. I try to read his emotion in his face, but the expression is stoic, the hacks steady and strong.

"Isaiah looked good in BP earlier, taking practice cuts. You think he's getting his first hit, Dad?"

"Maybe. But I don't care how he gets on base. I just want him to get there."

"I care. I need him to get a hit so bad," I say, glancing back at his mom, the overnight nurse at the local VA hospital.

I look at the old man, now motionless, waiting.

I notice my breathing seems to stop in my throat, so I try to breathe from my diaphragm, because that's a thing you're supposed to do, but if there's a change in my anxiety level, it's imperceptible.

"As long as you are breathing, there is more right with you than wrong with you, no matter what is wrong," said the mindfulness book. Fine. Fine. I'm alive and breathing and this is the state of me. I'm too nervous about Little League. That's one of my eighty-three problems, I think, remembering something Victoria had told us during a Monday night dharma talk.

The story she shared was about a farmer who went to see the Buddha. "This guy," Victoria told the group, "was seeking help for all the problems he was facing. The weather was bad for his crops. His wife was nagging him. His children wouldn't obey him. People owed him money and he couldn't get them to pay up. And so on and so forth. So the Buddha told him that he had eighty-three problems and said, 'I can't help you with any of those, but I can help you with your eighty-fourth problem.'"

Victoria pressed her palms into her knees, sitting in the lotus position, wild, curly hair jutting out at all angles. She leaned forward on her cushion, sitting on the center of the stage at the church. I leaned forward, too, sitting in the back pew.

"The farmer asked, 'What is the eighty-fourth problem?' And the Buddha answered, 'Thinking that you shouldn't have the first eighty-three.' See, it's an illusion that we shouldn't suffer. Problems arise and pass away, and others replace them, but the Buddha said all of us have eighty-three of them at any given time—things that cause dissatisfaction, stress, unease. That's the reality of being human."

If that's true, this season has put me in touch with some of my eighty-three.

My dad loves me, but he's also a buffoon.

We care about Little League way too much.

When I see Daniel coach our kids, part of my heart drops hard, like a Koufax curveball, because my brother's kids will never have their dad on the sidelines.

When I'm watching Nate, I live and die with every pitch, even though I wish I didn't. Because, for me, to watch kids play baseball is to experience the excruciating vulnerability of being a parent, and I can't shrink it down to size.

Oh, and I grieve too hard. Then I get mad at myself for it. Then I get even more mad, because, like Ruth says, "There's no right or wrong way to grieve." I still think it isn't fair that my brother died instead of me. The guilt is stitched into me now, like red thread into the cover of a baseball. When I try to begin again, to go back to the upper-left-hand corner, to take it from the top, like Ron told me to do, the music doesn't sound right and I don't think it ever will.

I hate losing. I know in my head it's good for kids to experience defeat, to practice tolerating pain and frustration, but I can't get my body on the same page as my head.

I'm too old to still be mad at my evil stepmother or feel happy that she's dead.

I didn't get to have the kind of mom I wanted. And I was kind of a crap daughter. I can't do anything about either of those things now.

And I can't stop thinking about my brother: his otherworldly patience, the way he rode out his pain, and all the gory slings and arrows of dying slow and hard. Snapshots of Morgan—with no time or date stamps—appear at unpredictable intervals, and I never see them coming, like the image of his daughter curling up next to him on his hospital bed, holding her lollipop. That little girl in the snapshot has no idea her strong, barrel-chested dad will fade away in the basement of her house and that when he's pronounced dead during a snowstorm, she will be too afraid to travel down the dark stairs and kiss his body goodbye. I think about that even when I don't want to. Sometimes I still reach for my phone to text my brother something about the Golden State Warriors or how Dad is chewing his Snyder's hard pretzels with his mouth open. Any talk of someone earning a pilot's license brings the grief spotlight right into my eyes and cranks it up to full wattage before I can brace. I don't trust doctors, and deep down I wonder if all that treatment was bullshit and if my brother would have survived for seven years just fine without any treatment at all. That seems paranoid and irrational, but I'm hung up on it. If a doctor asks me for my family medical history, I'm definitely crying on the exam table while thinking how I shouldn't be so sad about my dead brother anymore. *Goodnight Moon* shatters me. Father's Day makes me sad. Mother's Day makes me sad. Little League makes me crazy. These are some of my eighty-three problems today, and when I think I shouldn't have them, I have eighty-four.

"Why are they not starting?" Dad asks, checking the time on his phone. "The game should've started six minutes ago."

The players are introduced, one by one. They stand in a row on the third-base line.

"Please stand for the national anthem."

I know my dad hates corporations and nationalism and jingoism and the rote memorization of words written to celebrate a country with too many billionaires and too much strife for the working poor and pollution and high-fructose corn syrup. But it has also made baseball. I know he will stand. He rises without balking.

The boys put their hats over their hearts.

"You got eyes on Andrew?" my dad asks.

"Dad, look," I say, pointing toward the dugout, where Andrew's pudgy little hand is digging into his brother's bag of sunflower seeds. He puts down the seeds and stands, facing the flag across the field.

"He is so cute," says my dad. "In his happy place, the dugout with his big brother."

"I know. He is so *fucking cute*." I feel bad swearing during the national anthem. *"And the home . . . of the . . . brave."*

The boys move their hats from their hearts to their heads. "PLAY BALL," yells the ump.

Stay where you are. In this moment of now. That's what I tell myself to do. *Don't step in the goddamn bucket.*

Team Gray's infield whips the ball around one last time.

Ethan bats first and hits a hard grounder up the middle, like he seemed to do every time in the postseason, our steady leadoff hitter. He's safe at first base. *Thank you, baseball gods.* Nate steps up, then swings at the first pitch, lining a hard ground ball just inside the third-base line, all the way to the left-field corner. As Team Gray's outfielder scrambles to track down the ball and find his cutoff man, Ethan rounds third, then slides home, and Nate follows. The team explodes out of the dugout, and the Pinstripes are on the scoreboard, off in the distance. The red numbers flashing way above center field say we're up 2–0.

"Did that just happen, or was it a dream?" Dad asks. We are still on our feet.

We slide back into our chairs and I pinch his forearm, but the adrenaline juices my pinch and Dad screams, "OUCH!"

"At least you know you aren't dreaming. But, Dad, we have only two runs. We have to stave off irrational exuberance."

When it's time for the Pinstripes to take the field, Jackson gets a hit straightaway. But Nate mows down the next three batters. No runs allowed.

"HE IS DEALING," mouths Kai's dad from way behind the bleachers, where he is pacing, his hands jammed in his pockets.

From there, we just keep hitting. Gavin and Leo hit back-to-back inside-the-park home runs. Their pitcher is solid but hittable. And our bats are alive. I looked it up earlier in the week, whether or not good hitting is contagious. I found evidence of a "statistical contagion effect," with theories about mirror neurons and neural pathways. Maybe it seems possible to get your bat on the ball because the kid ahead of you just did it.

Isaiah swings at two pitches but misses both. "Good cut," we all yell. And Coach bellows, "Two strikes on you now, kid. Swing at anything close." The bleachers call out, "Now you've seen it," and "Gotta protect" and I hear myself, too, a bit restrained, but still trying to add my voice to the chorus. "Give it a ride!"

He swings hard and connects, not with the meat of the barrel, but he does make contact. A ground ball hobbles toward the mound, and by the time the pitcher fields it and fires it toward first, Isaiah is safe. His first hit ever.

Daniel tries to keep it cool, but I see him pump his fist and smack the kid too hard on the back. And Isaiah is already creeping off the bag, planning to steal second base any chance he gets, and he does. And he eventually makes it all the way home. Not on a walk. On a hit. And I know now, based on all I've picked up from the parlance of the bleachers, and all I've seen from behind the first- and third-base lines, that he hit that ball because he didn't step in the bucket, didn't leak out. I know that nobody makes contact unless they override the urge to flinch, to step away from the pitch hurtling toward you. Nobody makes contact unless they can risk striking out or getting hit by a pitch. But if you can tolerate the possibility of every kind of pain, real and imagined, physical and spiritual, only then do you stand a chance of hitting a baseball.

If this kid could stay inside, so could I, so could we. So I don't hide behind the snack bar when it's time for Nate to pitch another inning. I can watch him pitch in the finals of the Arcadia Little League, alone on the hill, in front of a huge crowd, his friends, and even his teacher. The whole neighborhood is here, and I can watch and pretend to be normal, and feel woozy, and stay in my chair.

I'm clapping so hard every time he strikes a kid out that my palms sting.

Nate stays in for three innings without allowing a single run. And as the Pinstripes take to the field for the fourth inning, I desperately call out to Daniel as he walks by us along the fence. "DANNY!" He comes over to me at the fence and I whisper, "You're taking him out, right? Right? You penciled him in for three, and that was three!"

"No way," he responds breezily. "Can't. He's dealing." As much as I wish he would pull Nate, leave well enough alone, deep down I'm relieved Daniel is approaching his management of the Pinstripes, of Nate, with a mathematical detachment. He doesn't knock on wood or ascribe divine meaning to a pitching performance. He doesn't need his kid to succeed for the world to feel like a safe place. That's not one of his eighty-three problems.

In the end, Nate strikes out ten, walks two, allows two hits and zero runs.

Gavin comes in to stitch things up in the last two innings.

Final score: 7–1.

The kids rush the mound as Gavin throws the final pitch. They hug, tackle each other, high-five, tapping leather gloves in the air. It's a blur of moms taking pictures, boys grinning with trophies, hair splaying out under their hats, their knees deep brown and red with field dirt. Dads beam and pat their sons on the backs of their jerseys, maybe longer than they thought they would, then rest their hands on purple iron-on jersey numbers. Nate runs over to hug his grandpa, who has been hanging back by himself as I take a team photo. Child flings his arms around Grandpa, then gets self-conscious and stops, stepping back.

"You pitched a gem," my dad says.

"Thanks," Nate answers softly, smiling under his cap.

"And the hitting wasn't bad, either! Not a bad day at the office!"

Nate smiles harder, then runs back to join his team, packing up their bags in the dugout.

Dad and I fold up our chairs, the scoreboard still lit up in the outfield. And I know we are folding them up for the last time of this magical season, the season of the Purple Pinstripes, now champions of the Arcadia Little League Minors. *Our team.*

The stadium lights shine down on the diamond, now empty. All the red dust has settled back down into the dirt. The field is quiet and still. It looks so much like a snapshot now, it's hard to imagine it was ever animated. The old man grips the handle of the red wagon with his hairy knuckles and begins to haul it over the dirt between the fields, and then across the grass. The air feels like a warm bath and the moon is hung low. My dad doesn't look back at the fields as we leave them. He just trudges forward in his sneakers. I keep pace and, without slowing down, I glance backward.

———

The thrill doesn't leave my body for days, and I carry in my tissues and organs the leftovers of the championship game and all that preceded it. Every base hit and every strikeout, every circus catch and every long throw from the cutoff man to the infield—it's all on record somewhere inside, on some kind of box score written in adrenaline. There's a jittery, strung-out hangover from a feeling I never thought we would have: Dad and I coming out on top. Our team surviving so many wild pitches, passing through slumps and yips and, in the end, posing on the third-base line, cleats on white chalk, shoulder to shoulder, clutching hardware. It's almost too much at first, a triple shot of triumph after so much losing, jacking up my system for more than a week, until I'm almost relieved to come down.

Where I land, I know all seasons come to an end.

On the battlefield of parental love and longing that is Little League, Dad and I got reps, a season of practice swings and warm-up pitches. We had to learn to let things be on the field, because there was no other way. And I had to let him be, and see what was on the other side when I didn't scratch the itch to berate him about Carol, or the half-eaten avocado he left in the fridge, or the bumbling way he lived, or the goddamn irony of him coming down on other parents when he'd made so many mistakes himself.

By the end of the season, everyone knew my dad, and I wasn't trying to hide him.

He was mine, along with his greasy hat, workman's shorts, single-wide trailer next to a cemetery. And I'd come to appreciate that he'd done the hardest and most heroic thing you could do, on the field and off: He didn't flinch. When my brother was dying, he never stepped out of the box. Simple as that. He sat by every bedside at every rehabilitation center. He rode out the hard truth that sometimes there is no rehabilitation and there's no redemption.

But sometimes there is.

This crumbling old man was my dad, and in the present, in the now of the Purple Pinstripes, he never missed a single inning.

Baseball doesn't promise you a happy ending, but it always leaves room for one.

And that's why the season of the Purple Pinstripes was a grief group for us. Things can be bad and then good. We'd lived it, lived it on the sidelines in our beach chairs, praying and cursing and cheering. And only because we'd felt the losses so fully—too fully, you could argue—did we feel this championship rearrange and lift us.

Our grief group met exactly nineteen times at the Ingleside Middle School in Phoenix, Arizona. There were no therapeutically trained facilitators and no rules, other than those dictated by the Little League of America, and the human heart.

EPILOGUE

||||||||||||||||||||||||||||

Like my brother, Nate was chosen to be an all-star, the youngest one to make the team.

All-stars are chosen by the votes of players and coaches, and each local all-star team competes against the other teams in their district for a chance to go to state. The Arcadia All-Stars blew through the other teams in our district. That's how they made it to Arizona's state tournament, held at the Tempe Sports Complex. We ran out of pitchers and I saw Nate warming up in the bullpen.

After my son walked the first batter, I relapsed into a less enlightened state. I wandered away and found a crumbling cement bench behind the brick bathroom building, where I listened to bursts of cheering—*was that for our team or the other team?*—and checked my phone for updates from my dad.

It was their fans cheering, not ours.

After forever, he finally texted:

Rough. Inning over. Nate pulled.

Nate had walked seven batters. We lost that game, our second loss in a double-elimination tournament. So, *sudden death.*

As we walked to the car, my heart was heavy for my kid. He'd wanted it so badly, to help his team, to feel the exhilaration of his body at his mind's command, and I wanted it for him. And I just couldn't separate my wants from his that day. Rehabilitation might be possible, but even when it is, it takes time.

On the way home, I could feel Nate parsing the loss, tabulating it, all the batters he walked, how he couldn't get command of himself, not this time. "Mom," he finally said from the back seat, "what's that thing called where it's like you're asleep for a long time?"

"A coma?"

"Yeah. I want to be in one of those—and wake me up right before All-Stars next year."

From the passenger seat, I craned my head back and looked at my dad. He raised his bushy eyebrows at me, then looked out the window, eyes blinking, jaw twitching. There was nothing but the sound of our tires on gravel.

How we hated baseball. Stupid, heartbreaking baseball.

And we couldn't wait for next season.

ACKNOWLEDGMENTS

||||||||||||||||||||||||||||||

I was already writing these acknowledgments in my head long before this book even sold. You know, just kind of passing the time and fantasizing.

As I shoved baseball pants in the dryer, I would write poetic sentences in my head, all about Anthony Mattero, my literary agent at CAA.

But I can't really remember any of that internal laundry prose now.

So it's really a good idea to take notes.

The gist of my fantasy thank-you was always this: Without Anthony, *Making It Home* would not have made it anywhere. There is nobody with better taste, a softer touch with people, and a more encouraging and generous heart.

I love him so much for all he did to help make the story of this one griefy season into a memoir. It was all a fantasy, and now, thanks to Anthony, it's real. I'm especially grateful that he connected me with my editor, Tracy Bernstein, at Berkley. (Or, I should say reconnected me, as she also edited my first book, *Exploiting My Baby*.)

My only question in regard to Tracy is this: How does any human being write a book without her?

She expected, encouraged, and required me to be clear and go deep, two missions that are as essential for writing as they are for human healing. I will be forever grateful for the care and attention she gave every little bit of this story. She is shrewd, wise, and tireless and doesn't miss a single thing. Every note she gave me made this book better, even if they hurt, *especially* when they hurt. Without Tracy, this would've maybe been a collection of possibly semi-touching ramblings, but not a book. Her skill with words and ideas is otherworldly, even if we do disagree on the overall merits of Jewish baked goods.

And now I tip my cap to Ryan Isaac, who helped me speak baseball. A former Major League Baseball scout who loves the sport more than anyone I know, he helped me rephrase sentences about batting stances, base-running pickles, and line drives. He found and fixed many technical gaffes. And maybe more importantly, this salty veteran of professional baseball turned Little League softball coach wrote me an email after reading one of my chapters, saying, "I cried. *Because baseball*. People are going to like this book." And for that moment of unabashed cheerleading, which I desperately needed, and for all the rest, I'm deeply grateful.

Thank you, Swarm Baseball, Arcadia Little League, Arcadia Youth Basketball, Arcadia Sports Central, and the Kirk Gibson Foundation for Parkinson's. Also the Detroit Tiger great himself, Kirk Gibson. His innocent question "Where do you want to be in five years?" sent me here, now, having written *this book*. Thanks, Mr. Gibson. Oh, and also for two of the greatest moments in the history of baseball.

Ted Kamp, you nudged me about this book every week for a

year, even set an alarm on your phone called "nudge Teresa," and then you read the proposal, read every chapter, and listened to every meltdown, and you talked me off every ledge. Your belief is a fire hose of love and acceptance. I'm so glad I get to know you. You are a wellspring of creativity and brilliance.

My deep gratitude also goes to Laura Sanchez-Puerta; Julian and Clara; Nate and Andrew; Kathy; Danny Seckel; Michele Ku; Genevieve; Gabrielle; Sharon; my first editor, Rob Eshman; and one of my writing mentors and heroes, Yvette Lee Bowser.

Lastly, thanks to all the athletic coaches (especially Daniel) who have ever coached my kids. That includes youth baseball legend Bob Strachan, who always yelled, "INNING HALF OVER!" after one defensive out, ever the optimist. My dad and I still imitate his catchphrase, "Kid, that was the best hit ball of your entire life." Coaches, the kids are listening. And so are the parents. You are doing the Lord's work.

Making it Home

TERESA STRASSER

||||||||||||||||||||||||||||||||||||

TERESA STRASSER

READERS GUIDE

DISCUSSION QUESTIONS

||||||||||||||||||||||||||

1. Why was the season of the Purple Pinstripes a grief group for Teresa and her father?

2. Have you ever been an obsessed superfan, whether of a team, a writer, an influencer, or a band? How did this help you feel part of a community?

3. What kind of sports parent are/were you?

4. Is Teresa's dad redeemed for his questionable parenting by becoming a devoted grandparent?

5. Do you believe there's a connection to our loved ones after they die? Are we connected as in the example of quantum mechanics, or what Einstein called "spooky action at a distance"?

6. Why do parents get so intensely wrapped up in their talented kids, whether they're involved in chess, violin, tennis, swimming, or baseball?

7. Do you have a memory that seems to encapsulate your relationship with your sibling(s)?

8. If you've experienced grief, what aspect of Teresa's grief seemed familiar to you? Did any of it seem wildly different?

9. How much of Teresa's grief is about the deaths of her brother and mother and how much about other things?

10. Teresa feels she should have died instead of her brother. Based on what you learn in the book, why do you think she feels that way?

11. Would you characterize Tammy and Nelson Strasser as "bad" parents? Why or why not?

12. In the end, Teresa gave up on getting an acknowledgment from her dad about her dysfunctional childhood. How do you feel about that?

Photo by Jose Ochoa

Teresa Strasser is an Emmy-winning writer (Comedy Central) and Emmy-nominated television host (TLC). She has been a contributor to the *Los Angeles Times*, *USA Today*, the *Arizona Republic*, the *Jewish Journal*, HuffPost, and the *Today* show. Her first-person essays have garnered three Los Angeles Press Club Awards, including Columnist of the Year. She's appeared on *The View*, CNN, *Good Morning America*, *The Talk*, and *Dr. Phil*. Radio and podcast audiences know her as Adam Carolla's cohost. Her first memoir, *Exploiting My Baby: Because It's Exploiting Me* was a *Los Angeles Times* bestseller and optioned by ABC.

CONNECT ONLINE

TeresaStrasser.com

🐦 TeresaStrasser

📷 TeresaStrasser

🅵 OfficialTeresaStrasser